A Radical Inner Process

# DEEP CLEARING

Balance Your Emotions

Let Go Of Inner & Outer Negativity

Shifit To Higher Consciousness

## JOHN RUSKAN

author of *Emotional Clearing*

R. Wyler & Co.
New York, NY

# DEEP CLEARING by John Ruskan

ISBN: 978-0-9629295-7-1

Library of Congress Control Number: 2019900348
Ruskan, John
Deep clearing: balance your emotions, let go of inner and outer negativity, shift to higher consciousness / John Ruskan
1. Psychology 2. Emotions 3. Meditation 4. East / West Psychology
5. Mindfulness

Typeset in Sabon and Frutiger
Original tradepaper edition published 2021 by R. Wyler & Co., NY, NY
Contact email: rwylerpub@gmail.com

**DISCLAIMER:** The author of this book does not presume to offer psychological therapy or advocate the use of any technique for the treatment of any specific or traumatic psychological condition without the approval and guidance of a qualified psychologist. The intent of the author is only to relate his personal experience in the hope that it may help you in your quest for emotional and spiritual health. If you use any of the information here as a form of self-therapy, the author and publisher assume no responsibility for your actions.

*dedicated to
spiritual seekers
everywhere*

# Contents

# The Search

Throughout the course of history, mankind has been confronted with the enigmatic dilemma of happiness. We plan, we strive, we pursue what appears to be of value, but lasting fulfillment mysteriously continues to elude us.

Often, as we gain in any area of life, tragedy strikes elsewhere, and we experience loss in proportion to our gain. Happiness and sadness, pleasure and pain, love and hate, good and evil itself appear to be inextricably linked, keeping us on edge, unable to fully relax. Many of us today unfortunately resonate with the negative D's of our physical, mental, and emotional being: Delusion, Denial, Dysfunction, Depression, and Deterioration.

How we respond to the question of happiness differs widely. You may think the answer is more money, resolving issues with your spouse, or children who would behave. Or maybe it's more time off, recognition on the job, a different job, more or better friends, and so on. If you have a severe health condition, you just want to get better.

However, when you think any *thing* will make you happy, you are in a state of Delusion. "Thing" in this context means an object, possession, person, treatment, attainment, condition or circumstance, including love, wealth, and health, the big three of our modern acquisitive culture.

The more you want any *thing*, the more deluded you are, the more in Denial you are, and the more unaware you are of the real cause of your pain. Looking to the acquisition of things to make you happy is the basic mistake you make in pursuing happiness. If no *thing* is to bring happiness, how is it to be obtained?

*By a shift in consciousness.*

This is still big news today. Hardly anyone thinks what they need is a shift in consciousness. To speak in such terms would generally cause eyebrows to be raised. But this is *exactly* what you need, and if and when you get that shift, all those other things you want so badly would be seen to be only play toys in the sand – perhaps pleasing for a moment, but certainly nothing to make a fuss over.

So, after enough Dysfunction, Depression, and Deterioration, you come around to questioning your values, motives, and goals. Let's say you are one of those advanced souls who starts to suspect that no *thing* will make you happy, what then? Then, you are about to embark upon *the search*.

Disdaining material acquisition because you see it does nothing to solve your real problem, you might start by unloading possessions, but this would be your first mistake – of the many to come – as you seek that ephemeral, non-material solution to the problem of happiness. It's not possessions, but your *attachment* to them that holds you back, and getting rid of them does not necessarily eliminate this.

Possibly, on the contrary, as you continue to hold on to possessions and keep getting battered by your compulsive addictive attachments to them, this can be a means to your goal of *non-attachment*, *if you handle the pain correctly.*

That's what this book is about – how to handle the pain – all kinds of pain, not only that which results from material attachments. And not only that, but how to make pain *work for you*, in ways you never imagined. You think pain is bad. Not always so, as you begin to shift consciousness.

For most of you, this is not the first book you have read about *the search*. You have read metaphysical books, and perhaps meditated. You have studied psychology, and perhaps experienced some form of psychotherapy. You have been working on yourself. How is the program we will be exploring here different from other books and practices, why will it help you, and why do you need it? To answer this, perhaps I can share some of my personal story.

All my life, the fires of *the search* have been burning intensely for me. Although I have not entered the monastery, there are none who have more strongly heard the call to consciousness. However, for the first 20 years of this quest, something was missing. In the several spiritual traditions I avidly studied – Yoga, Buddhism, Theosophy, Metaphysics – my experience was that there was no in-depth guidance on *feelings*. Bad feelings, if discussed at all, were simply seen as bad. They were to be forcibly dismissed by the will. The goal was to get somewhere else, to a blissful, loving, higher, positive, "spiritual" consciousness, which would obliterate the bad energy. I was not aware of this shortcoming at first; it would take years before I noticed it. But eventually I realized that I had been neglecting an important part of myself.

And then, I was equally enchanted and well-read with Western psychology. Psychology, however, did not acknowledge the higher consciousness I was seeking, and I didn't buy into thinking that my childhood was the original cause of all the neuroses I might have packed away, as it glibly assumed. In the end, although psychology did ostensibly deal with feelings, I felt it was largely confined to an intellectual level and not especially effective or relevant for *releasing* feelings. I could not interface it with *the search*.

So I was on my own. I needed a *feeling-based* approach, some way to resolve the neurotic feelings and emotions I still harbored in spite of all those years on the spiritual path: Too much anger, compulsive acting-out, sexual compulsiveness, being driven for success, relentless feelings of failure and loneliness, and of course the love-hate relationship carousel that remains a mystery to most of us, but which I will attempt to clarify in part III.

Gradually, I put together my own system. That's what I will be talking about here. It's a synthesis of many traditions, psychological and metaphysical, with a fair amount of original insights thrown in. It's a way to understand the emotions – why they come up, where they come from, and most importantly, how to handle and release them and not be controlled and tormented by them. It's a new putting together of powerful routes to resolving negativity by means of a *shift in consciousness*. It may present and challenge you with ideas you have never quite considered – about emotional self-rejection, for example. But if you stay with it, and if you have the *capacity*, it will very likely give you an unsurpassed method of working on yourself to which you may never have been exposed. That's how and why I believe it can help you. You, just like me, just like everyone, need to work on a *feeling level*.

This work has never been more important. Today, we see vast negative energies undermining, dominating, and contaminating life on our planet. One central purpose of this chaos is to keep you preoccupied with external conflicts. When we are fighting each other, when politics, news, and controversial social reform issues become our main focus, attention is diverted from the important life tasks we should be expending our energy on. We should be using life's experiences to work on ourselves, to go within, to advance our personal and collective consciousness evolution. Instead, we see just the opposite, ranging from mindless absorption with electronic trivia to serious issues threatening our way of life that are difficult to ignore.

It's easy to feel powerless in the face of such threats. We may try to fend off negativity by putting up shields, or by fighting what appears to be outside. However, the real battle is on the inside. The outer is always a reflection of the inner. Our approach is based on the premise that inner disharmony, and the perceived outer disharmony that results, is due to the accumulation of negative "energies" within, which become known to us as *feelings and emotions*. If we work on an inner feeling level, we can calm and resolve the inner *and* outer chaos and advance our personal evolution as well.

*Raising your vibration* and working on yourself is the *only* way that lasting outer change can be achieved, the only way of confronting and rendering yourself impervious to apparent "outside" negativity, and that's what you can learn to do here. You can't raise your vibration when you are carrying around suppressed energetic negativity. Releasing it is the first step to freeing yourself from outside tyranny.

The format we will be discussing is one of *inner awareness*. It starts with closing your eyes and looking inside. The principles involved give you a road map and an innovative, effective means to handle negativity found there. This is not a quick-fix intervention; it is a serious, long-term commitment to regaining inner health. You will see that some skills are needed in this approach, as in any worthwhile endeavor. If you already have an ongoing interest in alternative healing, Eastern spiritual practice, Western psychotherapy, or right-brain activities such as the arts, you will most likely be able to easily apply the principles because you have already developed some of the required skills. If you are new to this type of work, don't consider yourself disadvantaged. You will develop the skills as you practice.

What are the skills? They are *inner* skills. They include an openness to non-materialistic thought and values; the ability to quiet the mind and enter the right-brain *Alpha-State;* the ability to focus inside and hold your attention on an inner object, usually an energetic feeling; the capacity for transcendental *Witness* consciousness, and more.

The deep healing you want, whether emotional or physical, can only come about through your deep participation. You need wisdom. You need to understand the rules of inner healing and not blindly apply a simplistic remedy. You need to go beyond the temptation of the quick-fix. You need to be an active participant; and you need an in-depth program that enables you to go deep into yourself, where negativity is held, in order to release it. This book attempts to present such a program in the most concise way possible. Most people remain ignorant of the basic rules of their emotional selves and mistreat and abuse themselves. Feelings are not cleared, but build and result in tragic life circumstances.

Many, if not all of us, are in pain, and don't know what to do about it. My sincere hope is that this book will reach those people, that they will see the Light and begin to earnestly work on themselves, because we are all one. If you are in pain, I am in pain. If you heal yourself, you heal me. Conversely, in working for the benefit of all, we heal ourselves.

*Emotional Clearing,* my first and previous book on the subject of emotional healing, was self-published in 1994 and subsequently released by Random House in 2000. It was based on a system of self-work I had developed over the years, derived from Eastern and Western psychological and philosophical principles. The original *Emotional Clearing* book was intended for spiritual seekers who came up against emotional issues as they worked on themselves. It was my contention that lasting advancement on the path to higher consciousness was not possible until the emotional levels had been resolved. Too often, we bypass the emotions in the name of inner growth; too often, genuine guidance is not available. We are continuing that emphasis in this present book, and possibly going further than before.

I have not published any follow-up books – as authors are usually inclined to do – until now, because I felt *Emotional Clearing* was a complete statement, not in need of revision or development. I did not feel there was anything else to be said, and I felt I could never equal the depth of the writing in another book. Besides, my goal was never to become a professional author – I wanted to work as a healer, counselor, and esoteric psychotherapist. Writing the book was my way of establishing credentials.

When I wrote the book, I had limited experience in testing the system on other people. With its publication, however, things changed. I immediately received correspondence from readers describing their success in working on themselves with the process, and also inquiring about personal counseling. I started working with clients, and after five years, when I felt I was ready, I began training others to act as *Emotional Clearing Facilitators.*

Now, after 25 years as an active professional counseling therapist in the field, I am publishing this new book on inner emotional healing. Times are changing dramatically, and I am hoping that a contemporary restatement of the work will reach new people and places. I am still concerned with emotional healing because I believe it is crucial to any wellness program, whether focused on psychological or physical health, as well as being essential on the inner path of consciousness development.

In this book, I have distilled my life's experience on the higher-consciousness path, combining it with insights gained from my counseling practice. I have tried to tell you everything I know about how to move forward with inner work and not get stuck on the feeling-emotional level, how to incorporate it with any spiritual path you may be on, and how to use the system as a *self-therapy* that can resolve any painful, traumatic issue you may have, without the need for outside help.

The interesting thing to me is that there have been practically no changes, modifications, or evolutions of the *Emotional Clearing Process* over the years. Everything I wrote then is still the way I understand and apply the system, both on myself and on others. I still see it prove itself everyday as a superlative method of inner growth – no changes are needed. The few minor aspects that have evolved over the years have been a matter of *emphasis*, not changes of content, in response to the needs of my clients as we have worked together.

For example, I have seen that the *Emotional Clearing* deep relaxation induction used to evoke the *Alpha-State* in preparation for processing feelings is unique, powerful, and highly beneficial in itself. At first its purpose, in my mind, was only to set the stage for emotional releasing, but now I have seen that it is valuable as a stand-alone technique, which can by itself bring about significant healings.

However, perhaps the most noteworthy development has been in my understanding of the importance of *Emotional Clearing* work and its range of usefulness. Experience with the process over the years has led to the realization that although it is primarily feelings and emotions we work with, the results obtained are by no means limited to that level. We experience clearing on the:

- **Feeling-Emotional level.**

- **Physical level,** since a large part of physical health issues are due to the overflow of inner negativity.

- **Mental-Behavioral level**, where compulsions, addictions, attachments, and unconscious, dysfunctional, ingrained, self-limiting patterns are outgrown.

- **Psychic level**, where energetic, Karmic influences are dissolved.

- **Spiritual level**, where feeling-based inner process work becomes the basis for transcendence of lower-self identification and activation of Higher-Self Witness consciousness.

In other words, it has become evident to me that a *feeling-based* personal practice naturally leads to the development of higher consciousness and realization of spiritual goals. I have found such an approach to be equal, if not superior to, any Yoga or Buddhist discipline with which I have been involved. The *feeling self* is what has been overlooked on the traditional paths, and its cultivation becomes the foundation for building a stable, integrated, fully functioning, evolved, aware, awake human soul. I would encourage you, therefore, to approach this work not merely as a means to get your feelings under control, or to feel better, but as a completely valid and unsurpassed pathway to enlightened personal evolution and genuine spiritual soulfulness.

Interestingly, I have learned from several sources that one of the important purposes of our incarnational journey on the three-dimensional Earth plane is to gain experience with *feelings and emotions -* to develop the capacity for, to learn how to manage, and to become enlightened, on a *feeling-emotional* level. Once we understand this, it can give us in our personal work on ourselves a renewed direction – a purpose. We don't necessarily need to cultivate extra-sensory abilities, or contact our past lives, or to have beautiful, other-worldly out-of-body experiences and visions to find fulfillment. We just need to face the conditions in front of us now, and realize that learning how to handle these conditions, *with all their negativity* – especially on the *feeling-emotional* level – is a prime reason we have incarnated, and that we are fulfilling a higher purpose by so doing.

The key to enlightened psychological work is to apply acceptance, presence, and detached witnessing to *what is* on the inner feeling level. This allows negativity to relax and dissipate. We will go into detail about how to accomplish this. On the contrary, if you mindlessly fight inner or outer negativity, it just gets stronger; negativity gets stuck exactly because it is consciously or unconsciously denied, rejected, resisted, and pushed away.

The methodology presented here is practically identical to the previous *Emotional Clearing* book. However, I have structured the discussion differently, in the hope of making it easier to immediately grasp and apply, and there are a few new elements. Part I is a stripped-down, quick-start guide that will enable you to begin effective emotional release work on yourself right away. Part II develops the discussion from a pragmatic, intellectual, psychological perspective without reference to esoteric concepts. When you are ready, Part III gets into the more advanced metaphysical aspects of the work.

The *Emotional Clearing* book, on the other hand, expands on several topics covered briefly here, especially on how Eastern spiritual practice and philosophy tie into Western psychological pursuits and has its own way of explaining the material that thousands of people have found beneficial. If you find yourself being drawn into the work, I therefore wholeheartedly recommend *Emotional Clearing*. It will give you another, more complete comprehension of what we are about.

If these introductory ideas resonate with you, you will find this work to be of immense, life-changing value. It was for me. Settle back, open your mind, and get ready to activate your *Feeling-Emotional Enlightenment Level.*

John Ruskan, 2020

# Foundational Principles

1. The subconscious is the cause of pain and suffering.

2. The judgmental, rejecting, make-wrong mind creates the subconscious.

3. The mind cannot heal itself or release the subconscious.

4. Healing and releasing occurs beyond the mind in the deeply relaxed right-brain *Alpha-State*.

5. Experiencing subconscious feeling energy from the *Alpha-State Witness* perspective releases it.

6. The *Emotional Clearing Process* goes beyond the mind and brings resolution.

# 1
# The subconscious is the cause of pain and suffering

*The Emotional Clearing paradigm: The cause of psychological dysfunction, depression, various mental/emotional disorders and self-limiting patterns of behavior is the containment of and unconscious defense against unreleased negative psychic-emotional feeling energy trapped in the subconscious body-mind.*

There is much talk these days about how to transform your life for the better. Often it is said that if you change your thinking, or beliefs, or just visualize what you want forcefully enough, your outer world will change accordingly. There is also discussion about feelings. We are encouraged to make an effort to avoid negative feelings, such as anger, and to cultivate positive feelings, such as love. The assumption is that by emphasizing the positive, whether it be positive thoughts, beliefs, visualizations, or feelings, the negative will be displaced and our quality of life will improve.

Deliberate cultivation of the positive can help to a certain limited extent, but those of us who have tried this simplistic approach long-term have come to the conclusion that it is not really workable for lasting fulfillment. If it was, complex schools of psychology would never have been invented.

The results obtained from simplistic cultivation of the positive will be inherently limited because such an approach does not touch the *core* of the problem. What's missing is an appreciation of the phenomenon known as the *subconscious*. Not taking it into account is the primary error made when trying to work on ourselves. The subconscious is the *core level* that determines our basic psychological make-up – if we are to be chronically dissatisfied, depressed, in poor health, and in general controls the quality of our lives.

Modern psychology can be said to have begun when the idea of the subconscious was first proposed by Freud and his associates. It was postulated that there existed irrational impulses, forbidden desires, neurotic complexes, traumatic memories, and self-limiting conditioned mind-sets on a level that the conscious mind was not aware of, and that these factors were instrumental in shaping sub-optimal human experience. The prevailing influence of the subconscious is one of the principles upon which humanistic Western psychology was founded, and that's why there has always been the emphasis on exploring and resolving the subconscious in psychotherapy.

But what is the subconscious? The formation of the subconscious is primarily due to the accumulation of unresolved negative feelings. Feelings have a natural cycle of building and dissipating. Humans have the capacity, however, of interrupting – or *suppressing* – a feeling before it has completed its natural cycle. When a feeling is interrupted, the energy of the feeling is not released but becomes stored within, pushed out of awareness, blocked, suppressed, unfinished and latent, relegated to what is called the subconscious. Most feelings are suppressed simply because they are dark and painful, and because we want to avoid them. The nature of the subconscious – sometimes referred to as the *pain body* – therefore becomes dark and painful, and that's why it is a major negative influence.

*The built-up negative feeling energy of the subconscious easily overrides your conscious will.*

Psychologists who recognize and study the subconscious estimate that it constitutes as much as 90% of our mind capacity. Have you ever been astounded with yourself and at a loss to explain why you acted irrationally in a certain situation? Or why you make the unfortunate choices you do? Or why you are attracted to the same wrong type of person, over and over, etc? These are all examples of subconscious influence overriding your conscious will.

Feelings are the main item that get stored in the subconscious, and feelings are composed of *energy*. As this negative feeling energy accumulates, it starts to act on us, coloring our perceptions, influencing our decisions, determining what kind of people we attract and are attracted to, even drawing negative experiences to us that correspond to the negativity trapped inside. And no matter how hard we try to do better – to not get angry, to be more loving, to find someone to love, to eat healthier, to exercise more, to be more understanding, to work hard and be a success – the negative keeps coming because the power of the subconscious easily overrules the conscious mind. It doesn't matter how hard you visualize or affirm positivity, prosperity, or good feelings, it's not going to change the subconscious, and that's what determines your experience.

Once you understand that negative subconscious feeling energy is responsible for your negative experience, and that the conscious mind is powerless to overcome it (much like the 12-Step affirmation of powerlessness), you are ready to begin serious work on yourself.

*It is the built-up negative feeling energy of the subconscious that determines your usual emotional state and the level of happiness you can tolerate.*

Is there any particular chronic, negative, painful emotion you can identify in your life? If so, it comes from an accumulation of that same feeling in the subconscious.

Suppressed feelings do not diminish over time, even over long periods. On the contrary, because we usually habitually suppress the same kinds of feelings, they tend to accumulate and get stronger over time. You try to keep pushing them out of awareness in the effort to feel better, but this does not permanently eliminate them. They keep building, eroding you away, jumping into awareness at the worst times, continually undermining lasting happiness.

One of the most insidious ways that suppressed feelings operate is that they will not allow you to maintain any significant level of happiness. Happiness doesn't reach you because the inner negative is not resolved and overrides any appearance of the positive, so that even when joy happens, you cannot feel it or maintain it or tolerate it for very long. Your capacity for spontaneous feeling decreases.

*It is the built-up negative feeling energy of the subconscious that keeps you blocked, unable to satisfy your drive for success or love.*

Often, we get the sense that we are "blocked" from achieving goals in career or relationships. We push ourselves relentlessly, believing it is only a question of effort, that if we just try harder we will eventually succeed or find lasting love. Many of the success programs on the market basically focus on giving you a pep talk and try to develop skills in order to make you into a success. But no matter how much enthusiasm you generate, or how much you improve your skills, you remain blocked, and your goal continues to elude you. You seem to go on bumping up against an invisible brick wall that keeps you at a certain low level of achievement.

If you have a reservoir of feelings of failure or loneliness, it will prevent you from attaining success in career or love because it is the dominating feeling in the subconscious that colors your experience. There is no room for fulfillment as long as there is that overriding negativity. Sometimes, you may come close to the goal, and you sabotage yourself, by acting in an inappropriate and self-destructive way. You may need to see this unconscious, self-undermining behavior clearly in order to really understand that it is you, yourself, who blocks you, who keeps you at your *comfortable low limit* of success.

Also significant is that your state of mind changes when suppressed feelings are cleared. You are not compulsive about achieving goals because you don't need them to make you happy. You are well-balanced, more content with what you have. You may find that it was not so much the goal you wanted, but the state of mind you thought the goal would bring. As a result, your goals become more reasonable and attainable.

*It is the built-up negative feeling energy of the subconscious that draws negative experiences to you.*

On the psychic inner planes, where feeling energy may be said to accumulate, the principle of *like attracts like* applies. As the feeling energy increases, it has instincts of its own, which is to merge with other similar energies. This is why, for example, an angry person will attract other angry people, and they will experience conflict.

You can extend this principle to include all of your experience. Everything you experience has been drawn to you by yourself, based on the principle of energetic attraction. The negativity you hold within attracts corresponding circumstances, and this becomes your life. Please understand that it is not your thoughts, or your beliefs that draws negative experiences to you. It is the built-up *energy* of the suppressed feelings of the subconscious that is responsible for continuing negative experiences. It is this suppressed energy that in fact *determines* your thinking or beliefs including your general emotional state.

The intention of the feeling energy in attracting similar energy is to perpetuate itself, but also to make itself known to the conscious mind, and to eventually exhaust itself. However, this in itself is not enough to clear negative feelings. It appears that until we gain conscious wisdom in handling feelings more effectively, we remain limited, confined as if in prison to a level of existence such as we see all around us, created by the collective subconscious, reflecting pain and ignorance. As we gain in wisdom, we start to manage our emotional experience correctly, and we approach higher levels of existence, joy, creativity and fulfillment.

*It is the built-up negative feeling energy of the subconscious that determines your state of physical health, including chronic disease, cancer, heart trouble.*

The built-up negative feeling energy of the subconscious is contained inwardly, in what could be called the *energy body*, where we feel emotions. It's important to realize that this energy is *toxic*. As it keeps accumulating, it starts to overflow into the physical body. We create our own personal toxic waste dump. Eventually, it manifests in the physical body as what is called disease.

It can take time for subconscious toxic energy to make itself known, possibly as long as what is now considered to be the normal life span. It may take forty to sixty years of continual unconscious suppressing to build the toxic energy to the point where it becomes life-threatening, and then we die. We have heard of references to other cultures and times where the lifespan has been hundreds of years. Are these just imaginary tales or could they represent a more normal kind of existence?

It's possible that as toxic energy continues to build in the subconscious over the course of a lifetime, not only do we experience disease, we experience pain with the disease, and when the time comes, we are likely to experience a painful death. I believe a certain balancing takes place before we leave the material plane. We have all seen or heard of people who have passed over peacefully, and those who have gone through an ordeal of pain. I don't believe this is accidental. If we have allowed pain to accumulate, if we have pushed it away into the subconscious, it may force itself upon us at the final exit.

Often, we contribute to the premature failure of the physical body by polluting it with nicotine, alcohol, poor food, or allowing ourselves to be exposed to environmental pollution. We appear to be helpless; we can't stop smoking, overeating, and so on. In New York City, my home base, it is astounding to me, at this point in time – especially with all the promotion there has been about the dangers of smoking – how many people I see smoking as I walk around on the streets.

The reason we can't stop polluting ourselves is because of the subconscious. Remember, *like attracts like*. Subconscious negative energy attracts polluted negative energy on the material plane. We are indeed helpless to reverse this trend until we start to work directly with the subconscious, releasing the negativity held there.

*It is the built-up negative feeling energy of the subconscious that creates and supports dysfunctional self-limiting behavior patterns.*

Much of psychological/psychotherapy work is concerned with exploring dysfunctional patterns of behavior, or *syndromes*, into which we unconsciously become locked and *act out*. These patterns and the subconscious motivation for them come directly from the suppressed subconscious.

For example, suppose you are suppressing and holding the energetic feeling of inadequacy. Since the feeling is mostly *unconscious*, trapped in the *subconscious*, you are likely to unconsciously attempt to *compensate* for the feeling by shows of bravado, or by being compulsive about always needing to be seen as the best. You may develop a compulsive drive for perfectionism or success. On a somewhat higher level, you may be obsessed with a compulsive urge for *significance*; you want to feel as if you are worth something, that you are valuable.

But the end result is that you can't relax in your work, you experience anxiety that you are always being judged and found lacking, you can't find satisfaction and stability, because in spite of any success you may achieve, the core feeling of inadequacy is not resolved. And then, the worst of it is that you unconsciously undermine your work, acting out, being driven by the uncontrollable instinct of the suppressed feeling energy of inadequacy to make itself known, attracting to yourself the very thing you seek to avoid.

*The subconscious is a huge energy drain.*

Suppressing feelings is a kind of fighting with yourself. It takes energy to maintain the fight, to suppress feelings, and to keep them suppressed. We are not usually aware of the amount of energy involved, but it takes its toll on us. We become chronically fatigued and depressed; we are often not at our best.

In contrast, when you are not consistently suppressing, when you adopt the mindset that is open, allowing all feelings to enter consciousness and complete their cycle, you feel relaxed all the time. You are not fighting, but simply *being present* with events as they unfold. This is all part of the *consciousness shift* that you are learning here.

*The subconscious is irrational.*

The subconscious is a huge reservoir of seething, tumultuous, irrational energies. When any particular type of feeling becomes habitually suppressed, it forms what used to be referred to in old-school psychology as a *complex*. The implication is that an entity of sort is created that continues to coexist with us on a shadow level, influencing and undermining our daily lives.

One of the curious yet troublesome qualities of this entity-complex is its absence of logical reasoning power. You, as a conscious ego, take for granted your logical mind that you use all the time. You may think you can reason with the subconscious, but that would be a mistake. The subconscious reacts in an illogical, emotional, knee-jerk fashion whenever it is activated.

For example, if we were to assume that a complex has been formed by a certain incident in the past, let's say when you were rejected by a sweetheart, all the trappings of that incident would tend to provoke you. If someone was wearing similar clothes, or you were in a similar place, or a similar song played on the radio when you were trying get close to a new sweetheart, you could feel irrational rejection.

*It is the built-up negative feeling energy of the subconscious that results in depression.*

Depression results when subconscious suppression has built to high levels. I have repeatedly seen in clients that depression lifts as we work to release suppressed feelings.

Suppression coincides with *inner blocking.* We cut ourselves off from parts of ourselves – the painful, suppressed, split-off feeling parts. The inner blocking occurs on a non-materialistic level of consciousness – what might be called the psychic, or emotional, or *feeling body* level. The blocking is so extensive that not only are we cut off from painful feelings, but that same blocking obscures positive feelings as well, including feelings of basic well-being. We feel lost, disoriented, alienated from ourselves, without purpose – in other words, depressed.

The energy required to keep feelings suppressed is a major factor in depression. We are not aware of this immense energy drain and how it contributes to the experience of depression. When depressed, we are always exhausted, energetically depleted, and not without good reason. Other important factors contributing to depression are poor nutrition and stress. We will explore depression in more detail in FEEL II.

2
# The judgmental, rejecting, make-wrong mind creates the subconscious

We need to look closely at how the subconscious is created. If we can understand and then reverse this process, we will be moving towards inner integration and emotional/physical health.

*Integration* is a term often applied to inner work. Before you start inner work, you are most likely in an unenlightened state, in the condition known as *fragmented*. Fragmentation means you unknowingly have split-off certain parts of yourself – in other words, certain feelings – abolishing them to their place in the subconscious through unconscious suppression. Integration is the opposite of this. Integration means to welcome those parts back and to become whole.

*Self-realization* is a term also used in consciousness circles. It has a similar meaning to integration. As you expand consciousness, you realize more of your true nature. This includes both elements of your Higher-Self, which is said to be composed of greater capacities; and your lower-self, the ego-mind, of which the subconscious is part. Realizing the subconscious means bringing the feelings held there into awareness, gently integrating them, moving into greater wholeness.

## the mind and pain

The mind is that part of ourselves which thinks and reasons. It's not clear exactly why, but in many ways we intuitively misuse the mind. Probably this has to do with our evolutionary growth. It is proposed by advanced metaphysical teachers that mankind is a work in progress, that we are steadily developing our capacities, until eventually we shall reach an indescribably elevated stage, merging with the *Absolute*. From this point of view, the purpose of life is the ever-onward expansion of consciousness, and realization of the deep fulfillment that accompanies it. We are now at the point of developing the mind, learning how to use it properly, and so we often misuse it as we make our way through life.

One of the important factors that contributes to this goal of consciousness expansion is *experience*. In fact, the need for objective experience is a central reason for our appearance on the material plane. We need experience in order to grow as well as meditative, reclusive times when we retreat from the outer world. But note that it is not necessarily pleasant experiences that advance inner growth; on the contrary, painful experiences can, and in fact do contribute more to growth than pleasant experiences.

*Pain occurs when the reality of* what is *conflicts with your conception of* what should be.

Our conceptions of *what should be*, most of which are unconscious, are usually ego-based, shallow, and defensive in nature. Our ego structure has become *crystallized* by our notions of *what should be*, and so whenever the reality of *what is* crosses our path, it jostles our crystallized, limited sense of self, and the result is what we call pain.

## the purpose of pain

For most of the world, pain is the only way that the limited ego can be loosened up, made less self-centered, the Heart opened, and evolutionary growth can occur. There is an unconscious higher part of ourselves that acts in our best interests and guides us into experiences that will stimulate our growth, and many times, it will bring us experiences we perceive to be painful. The more crystallized we are, the more pain we will need in order to grow.

If you can just accept pain without resistance, whenever it occurs, the pain will achieve its intention, and you will grow and move past the need for pain. But, the more you resist pain, the more it will come to you.

The mind, however, doesn't understand this. It's like that kid in the candy store. Not only that, it's like an undisciplined, wild, crazy kid in the candy store. It rushes around, trying candy after candy, being satisfied only briefly before it must rush over to the next new thing. All the while, its craving is for pleasure, excitement, taste, happiness, and it mindlessly turns away from – *resisting* – anything that makes it even vaguely uncomfortable.

If our *wisdom body* is undeveloped, we think that self-oriented happiness is all there is, and that the purpose of life is to get as much of it as possible. We fall into the habit of resisting any of our experience that is painful. This is the trap in which most of the modern world has ensnared itself, and one of the most consequential ways in which we misuse the mind.

## creating the subconscious

It is *we* who create the subconscious, by acting ignorantly and thoughtlessly. It is our *resistance* to painful experiences and feelings that interrupts their natural cycle and causes them to become suppressed, pushed out of awareness, trapped, relegated to that place we call the subconscious. From there they continue to act on us, shaping our destiny, creating the turmoil from which we seem helpless to escape.

What does it mean to resist experience? Resistance occurs in the mind, or *mental body*. Resistance is the equivalent of the inner act of rejection, of *making wrong*. We (the mind) judge something to be bad for us and then try to avoid it. We close down, shut down, we pull our energy inward becoming defensive and highly ego-motivated. The opposite to resistance is acceptance, tolerance, the mind-set that everything is OK, that we don't need to change anything, we can just coast with things as they are, and that we are *open* to anything that crosses our path.

What I am referring to here is primarily *feelings*. Resistance is most troublesome when applied to feelings. Feelings are where the pain is. That's what we want to avoid, that's what we push away. It is most important that you learn to see this tendency of the mind to resist feelings, and that you consciously replace resistance of your feeling self with *acceptance*. It is essential to cultivate acceptance in order to align with the evolutionary spirit, to reverse the trend of suppression, and to release already suppressed energies.

Inner resistance to uncomfortable, painful, or negative feelings is the same as *rejection* of the feelings. When you reject your feelings, you are saying "this is no good, I must be rid of it." This message of being no good goes deep into the subconscious, especially since we usually continue the barrage over the course of years. The self-condemnation takes its toll in a damaged sense of well-being and self-worth. Self-worth is that part of yourself that tells you "I have worth, I am worthy of respect, I respect myself, I am capable, confident, I can cope with the world." Continual negative self-statements to the contrary render you dysfunctional. I am talking about subtle feelings now. These feelings are just on the edge of consciousness. You may not be aware of them, but as you get familiar with yourself – as you expand your consciousness – they will start to become evident.

I can hear you saying "I don't care about expanding my consciousness – I just want to feel better." But that's the unenlightened attitude that results in pain. You are on the journey of consciousness evolution now, whether you know it or not. Quick fixes will not satisfy you any longer – literally. Once you enter the path, there is no turning back. The lamp has been lit, and mercifully, it will not be extinguished.

## 3
## The mind cannot heal itself or release the subconscious

Decades ago, Bill Moyers put out a book called *Healing and the Mind*. At the time, this was a step forward because it brought attention to the fact that healing in general is greatly influenced by factors other than physical. But strictly speaking, it's not the mind that heals; it's *going beyond the mind*.

The mind, or *mental body*, is that part of our individuality which thinks, reasons, plans, takes action, and from where conditioned behavioral responses originate. The mind is associated with the left-brain and the limited, lower-self ego. The common denominator of the various characteristics of the mind is that they all involve a sense of *doing*.

But these attributes of the mind, while essential for functioning in the world, are not what is required for psychological healing, or healing of the soul. It's true that a certain amount of mental, left-brain involvement is needed to get moving in the proper direction. We read books, we may get advice from counselors, we learn skills, but these resources are used correctly when they educate and point in the direction for healing, which is the right-brain, *feeling* mode of consciousness.

There are what may be called the *healing energies* of the body, and also of the Universe. They are one and the same; if you contact the inner healing force, you contact the Universal force, and vice-versa. These energies are very much akin to feeling. They respond to a feeling consciousness, that is, when the mind is relaxed and quiet, when you are body-centered, focused in the energy currents of the body, perceiving without thinking.

If you are to engage in psychological soul healing, you must learn to recognize and distinguish between left-brain thinking and right-brain feeling modes. You must learn how to engage feeling and switch off thinking. In our culture, this is a challenge in itself, because we are so totally indoctrinated with left-brain thinking that authentic right-brain feeling and functioning has practically become atrophied. Sometimes, we even try to feel through the mind, so convoluted our thinking has become. Just starting to function more in the right-brain feeling mode can spontaneously bring about inner balancing and restore health to a significant degree on the emotional and physical levels.

An argument can easily be made that the ruthless dominance of left-brain culture has directly resulted in the condition of the world today. Pollution, war, greed, can all be traced to the self-oriented, selfish, left-brain ego, fighting for more, more, more. Even the environmental crises we face can be seen as the Earth's reaction to the rampant negativity around us. But of course, such a holistic, shamanic viewpoint would be laughed at by the materialistic, limited, left-brained mindset of today.

Ancient cultures, in which the right-brain was more fully functioning, had access to realms of intuition along with deep experiential knowledge of the psychic worlds. This enabled them to control and maintain balance on the material plane and in the material physical body. We generally consider those civilizations to be less advanced than ours because they didn't have the gadgets we find so endlessly fascinating, but the truth is that we are now living in a dark age of the soul, an age where humanistic values, capabilities, and priorities are indeed scarce.

### thinking away bad feelings

In our modern left-brain society, we are often tempted to use the mind to control or eliminate negative feelings. We may believe that feelings are created by thoughts, and that if we can analyze our mental process and correct erroneous or distorted thinking, we can change our feelings.

*It's not distorted thinking that creates negative feelings. It's suppressed negative feelings that create distorted thinking.*

The large body of unreleased negative feeling energy stored in the subconscious is responsible for coloring your thoughts – how you perceive, the opinions you formulate, the incorrect and even irrational ideas you hold. According to your suppressed feeling energy, you perceive people, events, and circumstances to be reassuring or threatening, loving or hateful, pleasurable or painful.

Sometimes a thought can give rise to a strong negative feeling, but this happens only when there is a large amount of that feeling suppressed in the subconscious to begin with. For example, suppose you are a nervous type of person, easily frightened. If I ask you to close your eyes and think of yourself walking alone on a dark lonely road at night, surrounded by nothing but thick black forest, most likely all sorts of fearful feelings will jump into your awareness. This is because of suppressed fear in the subconscious.

If I asked the same of another person with no suppressed fear, but who was a dreamy, romantic type, they might add a full moon to complete the setting, and fully enjoy the rapturous solitude of the walk. Of course, they might also experience sadness that they were there without a love partner, as suppressed hurt in the Heart was stimulated. This is how subconscious feeling responds to thought, and how it can result in two different feeling experiences in two people from the same thought.

It's possible for you to still insist that you had the fearful reaction because you interpreted the suggestion in an undesirable, incorrect way. An advocate of the mind might say you held *irrational* fearful thoughts in your mind. If you saw it differently, and presumably more correctly, you would not have the fear: There have never been any wild animals in that area, no assaults have ever been made on people walking there at night, your fears are all just in your head, there is no real reason to be afraid. Furthermore, if you would only replace those fearful thoughts with thoughts of being safe, you would not experience the fear. For example, you might use an affirmation such as *I am completely safe at all times*, repeating it as you walked on the road and especially whenever you noticed any fear coming on.

If you tried all this, walking on the road, I think it could be confidently predicted that you would feel as if you had been dishonest with yourself, disvalidating your real feelings, and that it would only stir up resentment and more fear.

Sometimes seeing things differently can help. But in the long run, simply seeing things differently does not dislodge the suppressed subconscious, which accounts for how you see and feel in the first place. You may be able to talk yourself out of your feelings for a short time, but they will inevitably keep coming back to interfere with your happiness.

All this doesn't mean there is no place for the mind in inner work. We will use cognitive (meaning the way you see things) reasoning in our work; for example, in comprehending the philosophy of *acceptance,* or understanding how we are being motivated by negative feelings. But in our work, the cognitive aspect is only a preliminary. It sets us up to be able to process the negativity *on a feeling level* so it can release. The negativity will never release if you stay on the cognitive mental level.

The concept that incorrect thinking is primarily responsible for emotional distress and dysfunction, or that significant emotional health can be regained only by reshaping the contours of the mind denotes an intelligence with no real intimacy or experience with feelings; that doesn't distinguish between thought and feeling; that doesn't comprehend the most basic rules of the right-brain. In the mind approach to feelings, it's all about how to see things differently to overcome your problem and make you feel better. There is no notion of the need to uncover subconscious factors behind the pain, or that suppressed pain is the cause of the hardships you encounter, or even that pain can be beneficial if approached correctly. Pain is regarded as the enemy, to be anaesthetized away as quickly as possible instead of going to its core.

When operating in the left-brain ego-mind and trying to bring about healing, we engage on the dualistic mental level, trusting that mind power will bring change. But as we become more familiar with the workings of the human psycho-organism, we realize a deeper, more profound truth: That all effort of the mind is limited; that it can only have effect on the mental plane, and does not reach beyond to the feeling level to create something new and unknown; that it brings only horizontal movement, not vertical ascension; and that it often creates the exact opposite to what it intends because it stirs up contrary subconscious energies. The very activity of the mind affirms the limited ego-self, continuing the circumstances that contributed to the undesirable condition. Perhaps most importantly, the very activity of the mind prevents natural, innate healing forces from coming into play.

## reconditioning

Can you see that when you attempt to motivate yourself with positive thoughts, feelings, beliefs or visualizations, you are fighting yourself? You are resisting, trying to fight, or *recondition*, the negative subconscious part of yourself with the positive. This fighting in itself must be understood to ultimately not be in your best interests. Fighting is never the way to accomplish anything. Fighting very often makes your opponent *stronger*. Fighting is very likely to stir up the suppressed negative feelings so that they become active, *attracting to you* exactly what you are trying to fight, change, or avoid. But aside from the fighting itself, let's look at the first central concept about the subconscious that must be understood in order to have success in managing it:

*The subconscious cannot be reconditioned.*

While it may be possible to modify superficial behavioral habits with reconditioning practices, the nature of the subconscious is such that adding more of the positive will not alter the core negativity that is behind all serious psychological issues. All attempts at change, discipline, reform, substituting or reconditioning only incite the core negative subconscious and create a false personality, out of touch with its own deeper self, highly susceptible to backlash as the subconscious attempts to make itself known by attracting negative, undesirable events.

Reconditioning has been a central emphasis of the *New Age*, and may be the main factor that distinguishes it, in a negative way, from more serious psycho-spiritual disciplines such as *Yoga* and *Buddhism* as well as classic humanistic psychology. The *New Age* has been captivated by the same erroneous cognitive concept we have discussed. It blithely assumes that you just need to "change your thinking, change your life." It assumes that what you think determines what you experience. While there is a grain of truth in this viewpoint, as I have discussed, it is the power of suppressed negative subconscious feeling energy, not your thoughts, that draws events to you, and even determines your thinking. This subconscious feeling energy simply cannot be changed by attacking it with "positive" thoughts and feelings.

Similarly, there has also been the same kind of naive, ill-founded emphasis on "beliefs." It has been proposed that we create our life experience because of the "beliefs" we harbor in the subconscious, such as "I am not worthy." Reprogramming of the undesirable belief then may take the form of using positive affirmations to bombard the subconscious in the attempt to displace or change the old belief. This approach may have some very minimal value if there is not substantial subconscious negativity stored away, but it just cannot affect the deep core negativity that results in the serious issues with which most of us are contending, and is a misapplication of the principle of affirmation.

Beliefs are created by suppressed core negativity, not the other way around, and it's the core negativity that attracts negative experiences to you, not the beliefs per se. You can't get rid of that core negativity by simply affirming and repeating to yourself that it does not exist. Such a misguided psychological principle has never been part of classic psychology, and has only come into vogue lately. Core negativity becomes known to us as feelings and emotions. As you release those trapped feelings, your "beliefs" change spontaneously, and so does your life experience, but you can't touch that core negativity with efforts of the mind.

Reconditioning has been the mainstay of old-school hypnotherapy, which takes advantage of the suggestibility of the relaxed *Alpha* state to attempt repatterning of the subconscious. For example, if you had a difficult experience in childhood that appears to be still affecting you, you would attempt to visualize, and repattern, the memory with a favorable outcome. This does not work because negativity stored in the subconscious cannot be reconditioned – it must be released.

Once you understand that negative subconscious feeling energy is responsible for your negative experience, you are ready to begin serious work on yourself. After this negative energy is released, undesirable conditions automatically drop away and positive conditions take their place, perhaps with a minimal amount of positive thinking or visualizing, which will be effective now that the negative subconscious is not interfering.

## thinking and feeling

Let's look more closely at the difference between left-brain thinking and right-brain feeling. Suppose you lost your job and are stressed out. I ask you how you feel about that. You reply,

"There are just no jobs in this lousy town."

True, you are expressing dissatisfaction, but you have not really answered my question. You have twisted your feelings through the mind, and made them into a thought. Not only that, you reached an irrational conclusion, probably because of your stress. And even if there are no jobs in the town, you are blaming the town, and not taking responsibility for your situation. Blaming is a favorite ploy of the mind. I ask you again how you feel about not having a job:

"I tried a dozen leads last week, and nothing worked out."

Now, you're getting even further from the feeling, and into self-pity, another characteristic of the mind. It turns out there are jobs, just none for you. The mind has defended itself even more from the feelings by distorting and wallowing in the past. Of course, I might switch to a mind-based intervention pep talk, and ask you to reframe the situation by realizing there is just not a job for you *yet*, but this probably wouldn't fly too well. So I'll ask you again, how do you *feel* about that?

"I really don't know what to do. I'm thinking about moving up to Des Moines."

Now, you have switched to a mind-based behavioral-reactive mode, telling me what you might *do* as a response to the predicament. Perhaps moving away is a favorite way your mind deals with problems. At this point, it seems clear that you just do not function well on a feeling level. You don't understand what I'm asking. This doesn't mean you don't have feelings, you just can't connect to them and so, it is safe to assume, you are not really feeling them directly – you are suppressed. But suppose you were to respond to the question by simply saying,

"I'm scared and angry."

Now, there's no doubt that you are not dragging your feelings through the mind. You are in touch with your feelings, not blaming, not acting out, most probably feeling them acutely, the first step to resolving them.

*The mind must let-go for healing.*

The general principle to understand is that the mind must *let-go* of its normal mode of thinking, ruminating, clinging, protecting, accumulating, becoming, blaming, and *doing* in order for authentic healing to occur. But the problem is that the left-brain mind doesn't know how to let-go, and almost does not have this capacity. That's the nature of the mind, and it is difficult to teach it otherwise. This predicament is basic to all paths to consciousness, spiritual realization, and true happiness. The teacher is trying to teach the mind of the student how to do away with itself, or at least quiet itself down. Note, however, that if your goal is only to get the new Mercedes, then the left-brain mind is essential to planning, calculating, and striving. It is only when you start to expand your awareness of the possibilities of life that transcending the mind becomes of interest.

But if you want to let-go, here's another strategy that can be helpful: Don't focus on changing the mind, focus on bypassing (going beyond) the mind by *developing* the right-brain feeling center. This can save you from, or at least put off, the hair-pulling Zen effort of yourself trying to dislodge yourself. Work on the feeling level. What is that?

The right-brain feeling center is concerned with softness, with the Heart, with art, with the feminine archetype, with nature. A walk in the woods or trip to the beach is a right-brain experience. It's better if you're not thinking about the stock market as you tread on the leaves or bake in the sun, but even if you are, you're moving in the right direction. How about cooking a meal and putting feeling into it? Playing with your pet? Or your child? Have you ever played a musical instrument, or practiced a visual art? There you go – you just need to make time for it. Get reconnected. The Source – what we are seeking in the end – starts with the feeling center.

4
Healing and releasing occurs beyond the
mind in the deeply relaxed *Alpha-State*

*Accessing the deeply relaxed, altered-state, right-brained mode of
awareness that we call Alpha puts us in touch with subconscious
suppressed material. Left-brain functions – thinking, analyzing,
willfulness, doing – must yield to right-brain functions – feeling,
intuiting, surrendering, being – for the process to proceed.*

As I worked on myself over the years, I developed the capacity of
entering an altered-state at will, in which it is easy to contact deeper
"subconscious" levels. Perhaps I am biased, but because the altered-
state has been so meaningful to me as a means to contact and heal
myself, I tend to believe it will also be invaluable to others who seek
to work on themselves. It is a foundational element of the *Emotional
Clearing Process*. I see it as a prerequisite, moreover, for any type of
inner healing or even creative work, and I tend to view psychology
professionals as well as their clients who are ignorant of the potentials
of this mind-shift to be operating at a disadvantage.

What am I talking about? It's the ability to shift into the right-
brain *Alpha-State*. Normally as we go about daily life, we are operating in the so-called *Beta* range, characterized by a brain-wave
frequency of 14 to 30 *hertz* or cycles per second. *Beta* activity corresponds to *left-brain* activity: thinking, analyzing, reasoning, planning,
judging, worrying, and above all, *doing*. It's essential for functioning
in the world, but the problem is that if we are familiar primarily or
only with left-brain *Beta* activity, we are far from realizing our creative potential; we are unbalanced; we do not access essential parts of
ourselves, and do not evolve. The mind activity to which I have been
referring in previous pages is associated with left-brain *Beta* activity.
In order to let-go of the mind, therefore, we want to downshift out of
*Beta* level brainwave activity, and cultivate right-brain *Alpha-State* capacity.

As you consciously shift to the *Alpha-State*, brainwaves slow
down to the range of 8 to 13 hertz, or even deeper to the *Theta* range.

The slowing down of the brainwaves means that the functions of the left-brain mind are put on hold: There is, first of all, a sense of *deep relaxation*, in contrast to the somewhat hyperactivity that characterizes the *Beta* state. Thinking slows down, and consciousness naturally realigns to the right-brain feeling level, empowered to perceive the deep energetic subconscious, accessing a natural, spontaneous healing mode. Ordinarily the busy mind obscures the subconscious, but with the mind quiet, you are able to see and feel deeply into the subconscious, into the core feelings behind any disturbing emotion or circumstance, accessing and releasing them.

The movement is from *thinking* to *feeling*; from *doing* to *being*; dropping all sense of *striving* and coming into *the moment*. There may still be some thought present, but the *Alpha* right-brain feeling consciousness takes priority, and thinking moves to the background. Qualities of meditative mindfulness are accessed: detached yet alert self-observation from *the Witness* viewpoint; dispassionately noticing one's present, inner experience. The right-brain *Alpha-State* is essential in our work. We use it to access the subconscious and facilitate healing, which occurs easily and naturally on this level. Feelings are processed in the deeply relaxed *Alpha-State*, where brainwaves slow down and the mind becomes quiet.

An *Alpha-State* excursion can take anywhere from one minute to an hour, depending on your intent. Just going to the *Alpha* level in itself is deeply healing, as well as inherently enjoyable. This relaxed altered-state will give you considerable relief from superficial stress, and initiate healing on the emotional and physical levels. Your emphasis, depending on your needs, may be simply to bring yourself into *Alpha*, to give yourself the experience of the healing energies that are spontaneously invoked in this deeply relaxed state. This is to be considered a valuable, complete experience in itself. You need not always be set on pursuing emotional content.

### entering alpha

In all the FEEL levels you will begin the *Emotional Clearing Process* by self-inducing an altered *Alpha-State*. This is achieved by assuming a relaxed sitting position, either upright or reclining, closing your eyes, dropping any sense of efforting, coming into the moment, and working with a simple conscious breath. What you are essentially doing is entering an altered-state experience. You can think of it as a kind of *hypnotic meditative trance*, but I don't want to scare you with that terminology. There's nothing to be afraid of; all you are doing is relaxing deeply. You will never lose conscious control of yourself.

What's important to understand is that when you begin processing work, you are shifting out of your normal mindset. You are still, with eyes closed. Your body is relaxed and still. You are making an effort to *let-go* – to stop the mind from jumping around as it normally does. You are concentrating, focusing inward. This is a skill – you may have difficulty at first – but you must understand that the ability to enter an altered *Alpha-State* is vital on the path of inner work, and you will improve as you practice.

The key mechanism we use to induce *Alpha* is breathwork. This will be described in more detail in each FEEL section, but to start with, it can just mean breathing smoothly and easily, keeping your focus on the breath, letting the breath relax you and take you deeper. When feelings come up, you shift your focus onto them.

It's helpful to remember that the *Alpha-State* is characterized by a sense of *deep relaxation*, a quieting of mind activity, and a gentle inner focus. Any time you shift into this state and experience a *relative* sense of relaxation from your immediately preceding mind state, you can assume that you have entered *Alpha*, or are at least moving in that direction. As you keep practicing, your capacity to go deeper will develop.

Although the overall effects of the *Alpha-State* are highly beneficial, there is an aspect to it that you should be aware of and on guard against. In *Alpha*, you become susceptible to suggestion. This is because the *Beta* mind normally acts as a critical filter for perceptions. With this filter relaxed, you tend to uncritically take in whatever is presented to you. This characteristic can be used for both beneficial and malicious purposes. However, my stance is that even attempting to use beneficial suggestion in order to heal is misguided; it will not change or recondition trapped subconscious negativity.

Deliberate malicious programming of the mind is another matter and is something going on all around you. When you watch TV, you drift into *Alpha*. You become susceptible to anything you see. You take it in, it becomes part of your unconscious belief system, and it rules you. You become "programmed." In your use of *Alpha*, be careful to never expose yourself to programming or external stimulation of any sort. Attention is to be directed inward; *Alpha* capabilities are used only for positive purposes.

### difficulties

If you have obvious difficulty entering *Alpha*, your approach needs to be modified. Activating the right-brain with appropriate activities will get you moving in the right direction. You may need to reappraise your lifestyle, carving out more time to relax. You can work regularly with the breath. Your skills will develop.

It's common to experience difficulty in trying to focus the mind. Your mind will jump around, from thought to thought, with perhaps strong feelings accompanying them. This is typical for both new practitioners and also experienced practitioners of meditative disciplines. Don't be discouraged. You can do meaningful work even though your mind is not completely subdued. Just keep on, and you will improve with time.

In today's world, a major impediment to cultivating right-brain capacity is the absolutely rampant addiction to electronic devices. It seems literally everyone has their nose stuck in a cell phone at every minute. The obvious conclusion to be inferred from this is that, deprived of constant external electronic left-brain mental stimulation, severe anxiety is experienced. The suggestion to put the phone down, close your eyes and look inward is probably going to be difficult if not impossible for many people. It's all the more tragic in that no one appears to realize the extent of their addiction.

5

# Experiencing subconscious feeling energy from the *Alpha-State Witness* releases it

*Bringing subconscious suppressed energy into consciousness will affect the release. The release is caused by experiencing the feelings – not necessarily or primarily by expressing the feelings. Experiencing completes the cycle, and the energy is exhausted.*

The *Emotional Clearing Process* is not analytical; it is an experience – the experience of the suppressed subconscious in *Alpha*. It is primarily through total conscious acceptance of *what is*, on the feeling level, that you self-facilitate the experiencing, and allow change to occur spontaneously.

The reason any feeling does not complete its natural cycle, thereby releasing and dissipating, is that it has not been *experienced* fully and properly. The problem is not that the feeling has not been *expressed*, as psychology has sometimes proposed – it is that the feeling has not been properly *experienced*. In this work, we gently approach the subconscious and deliberately experience feelings that were never properly experienced when they first occurred.

But don't fall into the trap of dreading the idea of experiencing suppressed feelings. As you learn the technique and see what it's like, it will be something you will want to do. After entering a deep *Alpha-State* relaxation and activating *the Witness*, the inner meeting with suppressed feelings is easy and fulfilling. The *Witness* is intrinsically joyful and you are lifted above the negativity. You will experience contact with long-lost parts of yourself as a joyful reunion.

This understanding can make for a dramatic revision in how you approach your feelings. When you unconsciously try to avoid and forcefully change your feelings, substituting what you perceive as positive for negative, the message you send to the subconscious is that it is not OK as it is – that it must shape up to meet your agenda. You become opposed to yourself, rejecting yourself, fighting yourself because the subconscious is you. Nothing good can come from this adversarial posture.

But what if your intention was to recognize and understand the subconscious, to welcome it into conscious awareness, a little at a time, treating it and yourself gently, just being present with whatever feelings came forward. Doesn't that sound like it could lead to reconciliation and wholeness? In following such an approach, you move towards the ultimate fulfillment you seek.

## witnessing

Aside from the basic right-brain *Alpha-State* shift, *witnessing* is perhaps the most important element in successfully working on a feeling level. Witnessing is the key that takes you fully beyond both the feelings *and* the mind. We will explore the metaphysical state of witnessing in detail later in this book. To introduce the concept, however, I will explain a few things:

Normally you are *identified with* feelings. To witness a feeling means to break the sense of identification, to step back, to detach, to watch without an agenda, with a sense of *choiceless awareness*. You watch, but you don't have an opinion. Or if you can't get past having an opinion, you witness your opinion along with the feeling. There is always a stepping back, a detaching, a realization that you may have feelings as well as thoughts but you are not the feelings or thoughts; you are something greater – you are *the Witness*. Regarding painful inner feelings, you watch and *allow* the feelings but remain impassive to them. You *surrender* to the experience; you allow it without needing or attempting to change it. You understand that dropping ego-based interference with feelings as they are is necessary to complete the cycle of the feeling.

We have been discussing how activating the right-brain feeling center will lift you above being trapped in the left-brain mind, and how it is of the utmost importance to connect to your feeling self. But once you start consciously connecting to feelings, you want to be sure you are not going to be undesirably influenced by them. You want to maintain a level-headed, objective perspective. You want a strategy on how to handle the feelings. This is the function of witnessing.

When you are in witness mode, beyond the mind, another important factor kicks into your healing process. There is a transcendent healing power in the universe, and it will enter and bring resolution wherever needed, to both inner feelings and outer circumstances, now that you have put aside personal efforting. This is the same as the spiritual healing that has been available since time immemorial, but you don't have to tie it to any mainstream religious cosmology. Moving into *Alpha, witnessing*, and in effect, *surrendering* to *what is* on an inner, feeling level, allows this impersonal cosmic force to enter and bring about spontaneous change that our little ego-based minds could never conceive of.

If you are not comfortable with the notion of a transcendent presence, don't fret. Your work can proceed quite well without conscious recognition of it but at some point, perhaps as you approach FEEL III, I think it likely you will start to become aware of this cosmic influence.

## non-doing

How are we to enter *Alpha*, go beyond the mind, shift to *the Witness*, and access universal healing powers? The first step can correspond to the concept of *non-doing*. We are so wrapped up in *doing* that it is impossible to slow down, to just basically relax. We vaguely realize we are stressed from the continual pressure *to do*, to perform, but are unable to stop. We have lost the essential capacity to sit and simply do nothing.

In the left-brain ego-mind we are naturally inclined to believe that *doing* is what we need. We believe that we need to *do* better and more effectively to bring about healing. Shifting into the non-doing *Witness* brings about the healing.

6

# The Emotional Clearing Process goes beyond the mind and brings resolution

*The 5 steps go beyond the mind, accessing universal healing energies, providing a working matrix for the resolution of the suppression.*

## 1. DEEP RELAXATION

### BODY LEVEL / GROUNDING FUNCTION

Deep Relaxation, or bringing brainwaves to the *Alpha* level or lower, is a precondition to the *Emotional Clearing Process*. Entering *Alpha* coincides with the movement of consciousness from the left-brain, through the body to the right-brain, and ultimately, *the Witness*. As left-brain thinking slows down, it ceases to interfere with right-brain feeling, and suppressed feelings emerge into consciousness, where they can be released and resolved by the remaining four steps. Deep Relaxation is facilitated by sophisticated altered-state techniques that include coming into the moment, breathwork, and body focus points.

## 2. AWARENESS

### INTELLECTUAL LEVEL / WISDOM FUNCTION

Basic awareness of the inner feeling motivating a certain behavior or apparently "caused" by some other person or event in the outside world; recognition that the feeling has been suppressed but continues to motivate you into non-productive behavior, or that the feeling has been projected onto the outside event, even attracting the event; taking responsibility, without blame, for the feeling and the event; "owning."

## 3. ACCEPTANCE

### MENTAL LEVEL / BEHAVIORAL FUNCTION

Ceasing resistance to the feeling. Normally, feelings are unconsciously blocked from full awareness by the mental attitude of resistance, resulting in self-rejection on the feeling level. When you become aware of how you normally resist feelings, your experience changes. Self-acceptance is awakened leading to self-love, and the gate to direct experience of feeling is opened. The concept of acceptance is a key part of the *Emotional Clearing Process*. As long as you continue to unconsciously resist, the feeling cannot be integrated. Resistance is what caused the feeling to be suppressed in the first place. Acceptance is made easier if you understand how feelings have been projected; how the other is not really responsible for your perception. Working with acceptance begins to open you to the transcendental aspects of the work.

## 4. DIRECT EXPERIENCE

### FEELING / EMOTIONAL LEVEL

Entering the feeling center or being in the moment with the feeling; "processing" the feeling. Feelings are allowed "to be" without resistance, analysis, or blame. Any of these mind-sets takes you out of the feeling center and impedes integration of the feeling. Feelings are experienced on the body level until the energy is cleared. There is no need to outwardly "express" the feeling. Processing takes place in *Alpha*, modulated by the breath. You experience feelings in the present, including present feelings about past events. If images or fantasies spontaneously occur, you are encouraged to let them unfold in *Alpha*, to experience the feelings evoked, and to acknowledge them. If no feelings spontaneously emerge in *Alpha*, you may go back to a certain event, or introduce a certain thought, or work more with the breath in order to access feelings. You should give adequate attention to body awareness, and to all body sensations emerging in *Alpha*, breathing into them.

Care should be taken not to contend with more emotional material than can be comfortably integrated, but there is also reliance on the Higher-Self ultimately guiding the session and revealing only what is appropriate. Negative feelings and emotions are the prime focus of the experience.

## 5. WITNESSING

### TRANSCENDENTAL / SPIRITUAL LEVEL

In this step, your position becomes that of *the Witness*, simply watching feelings from a detached, passive viewpoint as they go through the various stages of integration. *Witness* consciousness is a psycho-physiological altered-state that can be brought about by certain esoteric techniques. It can be thought of as corresponding to a Higher Power, using whatever concept for this that may be appropriate for you. Having accepted feelings as they are, you turn their resolution over to the Higher Power. Personal agenda is set aside; faith and trust prevail. The Higher Power transpersonal intelligence guides the process of integration, resulting in internal catharsis and unexpected creative external change. Adjustment occurs spontaneously, without conscious control.

You will note that each step is associated with a different level of consciousness. As you work on yourself, it can be helpful to stay aware of the various levels, or *planes*, so you know where you are at any moment: Now, you're functioning primarily on the body plane; now, the feeling plane; now the mind, or mental plane, etc. Your consciousness can function on any of the planes, and keeps shifting between them in the normal course of the day. As you become conversant with the planes, you set the stage for their development.

The evolution of consciousness is concerned with raising your awareness to the higher planes. If you are predominately centered in the body, or material plane, you are a brute. If you have no body awareness at all, however, you are ungrounded and cut off from yourself. If predominately on the feeling plane, you have no common sense or willpower. If you are predominately in the mind or intellect, you have no Heart, especially if the transcendental plane is unawakened. If the transcendental plane is unawakened, you have no conscience, inner guidance, higher vision, or stability. Balance is required. The process engages all the planes so you can bring into balance those parts that are lagging behind. As you work on yourself, notice if you have trouble on any particular plane and then devote time to developing it.

In the rest of this book, we will get into an expanded discussion of the foundational principles covered in this section, including fascinating case studies, practical details and esoteric techniques on how to apply the *Emotional Clearing Process* for emotional rebirth and transcendence into higher consciousness. There is an abundance of information here and you want to be careful to avoid overloading yourself. Go at your own speed, with what's comfortable for you. You can start work with only FEEL I, without having finished the rest of the book. When you are ready, the next level will be waiting. My intention is to create a reference manual that you will go to for years to come. The presentation is divided into several sections in order to slowly activate your *Feeling-Emotional Enlightenment Level:*

**FEEL 0**: Ignorance of the fundamental rules of the emotional self. How you self-reject and create the negative subconscious.

**FEEL I**: A quick-start, streamlined, basic practice for emotional healing that you can easily learn and apply to any issue.

**FEEL II**: Going into psychological subtleties. Becoming psychologically enlightened and articulate. A deeper level of understanding. Psychological tools. Expanding your feeling vocabulary.

**FEEL III**: Transcendental. Getting out of the mind. Altered state work. Advanced Energetic Techniques. The importance of *Witnessing*. Feelings-based work as the foundation for the shift to higher consciousness.

# The Stream

There's a stream running through the woods. It has lovely, clear water gently flowing, guided by the banks on either side. There are places where the water flows smoothly, and places where there are naturally occurring eddies, or swirling energies. All in all, the stream forms a living, breathing, bubbling, constantly varied energetic entity happily expressing itself in the material world.

At one point, a tree has fallen across the stream. Debris has collected around the fallen tree, obstructing the flow of the moving water. You see the water accumulating, and notice it is creating a problem. There is flooding of adjacent land and stagnation. You would like to try to correct the problem. You talk it over with a forestry expert. He says to just take a bucket and bail out the accumulated water.

You try it, and you find that this idea, to a certain extent, works. You spend hours bailing the water from the upstream side of the tree and dumping it on the downstream side. But it's taking too long, and the water keeps building up at about the same rate as you are bailing.

You go to another expert. He says to not bother with bailing; just install a pump to draw off the water in front of the blockage. You try it, and this idea works too, but you find that the pump requires maintenance and electricity. Finally it occurs to you that if you could just remove the fallen tree the problem would be genuinely solved.

You go back to the experts and tell them about your idea. They say it would be great if it could be done, but the tree is too heavy to move. But you are not sure about this, and for the first time, you doubt the experts. You are jarred into starting to think for yourself. You think, for example, what if you were to cut the tree into manageable sections?

The water accumulating and stagnating represents the trapped negative energy you carry around. The bucket and the pump represent many of the suggestions you will find as you look for solutions to the dilemma of human existence, even those proposed by the "experts." These methods may appear to work for a while; they may lessen the congestion, and if you are relatively unfamiliar with the technical side of the human psychological system, you may even find them useful. Perhaps they all serve in that they provide some support for you, where you are at, until you are ready for the next level. But they will not provide the complete healing you seek.

What are these methods? In brief, any self-improvement system or therapy that does not recognize, address, and intend to remove the subconscious inner debris that has fallen across and blocks the free-flowing stream of your being; any quick-fix system that tells you that you can change your inner experience merely by changing or reconditioning your thoughts, feelings, beliefs, or memories, substituting "positive" for "negative," or by visualizing what you want; any system that would have you give away your power to an external authority.

So, at a certain point, you will become dissatisfied with any method of merely bailing out the water. You will set your sights on removing the tree. Then, you are ready for this book, and the deep, authentic work it will lead you to. Your experts are not entirely incorrect when they say the tree is too heavy to move. For the average person, with average knowledge, time, capacity, and resolve, this may tend to be the case, and that's why the world is as it is. But if you approach it correctly, with enlightened guidance, and are willing to concede that this endeavor is worthy of your full attention and dedication, and you are willing to recognize that major work like this takes time – then you will succeed. But probably, you will only arrive at this point after you have experienced major distress. If things are rolling along not too badly, there is no reason to make the effort to wake up and break out of the limited mindset that is the norm for most of the world.

Perhaps you are not particularly aware of the build-up of negativity within. You see it all around, you see it explode and you feel that you are being dragged down. You feel helpless. But you don't know why.

*You experience huge negativity outside because of the build-up of trapped negativity inside.*

And, the only way you can really fight the "outside" negativity is by going inside. And, when you go inside, the most important level of inner experience that you must address are what we call *feelings and emotions*. Feelings and emotions are how the inner negativity makes itself known to us. In order to release inner negativity, therefore, we must work on a feeling level. Many would try to avoid or discount the importance of feelings. That is the prevailing attitude in today's left-brain, materialist, goal-oriented, ego-driven world, but that's why we are in trouble.

The *Emotional Clearing* program is a way to handle this distress, to heal inner disharmony, and to grow and evolve instead of stagnating in the face of life's experiences. It consists of both a psychological philosophy and a practical inner process that can be applied when difficult experiences arise.

These difficult experiences happen everyday to us all. They range from minor inconveniences, frustrations, and unsatisfying interactions to major disappointments, loss, personal challenges, and emotional pain. Frequently, we find ourselves confronted with ongoing negative circumstances from which we seem to be unable to break free. Such experiences are difficult because of the distressing feelings they evoke. Therefore, working with feelings becomes our central concern. When we refer to *inner work*, we generally mean feelings work.

In order to work with feelings, you need to understand some things about them. It's not enough to blindly apply a simplistic technique that promises you instant relief. The more you understand, the better will be the results you get when you work with the feelings. Knowledge is power.

# Feeling-Emotional Enlightenment Level 0
# Disvalidation

*How you deny your true feelings and create the subconscious.*

You can be intelligent, a college grad, a Ph.D., an expert in your field, successful, popular, attractive, wealthy, healthy (for now) – or not. It has nothing to do with your *Feeling-Emotional Enlightenment Level*.

Your FEEL is the measure of what you know about the world of feelings. More importantly, how you operate on the level of feelings. Do you have feelings? Do you know what it means to allow for them? If you do, you tend to be flexible; if not, you tend to be brittle.

Feelings are what make us human. Of course, intelligence is a human attribute as well, but either without the other is a tragedy. In the world today, there are powerful sinister forces that operate against the liberation of feelings, that would like to keep you locked up in the world of painful negative feelings, because that's what breeds selfishness, distrust, conflict, and the backward evolution of humanity.

FEEL 0 is characterized by the absence or disregard of feelings, and the rule of the mind. This manifests in *denial of* and *resistance to* feelings. Denial and resistance are usually unconscious. We are not aware that we are mismanaging our feeling experience, which is the same as our life experience. We mismanage life, and hurt ourselves; then we think that "shit happens."

Shit happens because you are operating at FEEL 0.

## handling feelings

When difficult or painful feelings arise, there are basically two ways to handle them:

- You can *disvalidate* the feelings with denial, resistance, blame, and other subversive, self-defeating tactics which we all seem to intuitively understand and have at our immediate, eager disposal. You fall back deeper into ignorance and distress.

- You can *validate* the feelings and move forward to the next stage, which is to productively work with the feelings. To validate, you recognize that something important is happening which cannot be brushed aside, and you devote time and informed effort (what you are learning here) towards resolution.

What sometimes happens, however, is that part of us wants to move forward, so we validate feelings and start working on them, but another part does not fully get on board with the program and keeps resisting. In fact, you can expect this to happen. You need to keep constantly vigilant for the yes – no conflict that will begin as soon as you think about doing serious inner work. It's just a matter of being conscious of it, and then putting aside the part that continues to deny, resist, and disvalidate.

## feelings interrupted

As we have discussed, when feelings are disvalidated and not handled correctly, they don't finish their natural cycle of building and dissipating. The energy of the feeling does not release, but gets trapped inside where it builds and festers and influences you more than you realize. It colors the way you perceive experience. You react irrationally, alienating those close to you. It drives you towards goals that are counterproductive to your well-being. In the extreme, the trapped negative energy inside actually attracts negative circumstances, ranging from negative people, failure, violent accidents, and so on. This condition is the basic problem with which we are faced and the starting point of FEEL work.

We start with the premise that *feelings* that have accumulated and become trapped inside are the primary cause of psychological distress *and* outer conflict. As you resolve those feelings, the outer starts to change spontaneously and miraculously in accord with what is best for you. There is no need to struggle to bring what you consider to be the positive into your life. I have seen this happen countless times in myself and others.

## changing the outer

A favorite way to disvalidate negative feelings is by trying to change outer circumstances. We try to manipulate things around us in order to feel better. This is an instinctive, and not an unreasonable response. If we are hungry, we look for food to satisfy feelings of hunger. If we are lonely, we look for a mate to alleviate feelings of loneliness. However, with feelings that have become trapped and built-up inside, this approach does not work.

If you are hungry, eating a big meal will probably satisfy you. But if you have trapped feelings of loneliness inside, looking for and finding the perfect mate or surrounding yourself with friends will not satisfy the inner loneliness, although it may appear to at first. If you have trapped feelings of inadequacy, aggressively chasing after success and recognition, however you may define it, will not in the long run fix those feelings. You don't usually realize this. You assume that you only need to create the right conditions in the outer world – to acquire the right *things* – and then the painful inner feelings, whatever they are, will disappear. You don't yet understand that you've got it backwards:

*The inner creates the outer, not vice-versa as you assume; and inner feelings can be resolved without needing to change the outer.*

It is not easy to explain in psychological terms why trapped, built-up feelings are not resolved by changing the outer – by achieving what we think will make us feel better. We just know that this is the way the human soul operates. We will try to go deeper into this in the more philosophical final parts of this book.

But when we finally realize this truth, it can be said that we have attained an important beginning foothold on the path to illumination. We realize how we have been spending much of our life force in useless activity – activity that we think will make us happy when it has never had the potential to do so.

At that point, we are ready for serious inner work – we start thinking about how to move the tree. Often, this realization does not come until our later years, when we finally see the light – that inner pain is not going to go away just by rearranging the outer.

Being motivated by trapped inner feelings can lead to *compulsive* behavior. We feel the pressure of the trapped feelings, but no matter what we do or attain on the outside, the feelings do not go away. We become confused, despondent, fixated on getting, changing, acquiring, manipulating, controlling and protecting in order to be happy. In our self-oriented quest for more, we naturally come into conflict with others who are pursuing their misguided quest.

This conflict results in the ongoing personal crises with which many if not all of us are engaged. On a global scale, the urge for more brings about the international conflicts that never seem to end. That's what it's all about – getting more, in order to feel better, and there's no end to the struggle. Many times, this is when addictions take us over.

How might you personally get caught up in the trap of thinking that finding the *outer* solution will solve the *inner* problem? Here are a few examples:

**the issue:** Your spouse or romantic partner is not living up to their side of the bargain. They are not loving enough; they don't make enough money; they are dull; they don't inspire you anymore. Or, you are without a partner.

**your response:** You confront your partner. You make your needs known. You try to convince them to change. You sweet-talk, bargain, threaten and plead with them to be different – to stop doing whatever it is that drives you crazy. If they don't change, you look for a new relationship. You fail to recognize that something about you is being reflected by the dissatisfaction you experience. If you are without a partner, you make yourself more attractive; you become aggressive; you modify your behavior in order to be compatible with others.

. . . . . . . . . . . . . . . . . . . . . . . .

**the issue:** Your career is more a source of pain than fulfillment. You're not successful; you don't find this type of work satisfying; you're not making enough money; you are lost and don't know what you want to do; you don't get the recognition you deserve; you have conflicts with co-workers and your boss.

**your response:** You try harder. You keep trying new things. You put in long hours. You take self-improvement programs to develop skills. You are compulsive about being seen as successful. You start to use and manipulate people to advance yourself without even realizing it. You harbor resentment against people who disagree or appear to obstruct you. All the while, the struggle wears you down and frustrates you. If you can't make conditions improve, you look for a new job. While it's possible that you may not have found your true work yet, it's more likely that the same issues would present themselves no matter what line of work you chose. You avoid responsibility for your feelings and blame the circumstances.

. . . . . . . . . . . . . . . . . . . . . . . .

**the issue:** Your children are not behaving. They return your care with resentment; you did something that turned them against you; you just can't control them; they take part in activities you hate. Or, they are the most wonderful children on Earth and you become dependently attached, living vicariously through them.

**your response:** You respond with a strategy. You become stricter because they need more discipline, or you become more permissive because they need to feel you trust and love them. In both cases, it can be an attempt to control in order to satisfy your priorities. You encourage them to excel and you live your life through them, not realizing that you are sowing the seeds of major resentment by viciously draining their energy with your vicarious attachment. You fail to truly let your children find themselves, to rein in your emotional dependence on them and to start to work on your pressing inner issues.

. . . . . . . . . . . . . . . . . . . . . . .

**the issue:** You have major money worries. You are broke, in debt, and unemployed. You worry constantly about being thrown out on the street. You feel that no one cares and you are being left to die. You have constant anxiety.

**your response:** You don't have a response. You just continue to sink deeper into worry, fear, and hopelessness, assuming the outer circumstances are to blame.

. . . . . . . . . . . . . . . . . . . . . . .

**the issue:** Your health is a major worry. You have chronic illness; you have ongoing pain; you are in constant fear of getting sicker.

**your response:** You frantically pursue medical care; you blindly take medication. You fail to connect inner psychic energetic negativity to the outer manifestation of illness. You fight only the outer instead of marshalling your efforts with an informed approach to resolving the inner.

Each of these examples can be regarded as being merely *circumstantial*, meaning you think that you just happen to be faced with certain outer circumstances which you must fight, manipulate, control and conquer in order to achieve your goal of feeling better: If you can only get more love from your partner; if you can only get that promotion and more pay; if your kids would only behave; if you can just get out of debt; if you can just regain your health; then everything will be fine.

Your focus is on the outside. It's superficial because it does not take into account the inner reality that gave rise to your perception and experience of the outer. What it comes down to is that if there's trapped negativity on the inside, no amount of whatever you think you need will satisfy you. On the contrary, the more you acquire, the more insecure you become. You become perplexed because the outer is not satisfying the inner, and you live in fear that you will lose what you do have, even though it's not doing you any real good. Here are some other ways we disvalidate our true feelings:

## going unconscious

Trying to change the outer to fix the inner can be regarded as a *proactive,* albeit misguided, response to negative feelings. You try to make something happen in order to fix feelings.

In contrast, *going unconscious* when difficult feelings come up can be regarded as an involuntary *passive withdrawal* response. It is probably the next major instinctive way we disvalidate feelings. When you go unconscious, you freeze up, blank out, clamp down. You become disoriented, you're in mild or severe shock, you stop thinking rationally. All this prevents feelings from being properly released and they become trapped inside. Severe versions of this result in *trauma*.

## self-concepts / self-image

We all carry with us a kind of self-image, or concept about ourselves that forms our basic ego structure. This is not necessarily undesirable. If we did not have such an identity, we would probably be at a disadvantage in trying to function in the world. But often, if not usually, our self-image proves to be as limiting as it is useful in helping us define our individuality. Self-image is usually unconscious, and almost always the result of conditioning from society and our own subconscious. Here's how it can relate to feelings work:

You want to be a "good" person; this results in strong, unconscious resistance to "bad" feelings, thoughts, and impulses. You think you shouldn't be having them. You unconsciously filter out or negate them without realizing that the energy is not released but becomes trapped inside where it continues to affect you.

You are a "spiritual" person. You are religious, or attracted to the New Age. You take on the goal of wanting to become a beautiful, loving person. You form a corresponding self-image that becomes the mask into which you attempt to mold yourself. Anything contrary to this self-concept upsets you, makes you feel guilty and is pushed aside. You think you are working on yourself when you try to replace negative thoughts, feelings, and beliefs with positive ones. You don't understand that you are just driving the negativity deeper.

## replacing negative with positive

Often, we are told that whenever negative feelings arise, we should replace them with positive ones. This is one of the teachings you will find on most of the traditional Eastern spiritual paths, and which I have indirectly referred to in the opening pages of this book as not having provided me with the in-depth knowledge I needed regarding handling feelings when I was starting out. Many modern-day therapies will also advise the same.

I hope you will be able to see, after the preceding discussion, that such an attitude ignores and contradicts the concept of validating all your feelings, including painful ones, and working productively with them. When you assume that the negative must be replaced with the positive, you are mindlessly falling into the trap of rejecting the negative; this is the opposite of the acceptance that needs to be applied to the feeling for it to integrate. Your subtle assumption that the negative is bad suppresses it into the subconscious, and you are left compulsively seeking the positive, and in the state that we are trying to remedy. As we will discuss in detail, the way out is not to be addicted to the positive, but to *transcend* the negative/positive dualistic poles of any particular issue.

### blame

Blame is a knee-jerk, automatic response whenever we feel threatened and are at a loss in handling any particular situation. Blame is related to the ego – that sense of ourselves as being independent, separate islands of consciousness and identity floating about in the sea of the material world. We think we must defend ourselves from any perceived attack. We blame without hesitation; we unconsciously fall into the trap of maintaining our *self-righteousness*, which means we see ourselves as always right and others as always wrong.

We will explore in more detail what it means to take responsibility for your experience, but for now, to keep things simple, I would urge you to try to recognize and pull back on your blame, because blame is one of the key factors that disvalidates experience, preventing personal growth and success with the process you are learning here. If you were to stop and carefully evaluate how much you blame others, or conditions, or forces in the world, or even yourself for what happens to you, you would be taking the first serious, powerful steps to genuine personal enlightenment and success in this work.

### denial

How are you?
Just fine, thanks, and you?

If your thinking doesn't get beyond this level, you can hypnotize yourself into believing it's true. Some schools of "philosophy" advocate this: Don't admit, don't see, don't recognize pain and it will go away. It's denial and you are in the state of *repression*. Repression is generally considered to be unconscious suppression. Another clue to repression:

I don't really have any disturbing feelings.

### dismissing feelings

You think feelings are unimportant. They only get in the way. Because of your incorrect assumption, you have formed a thick shell around yourself so no feelings get through. You brush them aside before they get to you. For example,

What's done is done. Forget about it and move forward.

Intelligent people, even therapists, will give you this amazingly ignorant advice. When feelings are cleared, there is no need to struggle with them. If they are not cleared, the mind is simply unable to banish them from hounding and tormenting you.

## ignoring feelings

You stay busy, you distract yourself with TV, internet, the news, compulsive activities, work, and especially in today's horribly confused world, the cell phone. When you slow down, you experience anxiety.

## fixing feelings

You think that a painful feeling must be fixed. You do not know yet that's it's OK to let a feeling – any feeling – just be as it is. In trying to fix, you block.

> My boyfriend hasn't called me in two weeks. I need to go out with the girls and maybe meet somebody new.

## disciplining yourself

You make a valiant effort to control yourself, but in the end, the feelings win. Your mistake is in trying to control your behavior without addressing the feelings that motivate the behavior.

> I have big-time food cravings that I constantly struggle with. I tell myself if I can control myself for a week, I can reward myself with ice cream on Saturday night.

## mood-altering

Mood-altering practices are rampant and unconscious. You use food, coffee, alcohol, drugs, sex, thrills, religion, and prayer to mood-alter instead of just being present with your mood as it is and letting it shift on its own.

## time heals

Time does not heal the suppressed subconscious. On the contrary, unreleased negativity from the ancient past keeps building as it attracts and accumulates more of the same.

## going inside

As you grow in awareness, you start to intuit that there's something deeper going on.

*The outer is only a reflection of the inner.*

You will keep attracting outer experiences that correspond to the inner. If there's loneliness trapped on the inside, you will never connect to a partner on the outside. If there's inadequacy and unworthiness trapped on the inside, you will always attract failure – perceived or real – on the outside. If you are emotionally dependent on your kids, they will always be rebellious. If you neglect inner negativity, it will emerge as illness and disease. If you are unconsciously holding feelings of lack, you will attract poverty. If you try to push away negative feelings, even in the name of love, light, and spirituality, you are defeating yourself.

With this understanding, you now adopt a more enlightened approach to difficult feelings. You go inside and work with the feelings directly. This is where the FEEL program comes in.

*The FEEL program does not primarily involve substituting "good" behavior, beliefs, thoughts or feelings for "bad" behavior, beliefs, thoughts or feelings, or visualizing what you think will make you happy.*

For lasting change, you need to work on a feeling-emotional level. Trapped feeling *energy* is what creates your behavior, your beliefs, your thoughts, and your experience. When you work on the feeling-emotional level, you work directly on core negativity that is not affected by attempting to directly modify behavior, beliefs, thoughts, or with visualizations.

All the methods we have just looked at of attempting to cope with difficult feelings through taking action – an action of the mind –

result in disvalidation, mismanagement, and a *blocking* of feelings. We don't realize that it's this same blocking that prevents positive feelings such as love, joy, creativity, and fulfillment from happening. Ironically, we find ourselves cut off from happiness because of our instinctive yet uninformed habit of turning away from painful feelings in the quest for happiness.

How do we resolve feelings? By reversing the habit of trapping them. In the most simple terms, we *feel our feelings*.

### authentic feeling

When you don't know how to handle your feelings, you unconsciously clamp down on them, trapping them. They never complete their natural cycle and so you carry them around all the time. To have a healthy emotional life and get rid of trapped negative painful feelings, *all you have to do is feel them*.

Sounds simple, right? And maybe too good to be true. However, it's unfortunately not simple. You have to have the *capacity* for feeling, and in today's world, the capacity for feeling has been mostly lost. You are probably not aware of this. You will say you feel painful feelings all the time – you feel anger, fear, hatred, confusion, anxiety, heartbreak, depression, sexual frustration, and so on – that's the problem.

However, when negative feelings come up, you do not really feel them because of the automatic *unconscious resistance* you apply to them. In addition, you often approach feelings through the *mind* instead of sensing them directly in the *body*. What you do feel is then distorted. You never get to the place of *authentic feeling,* so the feelings never resolve. You don't see that most of your negative feelings remain trapped, inaccessible, yet still influencing you dramatically.

*Resistance amplifies negative feelings.*

Then, because you don't feel your feelings properly, they seem to be *much more* painful than they actually are. You create unnecessary pain which drives you further into non-productive, reactionary behavior.

Feelings clear when you approach them with wisdom instead of ignorance; when you bring full, relaxed, concentrated attention to them; when you open to them, accepting and not resisting them, experiencing them fully, without distraction or blame, in the moment, in the body, on an energetic level instead of filtering and distorting them through the mind; when you choicelessly *witness* them instead of being *entangled* and run-over by them.

These are the simple yet profound secrets to inner work. When you consciously approach a particular negative feeling in this manner it can vanish or integrate in seconds.

## what kinds of feelings do we work with?

Feelings are generally all handled the same way. As you become familiar with the rules and intricacies of the feeling world, you will gain confidence in facing any feeling, whether it is something that comes up in your current everyday life or something that keeps intruding from the past. You will know how to handle it, how to avoid having it handle you, and how to bring the feeling to resolution.

In some cases, resolution will mean a *clearing* or *lifting* of the feeling. It is gone. In some cases, resolution will mean successful *integration* of the feeling. It is not gone, but is no longer perceived as distressful. Integration often precedes clearing.

To start to get you more at home with and articulate about feelings, here is a short list of typical feelings you may encounter as you work on yourself. Any or all of these feelings can be taken through the *Emotional Clearing Process*. I would recommend going through the list slowly, trying to actually *feel* each one. I believe that emotional enlightenment includes the ability to empathically sense the complete range of human feelings, whether any one is of particular relevance for you or not.

# Feelings / Emotions to take through the Emotional Clearing Process

Fear, Panic, Anxiety, Tension, Stress.

Anger, Rage, Helplessness, Coercion, Distrust, Being Used or Dominated.

Sexual Compulsiveness, Impotence, Frustration.

Neediness, Clingingness, Emotional Starvation, Food and Substance Cravings.

Unworthiness, Inadequacy, Failure, Disrespect.

Sadness, Loneliness, Abandonment, Rejection, Jealousy, Hatred, Betrayal, Resentment, Heartbreak.

Not being heard, difficulty in verbalizing.

Blocked Creativity.

Confusion, Weakness.

Spiritual Despondency, Depression, Lack Of Purpose.

# the
# Emotional Clearing Process

## 1. Deep Relaxation – BODY plane

Sit comfortably, close your eyes, and let yourself relax. Let the mind come to rest.

Become aware of your body. Feel yourself in it. Allow a strong sense of *being in the body* to develop.

Drop all sense of striving – of needing to accomplish anything. Feel yourself coming into the moment.

Breathe smoothly and easily for 2 minutes. Stay aware of your body and the sensation of breathing. Relax even more.

Keep 15% of your attention on the breath throughout the remainder of the session, breathing smoothly and easily without being preoccupied with it. Do not allow the breath to become constricted or clenched, as it will tend to do when strong feelings come up.

# 2. Awareness – INTELLECTUAL plane

Open the door to the subconscious.

Bring the event or circumstance before you. See yourself in that setting. Let the experience take place in your mind.

Allow your true feelings to be activated.

Recognize or assume that you are projecting.

Drop blame; take responsibility; *own* your experience.

.............................................

To open the door to the subconscious, you just make that intention. If you want, you can visualize an imaginary door opening and then closing at the end of the session. You are training the subconscious to be available upon request, but to not intrude itself into your affairs at other times.

Bringing the event before you simply means to recall it, think about it, visualize it, see it as if it is happening now, see it as if it was a movie playing in front of you. Once you get the feeling, you drop the movie and focus only on the feeling.

Find the true feeling that has been activated. Be honest with yourself. You may feel angry, rejected, anxious, afraid, lonely, sad, depressed, tired, weak, inadequate, a failure, etc.

Blame gets in the way of releasing feelings. Try to put aside any blame you may feel as best you can, even if only for the duration of this processing session.

## 3. Acceptance – MENTAL plane

Find your inner resistance to the feelings.

Replace the resistance with acceptance.

· · · · · · · · · · · · · · · · · · · · · · · · · · · · · · · · · · · · · · · · · · · · ·

Look inside and find the inner sense that wants to push the feeling away. It's an action of the mind that judges, condemns, constricts, makes-wrong and closes you off from part of yourself. Replace the resistance as best you can with a sense of *allowing* the feeling.

It's OK to have any feeling, no matter what it is. Relax into the feeling. Make a place for it. Notice how you open up to yourself on the inside.

There's a part of you that intuitively resists pain and painful feelings. But dropping resistance to the feeling and shifting into acceptance of it is a crucial element of the process. Don't make the feeling *wrong* – it's a vital part of life, and resistance only prevents the feeling from resolving itself. Accept the feeling, but remember, <u>you're accepting only the *feeling* – not the associated circumstances</u>.

# 4. Direct Experience – FEELING plane

Stay present with the feeling.

Find the feeling in your body.

Experience the feeling.

Maintain a smooth breath.

Let the feeling develop.

........................................

Go to the most prominent feeling that comes up as you recall a particular event or circumstance. Allow yourself to have the feeling. Stay *unconditionally present* with it. Don't be afraid of it. Relax into it. Opening to the feeling can only help you. <u>Experience it without acting it out or extending it into the world.</u>

If you can get a sense of the feeling in your body, include that as well. If you can't easily sense the feeling in the body, don't struggle. Just feel whatever is present for you.

Keep breathing smoothly and easily, using the breath as a tool to manage the feeling: If the feeling intensifies, step up the breath slightly.

As you stay with the feeling, it will possibly spontaneously link to other related feelings and memories from the recent or remote past, including past traumatic events. Shift your attention to those feelings and apply all the steps of the process to them.

# 5. Witnessing – TRANSPERSONAL plane

Step back and detach.

Witness the feeling.

Remain conscious of yourself being present with the feeling.

· · · · · · · · · · · · · · · · · · · · · · · · · · · · · · · · · · · · · · · ·

Normally, we are enmeshed with our feelings. They overpower us and control us, often impelling us to do things we later regret. Training yourself to detach and witness feelings builds the capacity to remain cool and not be coerced by the feeling into non-productive acting-out.

Detaching and witnessing invokes a higher sense of peacefulness and makes it possible to be with strong negative feelings without distress.

Most importantly, detaching and witnessing plays an important part in enabling resolution of the feeling.

There is nothing you can do to directly make the feeling release. Do not try to push it away with the mind. Your intent is to accept and experience while maintaining distance and detachment. Waiting patiently, witnessing, just being present with the feeling will eventually result in the feeling lifting.

Stay aware of the feeling and of yourself in Witness mode simultaneously.

After you have spent enough time processing your issue (from 10 to 30 minutes):

# 6. End Processing

Start winding down, and get ready to come back to normal consciousness. Let any strong feelings that may be present pass away.

If you feel as if you had a productive session, thank the subconscious for its cooperation.

Close the door to the subconscious, just by willing it to be.

Gently bring yourself back to normal.

Open your eyes.

# Feeling-Emotional Enlightenment Level I
# Basic

*Learn the Basic Secret to emotional-energetic healing.*
*Get comfortable with going inside. Build feeling capacity. Unconditional Presence. Entering the Moment.*

## consciousness shift 1: opening to feelings

In order to begin inner work on the feeling level, you need to first become accustomed to feelings. You need to build your capacity for feelings. You need to start slowly. This is the intention of FEEL I. Nevertheless, with only the basic skills of FEEL I, you can get excellent, meaningful results.

For some, just going inside and looking at feelings is a major step, the potential difficulty and significance of which should not be underestimated. One of the goals of humanistic psychology is to simply get you "in touch" with feelings, meaning you recognize and experience them. The implication is that by not being in touch, feelings become trapped and lead to emotional disorders. After getting in touch with feelings, however, it's helpful to have an effective strategy in order to keep from being battered by them. You must know how to handle and *release* negative feelings.

Difficult, negative feelings come up as we go about our daily lives. They are activated by events or circumstances we encounter. We may not be aware that the feelings were originally trapped sometime in the past and are only reappearing now, but that's usually the case. The more severe the feelings and events connected with them, the greater the accumulated negativity. Working with feelings as they occur now, therefore, serves to release trapped negativity from the past.

The feelings became trapped, unable to resolve, because they did not receive the quality attention required when they originally formed. Most likely, you resisted the feelings; you pushed them away; you judged them as wrong and decided you did not want them. These are all *unconscious* reactions of the mind that influence your ability to assimilate feelings.

These kinds of reactions to feelings are understandable because negative feelings are painful, and the instinctive response is to try to avoid or rid yourself of them. However, in so doing, you hurt yourself and fall into a trap. In resisting negative feelings, in simply not being present with them when they formed, they never were resolved, and they continue to subversively act on you, limiting and distorting your experience.

In our work, we use a relaxed inner process that brings hidden feelings into awareness and releases them. Working with any difficult feeling is made easy, comfortable, and safe because of the nature of the relaxed *Alpha* state you are in, and because of how you approach those feelings. You detach from them, witnessing instead of being entangled in them, and you will use other subtle enjoyable energy techniques that will support and empower you.

To release negative feelings, you *process* them. Processing means to *be present* with a feeling in such a way that it completes its natural energetic cycle. *Being present* means to open to feelings, experiencing them *as they are* with no thought of changing or avoiding them. It implies a non-reactive, passive, unconditionally accepting, witnessing stance, even in the face of active emotions like anger or fear; keeping your cool; not being drawn into the feeling; not acting it out; dropping blame; just watching it with a sense of poise and *choiceless awareness*.

After a short while of being present with feelings, you will notice a shift. The feelings you are processing will be perceived differently. They will no longer appear so urgent; the intensity will lessen; it will seem as if they have lifted; you will no longer experience an impulse to act on the feelings. This means the feelings have released. Don't be afraid if feelings become intense or even wild as you stay with them. The process is enough to safely handle any kind of feeling. Just remember to stay focused inside, and don't let strong feelings motivate you into taking any kind of reactive action.

Often, when you successfully process an issue, something will magically shift in the associated external circumstances. I hope you will be able to experience this, because it will rock your boat with the realization that inner work does indeed go out onto the psychic planes and will significantly affect others, and that you are learning the true art of transformation and are acquiring genuine powers. The key to this is the *Acceptance* step. You can't accept in order to make better, to benefit yourself, to get even, or even to heal yourself. Your acceptance has to be genuine and total with no strings attached, then things will transform on their own.

*Getting in touch with feelings does not mean you are to express your feelings or vent or take action against others.*

The outward expression of feelings is not required for the process to succeed, and in most cases, will work against you. Trust that as you release negativity, the impulse to express or confront will diminish as well. However, this doesn't mean that there is never a time to confront and discuss circumstances with others, or to clarify your needs. The point is that if you confront before you have released inner negativity, you will most likely be coming at the other out of blame, even if you try not to, and the confrontation will usually not go well. If you process first, you release the inner negativity, and your confrontation will be much more reasonable and successful. Wait until you feel clear enough on the inside to confront, and by then the situation may have resolved itself anyway, as a result of your processing, or will need only a minimum of discussion.

As you process any feeling, other feelings may come up, sparked by the first feeling. You may focus on the new feeling, but be sure you haven't left the first feeling too soon. If it is an important feeling for you, some time may be required for its complete release. Inconsequential feelings can be released in a few minutes, but more important issues will require consecutive sessions. With very important issues, several – probably many – sessions will be required. You may have to process important issues over the course of a few days, weeks, or months. Don't be impatient with the time factor. You are doing permanent soul healing. Genuine deep clearing takes time – that's one of the reasons you have a lifetime at your disposal. Sensing that you are making headway will be enough to keep you going.

Subsequent chapters will describe the *Emotional Clearing Process* in more detail, expanding your understanding. The steps may seem simple, and you may underestimate their effectiveness. But subtleties are everything in this work. You can have significant success right at the start, and as you keep practicing, you will deepen and refine your understanding of the process, and your inner skills, at the same time releasing deeper levels of the emotional subconscious. These are inner skills that you will use for the rest of your life, I promise you. The purpose of life is evolution of consciousness, and these skills are directly related.

You will probably want to start with feelings that are not quite as challenging as those in the following example. Look at it as an experiment in consciousness. Play with it. Remember, the first step is *Deep Relaxation*. It's possible you may reject or even resent the suggestion to go inside and look at feelings. If you do, I hope another part of you will recognize that some resistance has been stirred up. As you keep moving forward with the process it's likely that, at some point, you will begin to appreciate its value.

To get the most benefit from this program, it's best to find a regular time to practice – ideally, twice a day, for a minimum of 15 minutes each. With regular practice, you will find that feelings will start to jump up to be cleared that you may not have been particularly aware of. By sitting regularly, you develop the skills that will enable you to process any disturbing event that may occur in the future. If you don't have any negative feelings that need to be addressed at that moment, just practice sitting quietly, stilling the mind. Keep your attention focused on the breath and try to quiet the chattering inside.

It's best if you sit quietly in comfortable, relaxing surroundings. After you develop skills, you will be able to process feelings to a certain extent during activity as they occur, but sitting, closing your eyes, and going deep into the experience will usually yield the best results.

Always remember that it may take some time to get accustomed to looking within. Our usual focus is outward. When closing the eyes and looking inside, it's normal to feel ill at ease at first. Anxiety, restlessness, or doubt may come up. You may not be sure what you are supposed to be doing. Just give it some time – I can assure you that you will never regret making the effort to contact yourself.

### connect to the negative

I want to be sure you understand that it is negative, painful feelings we are focusing on, in order to heal and release them. It's possible this may seem counter-intuitive at first. When you sit to process any event, you are not to try to generate positive feelings in order to counter any painful experience, or to try to discover "what the feeling can teach you." You are not to sit and think about what you must do to make things better, etc. You must bring your attention to the negative, painful feeling itself and be fully present with it with no thought of changing it. It is this *unconditional presence* that results in the resolution of the feeling.

As you start to go deep into your true feelings related to any event, circumstance, or other person, it is likely you will encounter strong negative feelings. Some of these feelings will have an apparent logical basis, but some can seem to be irrational. You may feel resentment or hatred towards loved ones, for example, or fear when there is no reason to be afraid. As you get into FEEL II, you will see how projection and the dualistic nature of feelings can result in what appear to be irrational reactions. The key is to accept these feelings without buying into them and without being drawn into acting them out. This is one of the key lessons to be learned in psychotherapy – that you have an irrational side, and that it must be accepted without being motivated by it. Those irrational feelings are likely to be a major component of the suppressed subconscious.

# Jean

Jean is a woman in her late 40's. She and her husband live in the suburban hills of Southern California. Her marriage is basically good with her two kids successfully raised and out of the house. She and her husband are financially secure. He works, she does not.

Jean's issue is anxiety. All her life she's been anxiety-prone, finding it hard to relax and sit still. In the past, she's managed the anxiety by staying busy. As she was raising the children, she had plenty to do and was able to keep the anxiety in control.

Now, things are getting worse. There's nothing for her to do at home, so she can't as easily distract herself. A few years ago, there was a brush fire that came close to her house. Some nearby houses burned to the ground. She has become obsessed with the idea that the next fire will destroy her house and she will be unable to get away in time.

She dreads the approach of the dry season, when the fires may break out. As her fears have been compounding, they have extended to the general idea of safety. She researched police records and found that several houses in the area have been broken into and burglarized in recent years. She worries that her house will be broken into during the day when she is at home alone and she will be attacked.

Her husband has been understanding and supportive, and they have installed a security system in the house, and even hired a private security agency to patrol the house and be on call. In spite of this, however, her anxiety has become only greater. Nothing that is done on the outside seems to have any effect. On the contrary, she now worries that the security system will fail; she worries that the guards will not come in time; she continues to obsess about the fire hazard. She exhibits all the signs of classic *obsessive-compulsive disorder*.

Jean is an intelligent woman with a master's degree. She understands that her anxiety is an over-reaction and that there's no rational reason to be so afraid. Still, she is helpless to change how she feels and she lives in constant dread.

One of Jean's friends gave her a copy of *Emotional Clearing*, which describes the same process you are learning here. She read the book and started to do the work. Over the course of a few months, she was able to dramatically turn things around. Here's how she worked, in her own words:

> In the past, whenever I got anxious, I just tried my best to feel better. Getting busy seemed to do the trick. I would get involved with what my two children needed. I would call up friends and talk about their problems. I would read or watch TV. I had a problem with food, and now I understand that I would try to bury my feelings with the food.

> When I learned how to process my feelings, I found a way that worked that helped me resolve the feelings without needing to try to change things in my world so I would not be anxious.

> I started to devote a part of the day to what I called "my time." I had two "my times" on every weekday. I have a lot of free time so it was easy to structure. What was hard was forcing myself to sit down at regular times because usually the anxiety would get worse.

> I was able to understand that it only appeared to get worse because I was now not running from it but facing it, which I needed to do to get better.

> So, I would take "my time," and sit down to face my feelings. John's book gave me the confidence and knowledge that it was possible to get better if I just followed his process and faced my feelings instead of running from them by getting busy. I was determined to get better. I would sit down and start to do the steps of the process.

> Step 1 is *Deep Relaxation*. I close my eyes. I breathe in and out, slowly and carefully, filling all the way up and exhaling, keeping my attention on the breath, for 2 whole minutes. When thoughts take me away, I refocus on the breath. It was amazing

that something so simple could affect me so much, but I found that just doing the breathing would start to make me feel better and more relaxed.

Step 2 is *Awareness*. I think about the fires, and immediately the anxiety comes. I look deep inside to find the feeling behind the event, and I see that there's a deep fear. I eventually see that the fear has been so big that I have never really seen it. I have been like a fish at the bottom the ocean, never seeing the water. The fear has been responsible for my general anxiety and timidity.

At first I was petrified of the fear, if that makes any sense. I was afraid of the fear, I wasn't sure if coming into contact with it was the right thing to do, but I remembered John's words, and I became more determined to have faith and move forward.

Step 3 is *Acceptance*. This step really threw me for a while until I got the hang of it, but it's amazing and far-reaching and has resulted in the new person that I can say I am today. The idea is that there has been an unconscious part of me that has been pushing away the fear so it can never fully heal and release. I need to instead welcome the fear! The act of welcoming is an important part of what heals it! It's an amazing idea that works.

In John's terms, it means to find the inner resistance that I have to the fear and replace it with acceptance. So I look deep within and I do that.

I sit quietly, relaxed even though the fear is there, and I accept. I'm OK with the fear. It's such an amazing relief just to accept it that I can't describe it, but as I bring the idea of acceptance more and more into my life, it changes me for the better every day in other ways as well, in all parts of my life.

Step 4 is *Direct Experience*. Now that I'm at peace with the fear, I can truly feel it, which is what the fear needs and wants in order to release. So I just sit and feel the fear. After a few weeks, I was able to feel the fear in my body, which I thought was amazing. I realize I have never done this, as strange as it will sound – I have never really felt my fear. It's not at all a problem to feel the feeling even though it is this intense, throbbing fear. I'm able to do this because of the next step where I become detached from the feeling.

Step 5 is *Witnessing*. I make an effort to step back – to detach – from the fear. I'm watching it as if it is no longer me. I'm no longer sunk into the fear and overwhelmed by it like I used to be, when I would get busy to try to get myself out of it. I sit in this place for 20 minutes. It's beautiful.

At first, I couldn't really get to the stage where I am now, but as I kept trying, I found I was developing the skills that were required. I found I really liked the peacefulness of sitting and relaxing. I found that it was no problem to face my feelings, and that the simple act of truly facing my feelings was all I needed to do to resolve the crises that I had been in. It has been amazing!

As I worked with the fear over the course of time, other memories would come up where there was intense fear. I applied the process to those memories, and healing occurred.

I am convinced that the healing I have experienced is permanent. The fear is just no longer there. I'm so grateful to my husband for loving me and humoring me all through the entire episode. We have stopped the safety patrol, and we only use the security system when we go away.

As for the fires, the fear is just not there like it used to be. I know the fires are still possible, but like everyone else who lives here, I love the hills so much that I'm willing to put up with the risk. I've accepted the risk, and I was only able to do that because I released the fear.

As John says, the positive and negative always come together. I'm at peace with them.

As you can see, the core feeling behind Jean's anxiety is fear. Her fear was activated by the prospect of fire, but of course, fear can be associated with many different conditions and events. Fear is rampant in today's world, and each of us will probably be able to identify at least a certain amount of it in ourselves. Current events, news broadcasts, war, the economy, climate crisis, immigration, racial tensions, etc., all converge into the collective subconscious to produce a blanket of fear, which permeates life as we know it. If enough of us – individually – start rising above disvalidation and start to work inwardly with our fear, it can be the beginning of a worldwide turnaround.

## the feeling behind the event

What kinds of feelings can you process? Any kind – but keep in mind that you want to go to the feeling that the event has activated. Look deep to find *the feeling behind the event*. Don't get caught up in thinking about what you must do to remedy the event.

When Jean sat and focused on the *feeling* of fear, the *thought* might have come up that she must get the alarm system installed, or worry if the alarm system is working, or if the surrounding woods are dangerously dry. As soon as she realizes she is being distracted by a thought, she re-focuses on the feeling. The thought may still be churning away in the background, but by not focusing on it, it starts to lose its momentum and wither away. You don't need to struggle to try to make the mind go completely blank – just focus away from the thought onto the feeling.

As you process whatever feeling you are having, you will link to the next appropriate feeling at the right time if that is what is needed, as long as you just stay focused and apply the steps. With Jean, anger could have come up as she stayed with the fear – anger that no one listens to her as she voices her concerns about the fire danger, for example. She then would shift to processing the anger, applying the same principles. After a few minutes, the anger will subside, and another feeling may come up. She then processes that feeling. All these feelings are related to the issue.

It's always critical to remember that acceptance of feelings does not give you permission to hold anyone else responsible for them, to blame, to vent, or to take action against anyone. You are learning a subtle, sophisticated method for inner healing that will resolve conflict without needing to engage in outer confrontation, controlling, demanding, or acting-out. Trust that in clearing inner negativity, outer balance will result.

### you can't hurt yourself

You may question if it can be harmful to keep negative feelings in awareness as they are being processed. Don't we become or attract to ourselves what we think, and so shouldn't we be trying to get rid of negative feelings and think positively? Doesn't accepting and focusing on them make them worse?

First, it must be understood that negative feelings represent toxic energies already trapped in the subconscious body-mind, already influencing you. They are attracting negative conditions to you right now, whether you are "thinking" about them or not. Just bringing them into conscious awareness does not increase their power. On the contrary, bringing the feelings into conscious awareness is the beginning of deflating their power and releasing them so they no longer influence you.

Second, we bring feelings into awareness within a well-defined, psychotherapeutic format, for a limited period of time, as we work on them. This is not the same as wallowing in the feeling or letting it overpower you – it is the opposite. Wallowing and being overpowered are where we normally are. When you bring full attention to the feeling, especially when you detach from and *witness* the feeling, you start to reverse this.

Third, humanistic psychology has always been founded on the general principle of getting in touch with feelings and thereby resolving them – not denying, turning away from or dismissing them. You now have a unique formula to successfully accomplish this complex task.

The only thing you might want to keep in mind is that when you apply the process to feelings that have been buried inside for ages, you are taking dramatic steps towards reshuffling your psychic self. Occasionally, this intense reshuffling can be experienced as a period of disorientation. It can seem as if you are getting worse. You may start to doubt whether you are going in the right direction. You are not getting worse, but are only bringing the suppressed contents of your mind into awareness. This is a phase you must go through. In the extreme, it can lead to a "healing crisis." It can happen not only with our work, but with all valid forms of psychotherapy. Take care of yourself, be moderate in your approach, use common sense, and you will be OK. Get help if you need it. Don't overdo your exposure to the negative but at the same time don't wimp out if negativity seems to kick up.

The foregoing ties into what Buddhists call *the Hindrances*. As you start to work on yourself, you may encounter opposition. Forces outside yourself, and forces inside, will try to interfere. It's because you're stirring up negativity as you prepare to release it, and it is making itself known and defending itself. Just be aware of this phenomenon and don't let it bamboozle you. Take it as a sign that you are doing effective work.

The *Emotional Clearing Process* is completely adequate in itself to manage and release distressing feelings; no other technique is required. It is the only modality I have used in my counseling practice, and it is what I train others in. However, if you are so inclined, you may combine it with other healing modalities.

Body-oriented energy psychology systems for emotional release, for example, are more effective when applied with the wisdom you are learning here. If you try to apply energy psychology and are still deep into resistance of feelings, you will self-defeat. Deep *Alpha-State* inducing CD programs will be more beneficial because you will be prepared to handle feelings that are likely to come up. Meditation practice can be expanded to include significant feelings work instead of naively turning away from difficult feelings when they arise.

The only restriction is that the other modalities should not be mental-intellectual, thinking-based, cognitive techniques which will jar you out of your feelings. For example, challenging beliefs, or trying to change thoughts to change feelings are mental, counter-productive efforts that take you out of your feeling center, as does intellectualizing or asking yourself pseudo-penetrating questions about what constitutes "enlightenment" in an effort to jolt yourself there.

## contraindications

Almost everyone can apply the principles you are learning here without risk. In all the years I have been teaching and counseling – since 1994 – there hasn't been a single report of anyone getting into trouble using this method. However, it's probable that persons who are right-brain atrophied, extremely disoriented, who the establishment would label psychotic or mentally unbalanced, those institutionalized, may not benefit from attempting to work on themselves in this manner.

A certain amount of *ego strength* is needed to look inside and detach from what is found. Without this, it could be overwhelming to face inner feelings head-on, even though I also believe that we are guided as we do this work by a higher aspect of ourselves that presents to us only that which we can handle.

Could children benefit from this work? Absolutely – a child easily understands that it's OK to have any feeling if they are so encouraged. In fact, it's likely that a factor in *ADD* or *ADHD* is the habit that children learn of not handling feelings correctly, by being constantly distracted by TV, video games, etc. As feelings build up, they keep intruding whenever the mind starts to slow down, so in order to keep the feelings at bay, a child learns to not stand still. Hyperactivity results.

Another factor regarding the success of the program relates to inherent right-brain feeling capacity. Over the course of the years, whenever I have had less than satisfying results with clients, I believe it usually came down to the person not being able to move into the right-brain. There was just too much left-brain dominance and right-brain atrophy for a feeling-based approach to work. For these people, talk therapy would be recommended until they could start to activate the right-brain.

## body practice

If you are unhappy but can't find specific feelings; if you are depressed and don't know why; if you can't feel all or parts of your body; or if you have chronic negative feelings that you can't go beyond, you need this. If you can add a body practice to your inner healing work, you give yourself a big advantage.

The basic problem a majority of us face today is being disconnected from feelings. Having lost the capacity for feelings, we are unable to resolve them, even if we know the correct steps. We flounder with ill-conceived strategies of the mind that we hope will solve our dilemma of Discontent and Depression.

A critical step in regaining emotional health is to contact your feeling self. You have lost your capacity for feeling because you are centered in the mind. But feelings occur in the body. If you have no connection to your body, you have no connection to your feelings. And this, unfortunately, is the condition that most people are in today. They don't know what it means to be in the body, to be body-centered. They are trapped in the head, out of touch.

Therefore, in order to get in touch with your feeling self, it's very helpful to get in touch with your body. It's fortunate and convenient that this option is available. All you need to do is get out of your head, and back into your body. Just by adopting a simple regular practice and changing your attitude towards the body, you can start regaining emotional health.

Connecting to the body is a foundational concept behind many Eastern spiritual practices as well as certain Western psychological approaches. The body is regarded as the entry point to higher, more subtle levels of consciousness that culminate in spiritual awakening and emotional adjustment. Working on a body level becomes a focus of the practice.

Almost any kind of physical activity – walking, dancing, sports, Yoga, breathwork, working in the yard, any kind of manual labor, etc. – has the potential of getting you back in the body, with one important exception: When you are pushing, striving, reaching for some goal, you tend to remain in the head, even in the midst of physical activity. You are driving your body to achieve some result, instead of merely being in the body, experiencing the physicality of the moment. This pushing with the mind negates the psychological benefits of any body-oriented practice.

For example, body-building. Usually, when you engage in body-building, you are intensely focused on results. You are driving the body. You are actually disapproving of the body as it is, and trying to force it to be something else. This amounts to a kind of self-rejection, which we will discuss in more detail, and works against you.

The same dynamic occurs in the Yoga studios of the day, which are almost all focused on some variety of "power" Yoga. Yoga is my favorite body practice, and I would recommend it as a superlative means of getting back into the body and triggering emotional release, but it has to be approached meditatively instead of as a form of exercise, intended to achieve results. Power Yoga does not allow deep relaxation into the posture flow that generates meditative benefits. I would advise you to seek out classic, meditative Yoga if you choose to incorporate Yoga into your body routine. I go into how to use Yoga as a means to get reconnected to the body on the emclear website:

http: / / www.emclear.com / WorkingOnYourself_yoga.html

### begin work

You can begin work with the *Emotional Clearing Process* as described and the information contained in FEEL I. Don't hesitate to start to experiment with negative feeling states. Prove to yourself that owning, accepting, experiencing, and witnessing any negative feeling can have dramatic positive repercussions. When you are ready to deepen your *Feeling-Emotional Enlightenment Level,* FEEL II awaits.

# EMT
## Emotional Management Technique

Sometimes we experience tremendous emotions surging up in the midst of personal interaction, and often we allow ourselves to be reactive to the emotions, doing or saying things that are counterproductive. The EMT is the first line of defense for handling strong emotions that jump up in these situations.

**EMT** has 4 steps:

### 1. Recognize that it's happening.
The negative subconscious is emerging, activated by circumstances or interactions with others. If you don't realize this, you will most likely be reactive.

### 2. Own it.
Take responsibility for your feelings. Pull back on the natural urge to blame.

### 3. Go to the breath.
Conscious breath can prevent you from acting out the emotion, and give you control over expression. Conscious breath immediately starts to modify the emotion because emotions are closely linked to the breath. Breathe smoothly and easily into the full body.

### 4. Remain non-reactive / Witness.
As you are breathing, remember the most important thing right now is not to react, unless of course, there is immediate danger. Be calm, keep breathing, stay non-reactive, in *the Witness*. Just keep watching, detached and relaxed, even in the face of difficult emotions. Defend yourself, but don't attack. At the earliest opportunity, sit down by yourself and go into a full processing session with the incident.

Feeling-Emotional Enlightenment Level II
# Psychological

*Get psychologically enlightened. Go to a deeper level of understanding. Become psychologically articulate. Employ psychological tools.*

## consciousness shift 2: reframing your experience

Something happens. You're upset, angry, fearful, depressed. In consciousness shift 2, you reframe your attitude towards the event. Previously, you regarded it as an annoyance or worse. Now, I want you to regard it as an *opportunity*. Instead of recoiling, retreating, fighting, blaming, anaesthetizing, or disvalidating, you walk towards the event as an opportunity for releasing negativity that you have been unknowingly carrying inside. You recognize that this is a major purpose of your life on Earth – that events happen *in order* to give you this opportunity. You welcome the opportunity and approach it with a sense of *reverence*.

# Awareness

In FEEL II, we focus on the psychological aspects of transformational work. You will find here a concise outline of how I would suggest handling the dynamics of inner life. Understanding how feelings operate is of the most basic importance in successfully working on yourself. In this section I have drawn from and built primarily upon the Western schools of psychology, with a touch of the East.

The FEEL II *Emotional Clearing Process* is completely adequate to bring about meaningful psychological-emotional healing. Although the following discussion of specific feelings and emotions is brief, if you have any aptitude for inner psychological work, you will be able to identify inner conditions and apply the process. If you are not entirely at ease with metaphysical thinking, whether you are practicing on yourself or are a therapist considering expanding your practice to include experientially working with feelings, you will be able to do satisfactory work releasing the negative subconscious without the erudite concepts of FEEL III.

> Are you ready to take a closer look at that? Bring it before you, as if it's happening now. See yourself in that setting, and let the feelings come up.

### consciousness shift 3: left / right brain

Let's look again at one of the most basic psychological concepts. It has been observed that humans have dual operational modes, corresponding to the dualistic world in which we live. Science has coined the terminology of the left- and right-brain in describing these modes. These terms are as good as any, except to note the subtle, erroneous, materialistic implication that the brain is responsible for these two types of behavior. The brain is only the transmitter of consciousness to the physical plane, not the originator, as modern day science would have you believe.

Left-brain functioning is concerned with *thinking*; right-brain functioning is concerned with *feeling*. In our modern world, the left-brain is usually dominant, and the right-brain is usually subdued, if not dormant or atrophied.

In the left-brain, we are concerned with results. We are *doing-oriented*. We use the mind, the organ of thought, to achieve. Of course, we need to accomplish many things in order to survive and prosper, but the point is that the left-brain is out of balance, and the right-brain needs to be developed for us to be fulfilled as fully-functioning human beings.

The right-brain, in contrast to the *doing* orientation of the left-brain, is focused on *being*. *Being* is closely related to the feeling capacity. *Being* is the sense of being here now, in the moment, instead of caught in the labyrinth of the mind, planning, evaluating, worrying, trapped in time.

Right-brain beingness is also closely connected to higher consciousness, but from a more practical standpoint, it is the right-brain *feeling capacity* that is of primary importance in our work. If you do not have some degree of right-brain activity, you will have difficulty in this or any type of inner work.

Focus on the feeling *behind* the event. Stay in right-brain/body consciousness. Stop the mind and be present with the feeling.

The ironic thing about low right-brain activity is that it does not appear to limit the occurrence of feelings – it just seems to limit the *perception* of them. Feelings still occur, but they do not come into consciousness, so they build up and fester and eventually result in the negative experiences, conditions, and behaviors that we are in the process of addressing.

Often people come to this work saying they are unable to contact their feelings, even though they understand the importance of so doing, and are experiencing symptoms resulting from repressed feelings such as depression, addictions, and uncontrollable outbursts.

The starting point is always to just get active in the right-brain. I started life with a highly technical engineering background, but soon realized I needed to work on my underdeveloped right-brain in order to bring myself into balance. I went to the extreme of quitting my old lifestyle and becoming an artist. I have worked on the right-brain my whole life, as a primary occupation. I believe this is what enables me to see into the world of soul deeply and to guide others on this path.

If you find yourself with no feelings, blocked feelings, severe negative feelings, blocked creativity, addictions, and unexplained depression, you need to contact the right-brain feeling self as a first step. Make a conscious effort to include right-brain activities as a regular part of your everyday routine. What might some of these activities be?

### shifting to the right-brain

Put aside doing, planning, striving, worrying. Enter the right-brain world of feeling through:

- Meditation with a sense of being here now.

- Reading fiction or poetry.

- Get involved with art, music, drama, performance.

- Walking, jogging, hiking while putting the mind on hold.

- Performing any task guided by intuition, not logic: cooking, gardening, child-care, manual labor, etc.

- Getting out of your head and into your Heart.

- Service, taking care of others.

- Playing like a child.

- Get into the body: Yoga, bodywork, breathwork, manual labor, sports, dance.

The *Deep Relaxation* that we do at the start of a processing session is intended to shift your consciousness to the right-brain, which is inherently feeling-oriented and associated with the body. Make the most of this opportunity.

## thinking vs. feeling

To me, it's astonishing that many professionals in the psychotherapeutic world do not distinguish between thoughts and feelings. It's common to hear someone ask "What are you thinking? Are you angry?" This sloppiness indicates a basic lack of comprehension about the human energy system. We have separate, different capacities for thought and feeling, which correspond to the left- and right-brain. It's helpful to begin to cultivate a sense for the different capacities, and to be able to distinguish which of the two may be dominant at any time.

In this work, it's always critical to remember that we are aiming to bring feelings into conscious experience. It's possible to believe you are feeling your feelings, while in reality, you are thinking about your feelings. If you have relatively unexercised right-brain capacity, it's probable that this is what you will do when you first start this work.

Thinking means planning, analyzing, evaluating, worrying, blaming. You think about what the correct response would be to the situation. You think what a terrible person they or you are. You think about times from the past when the same thing has happened. You are in your head.

> You're getting too intellectual – you're looking for an answer. Let the answer come from the process.

In order to feel, you may start with a thought. You think about what has happened, and that thought triggers a feeling. If I ask you to think of a happy time, you will recall a certain event, and the thought of the event will evoke a feeling of happiness. If I ask you to think of a stressful time, the memory (a thought) will evoke painful feelings. You then put the thought aside, and you focus on the feeling. *The feeling is occurring in the body*. You shift to body awareness, staying present with the sensation in the body, breathing into it. If you start to think again, you catch yourself and go back to the body-based feeling.

> I'm sensing you're more in your head than in the body. Come back to your feelings.

We often use this characteristic of thoughts and feelings when doing the work. We bring up feelings that need to be addressed by starting with a thought. It's helpful to keep in mind, however, the distinction between thoughts and feelings.

> Here's a thought: I am worthless and no good.
> Here's a feeling: I feel worthless and no good.

Using a feeling appropriate for you, play with these two options until you can clearly sense the difference, and can maybe even switch between the two at will. With the thought, you're in your head. With the feeling, thinking has stopped, slowed down, or taken a back seat to body-centered feeling; you are focused in the body, feeling. If you can't get into body-centered feeling, it's just a sign that your right-brain is inactive or dormant which, as I have said, is likely. You need to work on developing its capacity.

*Emotional Clearing* is not about what to do. It's all about just feeling the feeling, without letting the mind get in the way – without thinking about it. You will keep re-learning this, over and over, as you proceed on the path.

## consciousness shift 4: suppression – projection

The *suppression-projection mechanism* is one of the foundational psychological principles of our work. We have discussed how feelings are interrupted when they are not validated and allowed their natural cycle of building and dissipating. When this happens, the feeling becomes *suppressed*, trapped in the body-mind, out of awareness, forming what we call *the subconscious*. From here it becomes a source of ongoing disruption, coloring our experience, making us react in unreasonable and destructive ways, rendering relationships impossible, making us simply miserable and susceptible to addictions in an attempt to feel better.

The trapped, suppressed feeling energy tends to have a kind of independent existence and intelligence of its own. It wants to be released from the subconscious, and in order to do this, it must first come within conscious view. Therefore, it cleverly finds ways to bring itself to your attention. The way the subconscious usually works is indirectly. Suppressed feelings attach themselves to appropriate current events in our lives and we are deceived into thinking that the current event is the cause of the feeling. The truth is that the feeling has been stored within, and is only now *reappearing* in association with current events.

Feelings trapped in the subconscious make themselves known by reflecting themselves on your experience in the outer world. This is what is meant by *projection*. When projection occurs, you do not perceive outer reality with objectivity; your perception is skewed by the suppressed feelings inside. Then, you emotionally react to those feelings, adding additional confusion and pain to your experience.

For example, it appears to you as if your boss at work has been critical of your performance. The objective truth is that there has been no criticism, only an inquiring into the reasoning behind a certain recommendation you have made. However, you *feel* as if you are being attacked; you *feel* as if you have failed; you *feel* worthless and inadequate. What you have done is to overlay – or project – negative feelings that are already suppressed inside onto the incident.

Understanding suppression-projection is of basic importance in our work because it shows you how your experience is formed, and enables you to get past the blame that is usually present when difficult experiences arise, and which interferes drastically with the healing process. You see that it is not really the other person or outside circumstance that has caused your pain. The pain was already inside and is just being reflected *and activated* by the outside.

## taking responsibility – owning – dropping blame – forgiveness

These insights relating to suppression-projection enable you to *take responsibility* for your experience. Taking responsibility is essential. If you don't take responsibility, if you don't *own* your experience, you continue to blame, and blame is one of the things that stops inner work dead in its tracks. If you don't take responsibility, you see yourself as a *victim* – a mindset that makes inner work impossible.

When you feel yourself to be a victim, you give your power away to forces outside yourself. You literally render yourself weak and helpless. When you take responsibility, you reclaim your power and make it possible to use it for self-healing. In today's highly misguided world, we see victim consciousness being actively promoted by various factions. Many people ignorantly and even eagerly buy into this warped mindset. It has become the foundation for a personal identity with some people, who are not able to let go and evolve beyond it. If you aren't able to see the tragic absurdity of this frame of reference, your success with inner work is going to be limited.

> I'm sensing you're heavily into blame about this issue. We've talked about the importance of owning feelings. Can you put the blame aside for the moment and come into the feeling?

Try right now to look at a difficult experience you have had and see how it might have been a projection of negativity trapped inside. If you can't see this, just make the assumption that a projection was in operation. Doesn't this consciousness shift make you feel differently about your experience? Don't you feel more in control? If it's coming from the inside, you can do something about it – you're not at the mercy of hostile outer forces. You're not a victim any longer.

But, I can hear you saying, what about experiences where I'm not projecting? What about when I really did get laid off from my job even though I was doing well, or what about when my girlfriend had that weekend fling with someone she had just picked up in the bar, or when someone ran into me when I was sitting at a red light, or what about when my husband gets drunk and starts hitting? These things really happened, I didn't imagine them, I'm not responsible for them, and they caused me a lot of pain. You're telling me these kinds of things are projections?

Yes, I'm telling you that these are all *advanced* forms of projection, where you attract to yourself circumstances, people, and events that correspond to the suppressed energy inside. Because you have not properly handled the more subtle forms of projection, it has intensified to the point of actually manifesting negativity in the material world. This attraction occurs on an energetic-psychic level, of which we are not normally conscious.

## forgiveness

Forgiveness is desirable quality, but it is often misunderstood. Forgiveness is required or possible only when you have mistakenly held the other person responsible for your experience in the first place. When you take responsibility, you bypass forgiveness. You have dropped blame, and so there's no longer the need to forgive. Forgiveness is only possible when you incorrectly believe that forces or people outside yourself are the primary cause of your experience.

Forgiveness can keep you on a low level of consciousness. It tacitly assumes you are a victim, but it encourages you to be "spiritual" or generous or "loving" enough to "forgive" in spite of your continuing belief that the other caused your pain. Such "forgiveness" is intellectual, pseudo, and self-deceptive. It puts you more out of touch with inner experience. It can even inflate the ego, because you think you have been generous enough to "forgive." True forgiveness mean understanding that the original blame was wrong; it is not the granting of a pardon for what we mistakenly believe someone has done to us.

### the stages of projection

It's important to understand projection, and I would like to discuss it in more detail. I recognize three main stages of projection. The first stage is the mildest. Because we have cut ourselves off from parts of our inner self, we become more sensitive to influences and character traits in others that remind us of those cut-off – or suppressed – parts. This is what is meant when it is said that *you see yourself in others*.

However, because we have essentially condemned those inner qualities through the act of suppression, we then usually condemn the outer reflection. We become judgmental, we become intolerant, we condemn the mirror. For example, sexuality. We are sexually suppressed, and then we condemn sexuality outside of ourselves. We suppress the anger within and then condemn and punish those who commit violent acts instead of treating them with compassion. At the same time, we are fascinated by whatever we have suppressed – just look at the sex and violence in film and on TV. We are in the position of resisting and suppressing vital parts of ourselves, recognizing and being attracted to those same qualities in others, and at the same time condemning those qualities in others. It's the beginning of crazymaking.

The second stage of projection is where our feelings become more directly stimulated. We think some situation or person is making us feel a certain way – we assign responsibility for our feelings to others. In this stage, not only are we more sensitive to outside stimuli, but we overlay simple reality with the suppressed inner. We perceive things that are not really there.

Your partner has to work late one night, and all your abandonment fears come up. You feel helpless, angry, alone. You blame your partner, you have a confrontation and make demands. You don't see that the event is just triggering the feelings you hold within. You don't see the real world, you filter it through your layers of suppressed energy and think the cause of your feelings is outside. This is important and basic to understand in our work. Your levels of realization of how you have been buying into these kinds of projections will continue to deepen and amaze you as you go deeper and deeper into the work.

The third level of projection is when you actually attract events and people that correspond to your suppressed energies. You attract someone who really does abandon you, starting with your mother or father, continuing into your first and second marriage. And even when you become aware of the pattern, you seem to be unable to break it. You can't break the pattern because you haven't released the feeling energy behind it. And the worst part is that you will unconsciously create situations, undermine trust, and bring about your negative experience, all dictated by the subconscious in the effort to make itself known and released.

Becoming aware of a negative pattern is an important step in therapy. Often, we are unaware of what motivates us. Awareness starts to loosen the grip of the pattern, and we become more in control, less at the mercy of the pattern. However, simple awareness of the pattern, while an important first step, is almost always not enough to completely eliminate it, and we find ourselves getting drawn again and again into the same limiting, *neurotic*, self-destructive routine – we just don't recognize it at first. This is because the subconscious energy is not released by simple awareness of the pattern. The energy is still there, drawing events and people to us, dictating how we will act and react. In our work, we recognize this situation as a form of projection, where we attract people and situations to us that share a similar or complementary energy.

*You keep attracting the same situation in order to bring up that feeling energy from within for clearing.*

Because we have suppressed certain feelings, our unconscious inner guidance keeps bringing us situations that trigger those feelings, and it will keep doing so until the feelings are released. We could say the Higher-Self is bringing those events to us in order to bring up the energies for clearing, or we could say the feeling energy goes out and attracts events on the inner planes where we have no awareness. In Eastern spirituality, this phenomenon has been known for centuries and is called *Karma*.

If you are at all familiar with the New Age, I'm sure you have heard that "you create your experience." The build-up of suppressed negativity inside finally becomes so extreme that it results in what appears to be objective experience, instead of merely coloring your perception. You unconsciously attract unstable career opportunities; you unconsciously attract an unstable or even abusive romantic partner; you unconsciously attract contentiousness, anger, and violence; you unconsciously attract negative parental and childhood experiences.

However, from an emotional-metaphysical point of view, the purpose of negative events and circumstances is primarily to make you aware of corresponding negative feelings that you have been holding in the subconscious. It's not to punish you. If you can stop blaming the outside world and take responsibility instead, you use your situation to your advantage instead of being abused by it.

By the way, typical New Age "philosophy" might tell you that it's your *thoughts* that have created your experience. Change your thoughts, and you will change your experience, it says. However, it's not really your thoughts that attract negative circumstances, it's suppressed negative *feelings* that attract negative circumstances. Feelings are where the power is, feelings are based on energy. It's this energy that goes out on the psychic level and attracts corresponding energies. Thoughts do not have the same power as feelings. You must release the negative feeling energy suppressed in the subconscious to effectively change your outer experience. Just trying to replace negative thoughts with positive ones, including visualizing what you want to bring into your life, is an unrealistic, ineffective, and often harmful approach to working on yourself.

## outer conditions

The phenomenon of suppression-projection and how it creates our personal world experience must be tempered with a realistic understanding of how the world operates.

If we try to take an objective view of the world, it soon becomes apparent that vast negative forces are at play. I would not deny that these forces exist, that they act independently of us, that they have an agenda, that they may be attempting to attack, control, manipulate and exploit us, and that they do appear to affect us. To deny that these forces exist, or to ignore them in the name of "oneness" or "love" would be delusional, in my opinion. Some well-known spokespersons have advocated love as the answer to the dilemma of worldwide negativity. This is a step in the right direction – that we must work inwardly to rectify outer conditions – but it is highly simplistic and naive.

Negativity exists all around us, but the key to remember is that we are most susceptible to it when we harbor corresponding negativity inside. When you work on yourself, you become less influenced by the negativity outside. It may still be there, but you don't buy into it, you don't feed it, you shift to a place of *transcendence*. It doesn't touch you, or it touches you less.

That is why it is not incorrect to assume that, whatever your experience may be, you are projecting and attracting it for the ultimate purpose of clearing your subconscious. Even though it may be apparently caused by forces outside yourself, you take responsibility for the feelings that are coming up in you, not for the event itself, especially if the feelings are severe or chronic.

*Whenever you have a severe emotional experience in conjunction with external events, you can be sure those feelings have been trapped in the subconscious.*

If those feelings were not suppressed in the subconscious, you would not react the same way. You have not created the world, but you create your experience of it.

But, again, I can hear you say, aren't there simply feelings that don't have any connection to the subconscious? Do I have to always take responsibility? What if I'm doing a simple carpentry job and I bang my thumb with the hammer? It that the subconscious acting up?

Yes, that would most likely be the result of suppressed anger jumping out.

What if there's a flu epidemic and I catch it?

Our working assumption is that your immune system is low and susceptible to the flu because of suppressed negativity.

What if there's a worldwide financial crisis and I lose money?

Yes, again, you were caught in an unfortunate crisis because of suppressed negative feelings such as fear and greed. Not everyone will be affected.

What if there's a national emergency like war, terrorism, or weather catastrophes. Is that my responsibility?

Again, you will be most affected if you are harboring corresponding negative energies. You are not responsible for the events, only for your feelings activated by the events.

What about bad water, bad air, Wi-Fi pollution, aliens invading, and modern-day political correctness?

Ditto above.

## withdrawing projections

As you continue to build skills and capacity for inner work, your awareness increases, and you are able to spot projections in yourself, and others, more easily. Projection is an *unconscious* process, that's why you don't think you are doing it. Just by recognizing it, or even by making the assumption that a projection is in operation whenever difficult circumstances arise, you start to take the power out of the projection – you *withdraw your projections*.

You may find that just recognizing and withdrawing the projection is enough to head off a negative feeling. However, in most cases, the feeling will still occur, and will need to be taken through all the steps of the process. Recognizing and withdrawing the projection then becomes part of the *Awareness* step.

You should not fear, regret, or attempt to do away with projection, even though it is the mechanism through which your experience, both good and bad, is brought to you. Projection is a natural part of life. It's the main way you become aware of the subconscious, along with dreams. Just remember to recognize that pain is a projection from the inside. *Take responsibility* for your experience: The feeling is coming from inside you, only being stirred up by the circumstances. OWN your experience, drop blame, and then proceed with processing the feelings coming up.

## the kali yuga

An interesting concept in conjunction with the deplorable world conditions we see all around us is the notion of the *Kali Yuga*. Hindu Vedic scripture theorizes that human evolution moves through various vast cycles of enlightenment, ranging from highly advanced times when spiritual values and higher consciousness prevail; to degraded times when low-level consciousness takes over. In these dark times, known as the Kali Yuga, selfishness, ignorance, lust, materialism, violence, hatred, criminal leaders and evil in general are dominant. Such are the times we live in. It is entirely possible that we could be heading into even darker times than at present.

The Kali Yuga is said to last for several thousand years. It will not be ending in our lifetimes. But it is not to be regarded as a calamity or mischievous prank on the part of whoever may have designed the human experience. On the contrary, it is essential for human growth. It is only at a time of darkness when the sinister, hidden forces within us will be stimulated/projected into awareness for clearing. If you lived at a time of love and light, the negativity within would never rise to the surface. This could be a major part of why you have incarnated on the Earth plane now. Take advantage of the opportunity.

# Emotions and Feelings

We have been talking about emotions and feelings in a general way. Let's get more specific about what we mean. What is an emotion? What is a feeling? Are they the same or different?

*Feelings* are psychic perceptions of pleasure/pain. The kind of negative feeling with which we generally work tends to be distressful, painful, crippling. You feel pain when expectations, beliefs, needs, or desires are thwarted.

*Painful feelings occur when the reality of* what is *conflicts with your conception of* what should be.

Negative *emotions* are composed of inner feeling energy moving and being blocked. The inner energy is the feeling; the blocking occurs on the *mental* level, in the mind. The blocking is the same as the *resistance* I have mentioned, and is usually unconscious.

*Emotions occur when feelings are resisted. When inner feeling energy meets mental blocking resistance, an eruption results, which is the emotion.*

When your boss appeared to criticize your work, the projected feelings that came up for you were failure, worthlessness, and inadequacy. These are your core feelings, and if you can just recognize that a projection is in progress, take responsibility for the feeling experience, and then move it through the steps of the process, the feelings will start to clear from your subconscious. However, because of unconscious mental inner blocking/resistance, you react to the feelings with emotions: You become insulted, angry, and confrontational, or else you withdraw into yourself, hurt, sad, and depressed.

It's helpful to distinguish between feelings and emotions as you work on yourself. In general, you will apply processing steps to both, but there are some occasions when they will be treated differently.

What about happy emotions? Because of the principle of duality, happy emotions depend on the existence of negative emotions and are formed because of the same blocking. As we become more and more enlightened, we don't experience the same highs and lows, the same emotional intensity. A transcendental equanimity replaces up and down ego-based emotions. But you don't have to intellectualize about this now. Just do the work.

## core feelings and first-level emotions

A key insight regarding feelings and emotions is that there is a feeling behind every emotion; an emotion is always based on a resisted feeling. As you meet with any particular event or circumstance, often you will first become aware of the emotion, assuming you are reasonably in touch with yourself. However, in order to do lasting work on the feeling-emotional level, you must always eventually get to the associated core feeling.

In order to emphasize the distinction between them, we refer to emotions as *first-level,* meaning they are what you often first encounter as you look inward, and we refer to the feelings behind them as *core feelings,* meaning they are at the root of the issue.

*When negative core feeling energy meets unconscious resistance of the mind, it explodes into the first-level emotional experience.*

First-level emotions are usually active, closer to consciousness, such as panic, anger, lust, hatred, cravings, frustration, sadness, depression, compulsiveness, jealousy, or anxiety. Since the emotional experience can be intense, it often obscures the core feeling behind it. When you are faced with an emotion, you will feel the strong energy pulsing in your body. It can be a compelling, even wild force inside you. Don't be afraid of it – stay with it as you process it. It won't hurt you, especially if you remain detached and are careful to not act it out. As you stay with it, taking it through the steps of the process, at some point it will lead to the underlying core feeling.

The core feeling, in comparison, will feel cool, inactive, quiet. It is not as overly dramatic as the first-level emotion, but will include feelings such as inadequacy, rejection, frustration, heartbreak, loss, betrayal. There will be a sense of detached stillness, presence, and surrender as you engage the core feeling. This is what you are aiming for as you process any event. When you get to that still, calm place, even though you may be contending with a painful feeling, you have reached the place of optimal processing. This is the state I look for when I am facilitating a client.

There may be several levels of different emotions related to any event or circumstance; there may be several levels to go through before you get to the core feeling. Sometimes, there may be more than one core feeling. Usually, you will know when you are at a core feeling. It will feel like the basis of the issue.

Let's look at some examples of how first-level emotions are associated with core feelings:

Behind the emotion of envy is the core feeling of inferiority.

Behind the emotion of anger is the core feeling of rejection.

Behind the emotion of anger is the core feeling of being used.

Behind the emotion of anxiety, restlessness, or paranoia is the core feeling of fear.

These are only examples. Any emotion can have almost any feeling behind it. You must look inside and see what's there for you. You apply the steps of the process to both first-level emotions and core feelings. They are both energetic knots that can be suppressed and built-up and in need of release. They will both respond to *Relaxation, Awareness, Acceptance, Direct Experience,* and *Witnessing*. However, you want to keep in mind that your eventual goal is always to get to the core feelings.

At first, the core feelings may not be apparent. All you feel is a first-level emotion. As you process the emotion, eventually the core feelings will make themselves known. When you come upon a core feeling, it's usually a sign that you should move to processing it; you've spent enough time processing the emotion. But make sure you have in fact spent enough time on the emotion for it to start to dissipate.

Anger, for example, has built-up in many of us and in the collective subconscious to the point where it has become explosive rage that can be triggered by the slightest occurrence. Serious processing time must be allocated to its release, but still, it is a first-level emotion with deeper core feelings behind it such as helplessness, frustration, lack, disrespect, coercion, etc.

In today's world, a number of energy therapies are available, including tapping on the acupuncture meridians. It's my impression, both from my own experience and from speaking with clients who have tried these energy therapies and with several energy practitioners, that these therapies, if they work at all, would tend to be most effective with first-level emotions, since emotions are based on energies in the body. Deep core feelings represent another level of psychic congestion that the energy therapy format may not reach.

## reactiveness

There are yet other kinds of emotional responses to be considered. These occur *in reaction to* suppressed feelings that become activated in any stressful situation.

### 1. REACTIVE EMOTIONS

If you watch yourself closely whenever a stressful situation arises, you will see that you often have a secondary emotional reaction to your primary experience. We call this secondary emotion *reactive* because it occurs as an involuntary response to the initial experience. You might become angry about your anger, sad about your sadness, or afraid of your fear. You can also become despondent, depressed, impatient, blaming, vindictive, guilty or shamed about your anger, sadness, fear, or any other emerging subconscious feeling.

This second reaction is of *the mind*. However, it does have a quasi-emotional component. Since it is mind-based, and not part of the suppressed subconscious, it can be put aside by an act of will. Suppressed feelings and emotions, on the contrary, cannot be put aside by an act of will; they must be processed.

But if you are in the grip of a reactive emotion, by simply realizing it, you can often save yourself some grief. Dropping the reactive emotion does not affect the underlying first-level emotion and core feelings; it just makes them accessible. If you can't easily drop the reactive emotion, then process it.

If you process the reactive emotion, you can't get into trouble, but it's often not necessary. You will be spinning your wheels for a bit – until you wear out the reactive emotion and get to the first-level and core feelings behind it. Becoming aware of reactive emotions can be quite interesting from a detached, clinical point of view; it represents an advanced ability for inner work.

Guilt and shame are sometimes a major part of psychological work. They can become crippling, and can result in misconceptions such as thinking you must get/beg for forgiveness from persons you have "wronged." In my counseling work, I have had my share of guilt-paralyzed clients, some of whom have been unable to find resolution in traditional therapy. I have always had success with guilt or shame by regarding them as *reactive emotions*. The strategy is to put them aside as we look at the suppressed feelings associated with them. When these primary feelings are addressed and resolved, guilt and shame dissolve along with them.

## 2. THE REACTIVE EMOTIONAL IMPULSE

The next type of reactiveness is what I call the *reactive emotional impulse*. For example, suppose you have been hurt in a close relationship and feel vindictive towards the other person. It would be a mistake to simply stay with what you are feeling at the moment, which is primarily the urge to strike back. Although vindictiveness is a feeling, it is not the type of feeling we wish to take through the process. It does not represent a suppressed feeling; it is more of a *reactive emotional impulse* to the suppressed feelings being activated. Any response to retaliate, to return hurt for hurt, to take spiteful action, to blame, is a reactive emotional impulse and will be self-defeating in the long run.

Or, as extreme example, suppose you are deep in a quagmire and feel hopeless and suicidal. It would be a mistake to sit with these feelings because they are not suppressed feelings coming up; they represent an involuntary emotional reaction to your circumstances and the suppressed feelings being activated. You must look beyond the hopeless and suicidal impulse and find the emotions and feelings that are generating it.

You must diligently watch for and carefully separate reactive emotional impulses from valid emerging subconscious feelings. Put the reactive emotional impulse aside and go to the emotions/feelings behind it. If you were to attempt to process the reactive emotional impulse, you would get nowhere. Perhaps you would wear it out at some point, but it is also possible that opening to it would prove to be an undesirable influence. I know I just said it is permissible to process *reactive emotions,* but that does not extend to *reactive emotional impulses*, especially those of a violent or self-destructive nature.

> I can see you've been hurt, but I'd like you to understand that your feeling of wanting to return hurt with hurt is a counter-productive reactive emotional impulse and not a feeling that needs to be processed. Put it aside and look at the feelings behind it.

A reactive emotional impulse is actually as much a *thought* as it is a *feeling.* It's the impulsive *thought* to take action, in response to the feeling emerging from the subconscious. But since there is so much emotion associated with it, it's not inaccurate to call it an emotional impulse. The reactive mind has not yet learned that any action it takes to try to dismiss negative feelings is counter-productive. The mind needs to get out of the way and simply allow feelings *to be;* it does not need to intervene.

Sometimes, it may be appropriate to allow the reactive emotional impulse to motivate us, if we are in immediate danger, for example. But in most cases, the reactive emotional impulse will be only a knee-jerk, superficial, defensive, ego-based response that will eventually work against you if you allow it to determine your behavior.

Therefore, when you are processing, you need to make sure it is not a reactive emotional impulse you are processing. Don't sit with an image and emotion/thought of wanting to hurt someone to get even. Don't sit with a emotion/thought of how bad things are going for you and what you are going to do about it. Don't sit in blame, despair, guilt, or shame. Go deeper. Once you have addressed the first-level and core feelings behind any reactive emotional impulse, it will automatically dissolve and no longer be a factor.

The key insight about a reactive emotional impulse is that it is not part of the suppressed subconscious, and therefore does not need to be processed. You just need to recognize when you are in the grip of such an impulse, and you have the choice whether to yield to it or not.

Another type of reactive emotional tendency to watch out for is *emotionalism.* This is when we are overly emotional, easily agitated, reacting with what appears to be strong feeling or even hysteria, and possibly continual anguished crying. Emotionalism, or *drama,* is another way that we unconsciously react in order to defend ourselves from confronting core feelings. Continual emotionalism does not release feelings, as it may appear to do. It is only a diversion.

Crying can be therapeutic at the right time. It can coincide with emotional release, especially when you move into the Heart. Excessive crying, however, suggests that it is no longer performing this function, but has become a means of avoidance – turning away from the core feeling. Try to restrain excessive crying by looking with a clear awareness into the feeling level – look for the feeling behind the tears. Your awareness (intellectual level) can control the unproductive reactive emotionalism of crying as a defense on the lower feeling level.

## 3. REACTIVE BEHAVIOR

The other aspect of *Awareness* you will apply in FEEL II is to eventually identify and rein back on any habitual *reactive behavior* you tend to fall into when faced with difficult feelings.

Stop and identify your habitual response to negative feelings.

Recognize that it is an outward expression of self-rejection.

Do your best to stay *non-reactive.* Replace the *reactive behavior* with going inward and processing the underlying feelings.

The reactive behavior could include trying to change the outer in order to fix the inner as discussed in FEEL 0. It can include compulsions, addictions, withdrawing, getting depressed, confrontational, or rebellious, overeating, excessive drug or alcohol use, or any kind of mood-altering escapist activity such as TV, video games, internet and cell phone compulsiveness, and in general *acting out* feelings instead of containing and processing them.

It doesn't matter what the activity, if used to avoid unpleasant feelings, it is escapist, counterproductive and often downright self-destructive. Feelings are only suppressed, and build up more.

It can be difficult to modify this kind of reactive behavior by an act of will. As you develop an *Emotional Clearing* practice, however, you start to chip away at the core feelings motivating you, and your need to engage in reactive/escapist/compulsive behavior falls away without struggle.

## stay non-reactive

So when I tell you to stay *Non-Reactive*, it should be clear that I am not referring to the original emotion/feeling at issue. You want to allow your natural, spontaneous, uninhibited emotions and feelings to come up, but then you don't react to them in the ways discussed. You want to allow the original emotion/feeling to take place unhampered by mental interference and even to expand as you process it.

Remember that the urge to take action to remedy the emotional situation does not resolve it in the long run. The underlying feelings are not affected. Compulsive impulses can never be satisfied by taking action and pursuing outer acquisitions.

What about taking action to provide for basic needs and to function in the world? Of course, we need to do this. What I am talking about here are compulsive impulses undertaken with the intent to alleviate the built-up, suppressed feelings that are emerging. This is different from "normal" actions taken in the course of life.

## three types of feelings

Therefore, there are three types of feelings that we work with. You need to be able to recognize each for what it is as part of the *Awareness* step, and treat it appropriately.

1. **Core Negative Feelings** are at the root of the issue – this is what is to be processed.

2. **First-Level Emotions** may be what first comes to your attention. These should be processed, and when the Core Feeling behind them is discovered, processing shifts to that.

3. **Reactive Emotional Impulses** can be the initial unenlightened, ego-based, acting-out response to issues, often associated with habitual behavior and character tendencies. Put them aside and go to the emotions or feelings behind them.

# The Centers of Consciousness

We're going to get more specific now about the emotions and feelings you can encounter. This is quite important in that it will expand your awareness and vocabulary regarding the feeling world, enabling you to identify aspects of yourself of which you have been oblivious.

I find it works well in practice to assign feelings to 10 categories, or centers. I would encourage you to start thinking in terms of these centers. Not only do they give you a convenient way to organize your feeling experience, but later we will correlate the centers to the body chakra energy points, which adds another dimension to our work. Most of our activity is in the lower centers, so we'll talk about them first. The centers correspond to the needs, drives, and basic desires that are hard-wired into the human psychological system:

| | |
|---|---|
| 1. Survival | 6. Heart |
| 2. Power | 7. Expression |
| 3. Sensation | 8. Creative |
| 4. Nurturing | 9. Witnessing |
| 5. Significance | 10. Transcendental |

We all have a minimal amount of activity in each of the centers, but some may be relatively inactive and in need of development. If we are primarily focused in the lower centers, our consciousness is usually relatively low-level. If we are primarily focused in the higher centers, we exhibit higher-consciousness traits, but still, all the centers must be active and healthy for optimal emotional well-being. Sometimes certain centers will be especially important for a time, or even for our whole life. For example, we may be wrapped up in life-long Significance pursuits.

The following summary presents the *Core Feelings, First-Level Emotions,* and *Reactive Emotional Impulses* resulting from blocking in the various centers. Remember there is some flexibility in the correspondences. Don't try to rigidly apply the correspondences to yourself. As mentioned, an emotion such as anger can relate to various kinds of core feelings. Fear is another that can attach itself to a variety of feelings. Even though we consider fear to be a primary core feeling, it can also serve as a first-level feeling. We can have fear about the prospect of abandonment, for example. The key is to see what is there for you as you look inside, and to validate it all, taking the feelings as they come. Always aim for the core feeling, and assume you will recognize it as such when you find it.

I would suggest going slowly through the following summary of the Centers of Consciousness. As you read, try to self-generate each of the feelings, emotions, and impulses. Some of these may ring true for you if you have issues in that area. Some may be less relevant, but in order to cultivate your empathetic feeling capacity, it's an interesting exercise to make an effort to feel each of the items. It's very possible you will discover some areas that have previously been unknown to you and are awaiting your tender attention.

Along with *Reactive Emotional Impulses,* the following list includes some reactive types of behavior that *the mind* adopts as a response to painful feelings, trying to defend against them, resulting in self-rejection. I've tried to include typical reactive impulses, but the list is by no means complete. Once you get the idea, you will probably identify your own unique ways of reacting to your feelings, thereby suppressing them.

## 1. Survival

The Survival Center is the most basic to all living creatures. Its keynotes are safety, security, health, abundance, and life itself. When these instincts are thwarted, we experience anxiety, instability, and fear. We become fear-driven, compulsively clinging to any faint promise of security. It's normal and desirable to have a certain amount of caution to keep us on guard against legitimate dangers, but if you have large amounts of suppressed fear, you become unbalanced, irrational and obsessed. As you advance in feeling-based inner growth, you little by little come to the realization that you are indeed an indestructible spiritual being only temporarily housed in a 3D physical world; fear drops off without effort. To get to that point, however, you must first release the suppressed core negative feelings associated with the Survival center. If you are immersed in Survival issues, you are overly concerned with safety, money, and health.

> **core negative feelings:** Fear, Lack, Loss, Physical Pain, Sickness, Death.

> **first-level emotions:** Anxiety, Panic, Nervousness, Paranoia, Restlessness.

> **reactive emotional impulse:** Grasping for security and money, Survival struggle, Clinging, Greed, Self-sabotaging.

## 2. Power

The Power Center resonates with freedom and self-determination; the ability to control one's destiny. It follows the basic Survival Center in importance. After Survival, the next most important thing that people will fight and die for is freedom. If we feel restricted, enslaved, used, we start to contact the negative aspects of this center. This is where we unconsciously give away our Power to influences outside ourselves and allow them to dominate us. We see ourselves as a victim. Processing the core negative feelings of this center reverses this, and allows us to reclaim our Power and true independence. This is also the archetypal feminine sexual center, corresponding to *receptiveness*.

**core negative feelings:** Helplessness, Weakness, Feeling Enslaved, Used, Dominated, Manipulated, Taken advantage of, Cheated, Controlled, Restricted, Coerced, Invaded.

**first-level emotions:** Anger, Rage.

**reactive emotional impulse:** Fighting for freedom, Rebelliousness against authority, Victimhood, Thoughtless non-conformity, Control tendencies, Submissive tendencies, sexual or otherwise.

## 3. Sensation

Sensation is the center of sexuality and sensuality. The world is viewed as a source of *pleasure gratification* when this center is un-combined with higher, more refined feelings. Today's highly sexualized world paradoxically suggests widespread basic suppression of the sexual impulse, even with the excessive acting-out that seems to surround us; otherwise there would be no response to the sexual stimuli with which we are bombarded. We are trapped in compulsive seeking and acting-out, never to be fulfilled. Such is the nature of suppressed feelings; they can never be ultimately satisfied, but must be processed to release. If you have sexual issues, make a habit of processing sexual impulses and associated feelings such as anger, shame, or being blocked without yielding to them. This is the archetypal masculine sexual center, corresponding to *aggressiveness* and *assertiveness*.

**core negative feelings:** Unresolved Sexual Tension, Sexual hunger, Lust, Tension in General.

**first-level emotions:** Frustration, Anger, Shame, Being blocked.

**reactive emotional impulse:** Violent acting out, Sexual acting-out, Obsessively seeking release through sensual activities: Sex, Touch, Luxury, Entertainment.

## 4. Nurturing

The Nurturing Center has to do with emotionally receiving and emotions/feelings in general. It governs feelings related to being cared for, fed physically and emotionally, mothering and being mothered. Our hunger for these experiences, the pain of their absence or dysfunction, as well as cravings for food, alcohol, drugs, and smoking, and a general sense of emotional neediness and emptiness are what is to be processed to bring this center into alignment. Processing the pain of not being open to receive, not being nurtured, being hungry and needy, being emotionally shut down is how the capacity for nurturing may be developed. As the neediness and emptiness are welcomed, accepted, and experienced, you break the blocks to self-nurturing.

> **core negative feelings:** Emotional Neediness, Emptiness, Psychological hunger for Nurturing, Warmth.

> **first-level emotions:** Cravings for Food, Smoking, Drugs; Absent or cold mothering.

> **reactive emotional impulse:** Indulging in substances, Seeking a mothering figure, Emotional dependence, Vicarious attachment, Clinging, Energy siphoning, Dependency on children.

## 5. Significance

The Significance Center is the psychological home of the ego, having to do with needs for recognition, self-image, self-esteem, status, worth, success, achievement, authority, competence, identity, and the fathering experience. The drive for Significance is very powerful and may be considered to be one of the three primary drives, along with Survival and Sex. You may become driven for success, accomplishment, and recognition because you feel a deficiency, but no level of attainment can satisfy you. You always feel the need for more and continue to compulsively pursue the non-attainable. In this center, typically you are driven by a diminished sense of self. You feel inadequate, worthless, not good enough, insignificant, empty – these are the feelings to process.

> **core negative feelings:** Insignificance, Inadequacy, Worthlessness, Disapproval, Disrespect, Failure, Not being good enough.
>
> **first-level emotions:** Anger, Frustration, Envy, Absent or cold fathering experience.
>
> **reactive emotional impulse:** Compulsively seeking Approval, Recognition, Success; Overly ambitious; Compulsive need for Structure; Emotional dependence on authority or Father figure.

## 6. Heart

If the Heart is shut down, we are cold and inhuman. When the Heart opens, we start to activate higher human potentials, but we also become subject to the unavoidable vicissitudes of love. On a lower-self, dependent, dualistic level, where most of us operate, love is always painful. Loss, fear, and resentment always accompany love. It is the ultimate ambivalent dichotomy, forever tormenting us. You may bumble through life, perhaps lucky to find a temporary liaison that seems to carry you through. But in the end, there will be the pain of separation. The goal is to become a warrior of the spirit, so strong inside that you are beyond the need for dependent, attached "relationships." You are complete unto yourself, you have joined male and female within. You do not seek to be coupled to another in order to become whole. How do you become complete unto yourself? By facing and processing the inescapable, inevitable pain of the Heart. There is no other way. Acceptance of heartbreak de-crystallizes the frozen Heart and matures the young naive Heart. This is the opportunity.

> **core negative feelings:** Heartbreak, Hatred, Rejection, Betrayal, Abandonment, Loneliness, Isolation, Abuse, Loss of Love, Alienation, Coldness, Grief, Breach of Trust.
>
> **first-level emotions:** Sadness, Hurt, Resentment, Longing, Remorse, Humiliation, Embarrassment, Jealousy.
>
> **reactive emotional impulse:** Dependent attachment, Possessiveness, Vindictiveness, Shame, Guilt, Self-pity, Excessive emotionalism.

If you discover intense hatred in the Heart:

Withdraw the hatred from the object, whether it's another person or yourself. Allow the hatred *to be*, without an object. It's normal to have hatred. It's part of the Heart. Relax into it. Feel it in the body, without extending into the world.

It doesn't really matter whether hatred is directed towards another or towards oneself; this is a somewhat arbitrary choice determined by other factors. For example, a child usually directs negative feelings inwardly – a tendency that may carry over into adulthood. The important factor is the hatred itself, which can be processed, released, and brought into balance.

Most of the suppressed energies we carry are confined to the six lower centers just discussed. This is where our work will be focused. After we get clear in these centers, we start to spontaneously activate higher centers. However, it is possible to be active in the higher centers without the lower being entirely integrated; but if the lower centers are holding substantial negativity, the higher centers will be unstable. For example, we have artists who are talented, but liable to drug addiction; leaders who may be charismatic speakers but whose motivation is based on self-interest.

## 7. Expression

The capacity for Expression, both verbal and through other means, is acquired as we clear the lower centers. We gain the ability to influence others, to make ourselves heard. The negative feelings of this center to be processed include not being able to express yourself or communicate effectively, or not being heard.

**core negative feelings:** Blocked expression; Can't speak, Can't be heard, Ignored.

**first-level emotions:** Frustration, Resentment.

**reactive emotional impulse:** Withdraw, Argue, Gossip, Excessive talking.

## 8. Creative

When the Creative Center comes into play, we express our higher selves. We experience the joy that comes from creative endeavor. Being active on the creative level is one of the best ways to raise your vibration. You experience a level of consciousness unknown to the average person, who is primarily concerned with survival, sex, and other lower-level, ego-centered pursuits. This is why the stereotypical artist, inventor, or entrepreneur is unconcerned with materialistic needs – they function on a higher plane of being. There are pitfalls to the artistic life, however. Since almost all my time is spent in creative activity, this is an area of prime importance for me. Some years ago I wrote a book I would refer you to for a detailed discussion of the creative life if you are interested. It's called *Emotion and Art: Mastering the Challenges of the Artist's Path*. One of the key pitfalls is self-criticism, which everyone, not only artists, experiences. Regard self-criticism as a *Reactive Emotional Impulse;* put it aside and go to the core feelings behind it.

> **core negative feelings:** Doubt, Being drained, Isolated, Feeling untalented, Unrecognized, Unfulfilled.
>
> **first-level emotions:** Dullness, Boredom, Blocked Creativity.
>
> **reactive emotional impulse:** Self-criticize.

## 9. Witnessing

The *Witness* Center marks the beginning of the higher consciousness experience. We will discuss this later at length.

> **core negative feelings:** Ungroundedness, Airiness, Disconnection, Boundary issues.
>
> **first-level emotions:** Distress, Confusion, Clinical Disassociation.
>
> **reactive emotional impulse:** Overemphasize logical thinking as the means to resolve issues.

## 10. Transcendental

This center marks the authentic higher consciousness. We shift beyond lower-self ego orientation and start to connect with our Higher-Self.

**core negative feelings:** Isolation, Cut off from Source.

**first-level emotions:** Despair, Depression, Despondency, Selfishness, Longing for completion.

**reactive emotional impulse:** Acting out of self-interest, Compulsive searching, Reckless behavior.

# Acceptance

At the start of this book, we briefly looked at how resistance and rejection of our feeling selves leads to disvalidation of feelings and creation of the negative subconscious. Let's continue that discussion.

### consciousness shift 5: understanding self-rejection

We seem to have an intuitive, built-in instinct of how to disvalidate feelings. We could speculate that becoming aware of this counterproductive tendency and eliminating it is part of what we are here to learn. Life is, indeed, a journey through experience that is intended to impart wisdom. Until we gain wisdom, however, life continues, largely fueled by the suppressed energies we hold within. These energies project themselves, coloring or dictating our life experience, and we are presented with challenges we must master.

I'd like to suggest that you start to think of your mind as something you possess, but something which is not the real you. You are more related to *the Witness*, that part of you which detaches from and disidentifies with experience. You then start to use your mind as a tool, to accomplish what the higher part of you wants.

As you get to objectively know your mind, you are likely to see that it often works against your best interests. One of the ways it does this is to *unconsciously* engage in *self-rejection*. I'm sure you have heard of self-rejection, and know that it is considered undesirable, but do you really understand what it means, and how you do it, and exactly how much of your time is spent in self-rejection?

Self-rejection results from your unconscious disapproving attitude towards your negative feelings. Your feelings – of all types, positive and negative – are a vital part of yourself. When you align the mind against any of them, rejecting them, you are indeed rejecting yourself. This attitude of self-rejection goes deep into the subconscious and permeates it until you are filled with an overriding sense of inadequacy, doubt, despair, and depression.

Rejection occurs when you *make-wrong*, and self-rejection occurs when you make something wrong about yourself. What is it that you most often make-wrong? Usually, more than any other aspect of yourself, it is your *feelings* that you make-wrong. That's why they don't complete their natural cycle. Most of us don't recognize that we are in continual rejection of ourselves much of the time, but because we believe that certain feelings are bad for us, we make-wrong and reject those feelings and ourselves.

*When you reject or make-wrong any feeling, you reject yourself.*

Look carefully within, at any negative feeling with which you may be contending, and see if there is a subtle sense of making the feeling wrong. There's bound to be, because we instinctively assume that anything painful is bad, and that we must fight, control, conquer, and get rid of anything that appears to be bad for us.

But I can hear you saying, what? You want me to accept my fear, my anger, my loneliness? That's crazy, how will I ever get better if I accept my pain?

What I'm trying to *enlighten* you about is that the attitude of self-rejection is worse for you than the feeling to which it is applied; that when you make-wrong, reject, and disvalidate any feeling – including painful feelings of any sort – you are hurting yourself more than the feelings themselves could hurt you because you are building the suppressed subconscious and laying the foundation for ongoing emotional distress. When you accept the feeling instead of making it wrong, you start the process that will eventually result in resolution and release of the feeling.

Another way of explaining the make-wrong mindset is to trace it back to an inner *resistance* that does not want to open to pain. Again, there's no mystery why we feel this way. Our instinct tells us to be safe, and avoid danger. But the amazing and unexpected thing about resistance and making-wrong is that they *amplify* the pain. By turning away, the pain appears worse than it need be.

*Resistance, self-rejection, and making-wrong cause your feelings to be more painful than they actually are.*

As you apply the Acceptance step in FEEL II, you will look for the inner resistance that results in making-wrong and self-rejection; you will replace the resistance with a sense of acceptance, of being OK with the feeling, of relaxing into it, of *allowing it*. This becomes much easier when you are in a relaxed *Alpha-Witness* state.

### neutral acceptance

The acceptance to which I am referring is not the same as actively *being for* something. Resistance is *against*, but acceptance for us does not mean *being for*. It is more of a neutral acceptance, neither for nor against. *Neutral acceptance* is the simple, passive recognition and acknowledgement of *what is*. You don't have to force yourself to try to "love" *what is;* you only need to neutrally accept it. You don't fight *what is*, you simply admit that it already exists. You stay present with it. With regard to feelings, you stop fighting your feelings. You just see your true feelings.

Bringing the perception of *what is* to the *feeling level* is critical. While it is possible to focus on external events and circumstances and to struggle with applying acceptance to them, it is much more beneficial, and easier, to apply acceptance to internal feelings. This means your focus shifts to how you are actually, truly, honestly feeling now, in the context of those external events and circumstances.

The application of *neutral acceptance* is critical when considering painful feelings, as well as *physical body* health issues. When processing feelings, we align the mind by recognizing resistance and replacing it with *neutral acceptance*, and then go beyond the mind, to *the Witness*, a place where the question of resistance and acceptance no longer apply.

But before you can replace resistance with neutral acceptance, you must be able to spot resistance in yourself. It can be hard to recognize resistance because the sad truth is that most of us are so deeply immersed in it that we just can't see it. But if you look closely, you will find it. Try this simple exercise right now. Put the book down, close your eyes, and in your imagination:

Observe the difference in your inner sense of being when you visualize something or someone you like, and then something or someone you don't like.

You should be able to sense a kind of "opening" to the liked object, and a kind of "closing off" to the disliked object. The feeling may be centered at the Heart. If you can't feel anything, you might want to continue the exercise daily, stretching to feel the energetic sensations.

What you are feeling is on the level of the *energy body*. On this level, you sense energy currents, especially when they become intense and appear to you as emotions. These energy currents are just subtle inner sensations, but they have drastic ramifications, directly contributing to the accumulation of feeling negativity that is resisted, or to its releasing when accepted.

### circumstances

Note that the acceptance you inwardly apply is directed towards feelings only. I'm not asking you to accept the circumstances that gave rise to the feelings. Make a distinction between inner feelings and outer events and circumstances. You especially don't want to try to accept events and circumstances that are clearly harmful or life-threatening. However, the associated feelings are always to be accepted.

For example, if you are faced with money issues that are bringing up core feelings of scarcity, loss, impoverishment, etc., it is these *feelings* that you accept, not the circumstances. You will continue to *prefer* that you have ample material resources at your disposal; this is a basic requirement of life, and you will continue to take whatever steps possible in order to achieve financial balance. You do not become apathetic about meeting life's challenges. At the same time, you recognize that this is your opportunity to clear and release inner suppressed negativity that has built up and attracted these difficult circumstances. You maintain equanimity in the face of difficult feelings, applying the steps of the process to them, releasing them and eventually eliminating the need for the circumstances.

However, that said, I believe you will find that as you apply acceptance to the feelings behind any difficult circumstances and not the circumstances themselves, your attitude towards the circumstances is also modified, and a kind of acceptance of them results also. So, you are accepting and allowing your feelings, which results in a more relaxed attitude towards the difficulties, but you continue to persevere in correcting the difficulties. You do not cave in, negate, ignore or get run over by life's challenges.

> Look within, and find any resistance you may have to the feeling. Resistance is often unconscious, so look deep within. You may find it in your body, or perceive it as a mental impulse that wants to block or push away the feeling.

> Replace the resistance with acceptance, to whatever extent you are able. It's OK to have the feeling. Gently drop the resistance, even if it's only partially, just by making the intention.

> We are only accepting *feelings* that are present now. We are not accepting, condoning, or giving permission for negative circumstances to continue into the future.

> Silently repeat to yourself, "I fully accept my feeling of _____."

Let's look at an example of applying Acceptance and dropping the associated reactive behavior pattern:

You lost your job, and feel as if you are a failure. The loss of the job is the event. You don't want to try force yourself to accept the loss of the job, in fact ideally you don't want to have any opinion about it. It happened, and although there may be some factors that appear to have contributed to the loss, in the end, we don't really know why things happen as they do. However, your feelings, *as they are*, need to be validated, honored, and accepted.

You feel like a failure – OK, that's a valid feeling that can be worked with. It's not an objective evaluation – it's subjective. We always validate and honor all feelings, at the same time recognizing that they are subjective and not necessarily "accurate." From a psychological-metaphysical point of view, the purpose of losing the job was to make you aware of the feelings of failure that you have been dragging around in the subconscious. If you simply ignore the feelings or try to fix them with a pep-talk and psyched-up pseudo-confidence, you will most likely repeat the experience in the next job.

However, your continuing reactive pattern is to try to control your feelings by giving yourself the pep-talk and trying to psych-up your confidence: You remember times in the past when you were successful; you list all your positive qualities; you envision positive outcomes. Then, when you wear yourself out, you retreat to your favorite bar where you mood-alter and attempt to get rid of the negative feelings still there by compulsive talking. All these efforts resulted in self-rejection – you resisting and making-wrong your feelings as they are, and being drawn into a non-productive reactive pattern of behavior. Is it possible you lost the job and there were no trapped feelings of failure that were responsible? Yes, but then you would not be taking it so hard, and you would not be incapacitated by those feelings. Whenever strong feelings are present, it points to a subconscious accumulation manifesting.

To work with this scenario, you process the feelings of being a failure, taking them through the steps. You recognize your reactive behavior pattern (the pep-talk and the bar) and put it aside, focusing your energies into an inner processing mode. The core feelings you work with include feelings such as the basic feeling of failure; fear that you are now financially vulnerable; feelings that you are incapable of taking care of yourself and others; and probably a lot of first-level anger, sadness, and depression about it all. These feelings will emerge, one by one, in no particular order, as you enter a processing mode. As you process, the feelings are lifted, and the urge to indulge in the reactive pattern is bypassed.

Perhaps the circumstances were different concerning the loss of the job. Perhaps you feel that you were treated unfairly for no good reason. Perhaps you feel as if you are up against forces impersonally aligned against you. While this may be true, especially in today's world, processing steps still apply. The first feeling you may encounter could be anger. You take it through the steps, cool it down, and then get to the core feelings, which could be Control center issues – being dictated to, dominated, being made subservient, having no say over your destiny.

## modes of self-rejection

All the feeling-disvalidating types of behavior we discussed in FEEL 0 can be considered to be forms of self-rejection. Here are a few more modes of self-rejecting behavior to add to the list:

### acting-out

You must be careful not to fall into the trap of *acting-out* feelings. When you act-out, you allow feelings to motivate you into unnecessary drama or actions. For example, in FEEL I Jean acted-out her fear by taking excessive safety precautions.

In acting-out, the feeling is expressed outwardly, usually in some type of behavior, instead of being contained for inner processing and release. A most obvious form of acting-out would be to carelessly vent anger on others or to try to get even with or hurt others who appear to be frustrating you.

But there are more subtle, unconscious forms of acting-out. With anger, you may unconsciously provoke others into anger, not recognizing or admitting to it in yourself. If you are lonely, you act-out by hanging out in the bar or the internet all the time. If you think you are a failure, you act-out by boasting about your "achievements" in the attempt to compensate. Acting-out is ultimately self-defeating because it is based on the false premise that you can fix the feeling by taking action.

### setting yourself up

One of the most common forms of *unconscious* acting-out is to set yourself up for the appearance of the negative. If you have issues with authority, for example, you set up a situation, usually provoking the authority figure upon which you are projecting with unreasonable requests or complaints, and then you react and rebel when they try to talk sense. If you have issues with abandonment, you provoke others into abandoning you. If you have significance issues, you act in such a way as to cause disrespect. You are acting crazy, and you don't realize it.

Once you develop basic psychological astuteness and become aware of this mechanism, it's hard to go through a day without coming across it repeatedly. You see it in others, and sometimes you will be the target. You will also see it in yourself, as you set yourself up to fall. If you can adopt the right attitude – detached, seeing the humor in it – you start to move beyond the need for it. If you catch yourself doing it, and it's too late to avoid repercussions, just take advantage of the situation and process the feelings that are coming up, taking responsibility. After all, that's what you wanted all along, isn't it?

### displacement

*Displacement* is another form of acting-out. It is the unconscious act of shifting a feeling onto another person in an attempt to get rid of it. You would have to be especially psychologically savvy in order to spot this in yourself. I once had a client who would humiliate her husband, making him feel he was not good enough, in the unconscious effort to get rid of that feeling in herself.

### expressing feelings

Sometimes expression is appropriate, for example, if you have an issue with *unassertiveness*, but in the end, it's not the answer to trapped feelings. You think the feeling will go away if you get angry, let that person know how you feel, stand up for your rights, get it off your chest, get rid of it, vent, explain, communicate, confront, share, defend or 'express' yourself, even in more refined forms such as art-making. These are all types of uninformed, self-defeating *blameful expression*. The feeling is just buried deeper and *reinforced*. You don't need to outwardly express the feeling, you just need to experience it.

### guilt

Guilt is the condition of blaming yourself. All the previously discussed components of blame apply, but now you direct them towards yourself. Sometimes there is fear of blaming others, so we redirect blame towards ourselves. Children often fall into this syndrome. If guilt appears, recognize that it is an inappropriate act of the mind, the ultimate purpose of which is to avoid the feelings behind it.

What if you appear to have really hurt someone, and you feel remorse about it? Remorse can be authentic and justifiable; however, it is subtly different from guilt. In remorse, you are coming from the Heart. You understand that your actions may have been unwise or selfish, but there is not the sense of self-condemnation that comes with guilt. You may have made a mistake, but from the bigger picture point of view, we don't exactly know why the other person, or you, needed to have that experience, or what kind of *Karma* is being worked out. Remorse can be considered to be a first-level emotion, and guilt a reactive emotional response, to be put aside by an act of will as you turn to the feelings behind it.

### shame

Shame is closely related to guilt. Sometimes others will shame us in attempts to control us. Especially as children, with undeveloped ego-strength, we can be the object of vicious shaming tactics from parents or other children and can be strongly affected. We see shaming as well as guilt tactics employed in today's politically correct arena. If you are weak, you are likely to allow yourself to be coerced into shame. Similarly, if you do not have a strong sense of self-definition, you can be dominated by society's conditioning, instead of finding your inner values. Again, this can be thought of as being a central goal of your self-realization quest. Learning to rise above being susceptible to shame can be one of the objects of your training on Earth. Shame occurs on a mental level, and so is not to be considered a true emotion, but more of a self-deprecating reactive emotional response. If it cannot be easily put aside, it can be taken through the steps of the process, especially detaching from and witnessing it.

### worry

Worry is the condition of thinking about feelings instead of feeling the feelings. In worry, you are deep into the left-brain. Since you are not accessing your feeling self, you don't clear feelings. When you catch yourself worrying, shift to the right-brain and take the feelings behind the worry through the process.

# Direct Experience

As you replace rejection with acceptance, even if it's only partially, you gain the ability to see and *be present* with your feelings, as they are. Previously, the busy make-wrong mind was getting in the way. You now sit and experience the feeling. If you've never done this, or if you are not at least somewhat activated in the right-brain, you may not immediately be able to find the feeling, or you may not fully comprehend what it is you are to do. Again, please allow me to emphasize the importance of cultivating right-brain feeling capacity.

Why do we need to experience the feeling in the first place? Because this is what was missing some time in the past when the feeling originated. It was not properly experienced; it was clamped down on. Resisted, rejected, made-wrong, the feeling became trapped instead of being allowed to exhaust its energy through the straight-forward act of being experienced by you. When the feeling is experienced fully, it finishes its cycle and is not trapped and held inside.

Why does it work this way? This is another characteristic of the human soul that we can't explain. We just know that this is how it works. When modern psychology began with Freud, a major part of the emphasis was on *re-experiencing* painful feelings in order to resolve them. It was called re-experiencing even though in actuality it was experiencing for the first time because the feelings were never originally experienced adequately, and so became suppressed. The idea of re-experiencing is still central to most humanistic psychologies that may be lingering in today's world, but with the current domination of "cognitive" based therapies, the importance of re-experiencing and the idea of the subconscious in general has been tragically, ignorantly, and perhaps even intentionally minimized if not denied completely. It's now: Change your thinking and you'll be fine. This is one of the key bailing techniques alluded to at the start of this book that the "experts" will advocate today.

So, knowing better, you experience. If it's sadness, you sit and feel the sadness; if it's fear, you sit and feel it; if it's hate, you sit and feel that.

Note that we do observe a certain protocol, which is summarized in the steps of the process, so you are not caught in one of the quagmires of feelings. You don't want to be overwhelmed by the feeling; you don't want to sit with blame as you stay with a feeling; you don't want to be embroiled in a reactive emotion or a thought and think that's the feeling, etc.

## be present with the feeling

*Being present* means to be focused on the feeling without the mind interfering. Thinking is put aside, or at least put on the back burner. Thoughts may be coming up but you're not paying attention to them.

> Focus on the feeling. *Witness* it. Send your breath to it. Find the feeling in your body. Feel it deeply, watching it from *the Witness*.

> Understand that the feeling is part of your lower-self, and must be accepted unconditionally. Shift your sense of identity to the Higher-Self, the witnessing self. Stay with the feeling, open to it, and experience it. Be in the moment, with the feeling, dropping any desire for it to be anything except what it is, right now.

> Let awareness of everything outside fade. Become *the Witness*, with only the feeling before you. Just you, witnessing the feeling.

Feelings occur in the body. A key way to stay on the feeling is to find it in the body, where it becomes an emotional-physical-energetic sensation, and latch onto that. You then have basically two options as you look inside: You can be in the mind, in the head, wrapped up in thoughts about the feeling; or you can be in the body, in the feeling center, where you should be. Keep cultivating the body sense as you practice, and you will develop your feeling capacity.

## let the feeling develop

As you process, feelings will keep developing. You will go to deeper levels of feeling. You will see and experience the feeling more clearly before it finally resolves itself. You may see how you have been acting the feeling out, for example, or how you have been unconsciously blaming instead of taking responsibility.

What's the feeling like now? Where is it in your body?
Can you see it? Breathe into that area.

It's possible the feeling may intensify, and may even temporarily become more of a problem in your life as you work with it. If this happens, have faith that you are on the right path, that negativity is emerging from its trapped place within, and that by continuing the process, you are doing lasting work on yourself, bringing into balance negative energies that have been with you for long periods of time.

As you look inside and stay present with the feeling, you may find that the feeling changes. If another apparently unrelated feeling comes up, you have to use your judgment about whether to go with it or stay with your central issue. You don't want to leave your issue of concern too soon. Sometimes, the mind will try to distract you by throwing up unrelated thoughts and feelings. If the new thought/feeling seems to be important, switch to that. If it seems to be only the mind wandering, go back to your issue.

## experience, don't express

It's worth re-emphasizing that our work with feelings and emotions is inner-directed. There is no need to outwardly express core feelings and emotions, including active emotions like anger, in order to clear them. Once you notice that you most likely have a trunk full of suppressed negativity, you may be tempted into *expression* as the remedy. After all, if it's suppressed, you want to express it to get rid of it, no?

No, I'm afraid this is one the wrong turns that classic psychology took in its attempts to save us and can be regarded as another bailing technique. Attempts to "get it off your chest" only lead to damaged relationships. You should be able to see at this point in our discussion that *you* are responsible for your projected experience. To hold another responsible and to take it out on them is just plain ignorant. And does not work.

Expression is not the remedy for suppression, but its *dualistic complement.* If you go from suppressing to expressing, you are falling into the trap of going from one polarity to the other, making no real headway. You're still caught in the same loop. This includes active expression such as beating mattresses with a tennis racket, etc. The way out is to transcend the suppression-expression dualism by moving to *experience.* When you inwardly experience your suppressed feelings, you are neither suppressing nor expressing; you transcend and effect real change.

Of course, we are not talking here about the non-blameful sharing of feelings when appropriate. However, it is easy to fall into the trap of thinking you are just sharing when you still harbor the secret motive of dumping your feelings onto someone else. The inner *containment* that is necessary for processing becomes weakened, and processing becomes less effective.

This applies as well to traditional talk therapy, where it is naively assumed, in my opinion, that just by venting feelings in a neutral setting they will be resolved. I'm basing my opinion on my experience and the testimony of numerous clients of mine who have been through the talk therapy regime. Any apparent relief of feelings through any type of expression is illusionary, and core feelings remain buried and untouched.

# Witnessing: The Major Shift

## consciousness shift 6

We have briefly touched on the importance of witnessing inner experience. We will now expand that discussion, exploring the subtleties involved.

We are normally *identified with* our moment-to-moment, day-to-day experience. *Identification* occurs because we feel isolated, insignificant, weak, anxious. When we identify with objects outside ourselves we gain a temporary, illusive connection to something bigger than ourselves that tricks us into a false sense of security or worth. Identification is a lower-consciousness attribute. It is a highly limiting yet natural, unavoidable stage of human development that is not to be regretted, but as we start to wake up, we spontaneously become *disidentified*. Identification can be understood both intellectually and experientially.

Intellectually, identification means there is an *unconscious assumption* that we are the same as the object of concern. For example, most of us identify with the physical body. We think we *are* the body. Many people, even intelligent people who, however, are lacking in higher awareness, believe that when the body dies, they will die.

You can identify with other physical objects as well. Usually, if you feel you *own* something, you are identified with it. Your car, your house, or any possession becomes an extension of yourself. An attack on your possessions is felt like an attack on you. Possessions serve to define you in terms of social identity. You are a person with a big house, so you have succeeded; you don't have much money, so you are a failure. Becoming aware of and seeing the absurdity of these kinds of socially conditioned, unconscious identifications upon which we foolishly base our lives is a large part of enlightenment – some well-known authorities have asserted it's the main part.

Identification extends to more subtle levels. We identify with our job, skills, or role. We identify with other people, not only loved ones, but also people with whom we are in conflict as they receive our unconscious projections. We identify with our self-image: smart, dumb, success, failure, beautiful, ugly, spiritual, evil.

But the most insidious, pervasive, unconscious form of identification is with feelings. From the normal, unenlightened, unaware, don't-have-a-clue perspective, we unconsciously assume that we *are* our feelings. We ignorantly and obliviously keep reconditioning ourselves into the feeling identification trap when we say:

I am happy. I am sad. I am strong. I am weak.

More accurate would be to say,

I'm feeling happy now. There's sadness now. I have strength.

## breaking identification

*Breaking identification* occurs when you become aware of your identification. Of course, you must understand – and have an *aptitude* for – the concept of identification to begin with. As you spot it in yourself – as you *sense* your identification – you also recognize that it is not in your ultimate interest to hold on to it, and so it dissolves in accordance with your enlightened preference. You drop it. Just bringing simple, non-judgmental, conscious awareness to an out-grown psychological mechanism can bring about resolution, similar to *withdrawing projections*.

*Pain is the signal of identification – use it.*

Similar to the condition of attachment that we will discuss in the next section, identification brings pain. Pain occurs when the object of identification is threatened or lost, which is bound to happen. If you cannot easily get past identification after becoming aware of it, just process the pain that it brings. This will result in lifting the identification.

For example, you finally notice that you are probably identified with your self-image of being important. Any experience that reminds you that you are really not so important, when you are snubbed or disrespected for example, will cause you to feel anxiety. So, now that you are advancing in your *Feeling-Emotional Enlightenment Level,* you sit with the anxiety instead of disvalidating it. You are using the experience, and your identification, as a means of growth. Soon, you come to the core feeling behind the self-importance, most likely a sense of inadequacy. You process that. The identification with the sense of importance has withered away.

## experiential disidentification: witnessing

So far we have been talking intellectually about disidentification. It does take something of a psychological flair to be able to follow these ideas, through which we are moving swiftly. But the most powerful form of disidentification involves a *consciousness shift* – going *beyond* the intellect – and that's what I want you to experience. That's when you are really witnessing.

You may not get this right away, but I'm hoping that knowing about it will be enough to keep you on the path, developing your higher awareness until the day it becomes second nature. In fact, what we are talking about now is no less than the goal of consciousness expansion through spiritual practice. It's one way to describe the enlightenment experience.

The essence of witnessing is when the inner sense of you – the true, inner person you feel you are – the sense of yourself, in whatever place in the world you are now – *somehow comes alive.* You become more aware of yourself, more conscious, and at the same time, less connected in an unconscious identified way to all that is around you.

You start to become aware of a strong sense of individuality, and are less emotionally/psychically dependent upon objects and people, but this is different from the unconscious sense of separation that forms the basis of what could be referred to as *existential anxiety.* You become consciously aware of being a separate, self-functioning, self-fulfilling human unit, and you start to let go of all the countless ties that result from the unconscious identifications you have been holding. Paradoxically, the experience of *oneness* that is spoken of in spiritual texts is reached by going through this stage of heightened, independent individuality.

*Identification* is the unconscious assumption of being the same as, or connected to, or linked to other objects, concepts, and people on the outer level, and your body, thoughts, and feelings on the inner level. Witnessing is the opposite of this. So, when I say *step back, detach, witness!* I'm trying to describe a new state of consciousness that will expedite your self-work 1000%.

However, it is still possible to work with feelings and emotions to a certain extent in an identified state. This is how practically all of psychotherapy works. You identify with your abuse, and your anger, and your blame. If you talk about it enough, or think differently about it, or maybe hit some pillows, or do some acupressure tapping, or try to recondition yourself with hypnotic suggestion, eventually you get a little better, even though you're still basically bailing out the water in front of the fallen tree. But that's the direction the human race is heading – we're all slowly getting better. The work you're learning here is a direct route to emotional liberation and well-being.

## shift consciousness to the Witness

### STEP BACK, DETACH, WITNESS!

*Feel* as if something has changed. You're not the same person you were seconds ago. You're more awake, more aware of yourself. Your awareness is sharper. You're in another zone. It feels different. Stop reading for a minute and try to jolt yourself into this altered-state, super-aware and awake consciousness zone. Then, you might want to experiment with other ways to do it:

Become aware of yourself as you do any simple task.

You're walking. You become aware of, conscious of, yourself walking. In contrast, if you are not aware of yourself performing any such task, you become a zombie. If you are sitting quietly and your task is to watch the breath, be aware of yourself sitting quietly, watching the breath. You are now conscious. You go unconscious, out of *the Witness*, identified, when you forget yourself, when you forget what you are doing even as you do it, when you get lost in the mind. You probably have had the experience of going unconscious when driving. You realize that you don't remember having been driving for the last few minutes or how you got to where you are. You went unconscious – the opposite of remembering yourself and being in *the Witness*.

**Remember yourself.**

Remember that you exist, while you sit quietly, or while you perform any task. As you remember yourself, you are aware of yourself – you have become conscious of yourself. This one simple technique was the primary tool for awakening used by the legendary Gurdjieff school back in the early 1900's. Remembering yourself implies and generates *self-awareness,* which is a prime distinguishing feature separating humans from animals. Some metaphysical authorities have suggested that acquiring self-awareness is the main reason we incarnate on the three-dimensional Earth plane as humans, and once accomplished, no further Earth lifetimes are required! Don't overlook this opportunity. Self-awareness is the same as witnessing.

**Come into the moment.**

If you intuitively understand what to do to bring about the sensation of being *in the moment*, you are also witnessing.

**Emphasize the sense of "I AM."**

Mentally repeating and allowing the I AM mantra to work on you is another traditional pathway to detaching from the lower-self and stimulating higher awareness.

Learn to distinguish between being conscious (the same as witnessing) and going unconscious. Eastern spiritual practice is basically about staying conscious – or in other words – to be in *the Witness* all the time. When you sit and practice this, it is called *meditation.* When you are not witnessing, in the moment, you are said to be asleep.

If you have been able to sense anything at all during this discussion, regard yourself as fortunate. You have experienced the beginnings of the altered-state *Witness.* Keep practicing. Try to meditate 24 hours a day by being in *the Witness* all the time.

How long can you stay conscious? When you're starting out, it's usually for no more than a few seconds. But try: As you perform any simple task, remember yourself – witness yourself doing it. And then, whenever painful feelings come up, extend that same consciousness to the feelings. You want to be able to witness feelings during activity, when they come up, as well as during special times of sitting quietly.

**Break the identification with the feeling.**

**Remember yourself, stay separate as an emotion erupts.**

**Step back, detach, wake up.**

*Witness* **the feeling.**

Note that I'm not telling you to try to change your anger or any emotional pain, except for the important point of not acting it out or extending it into the universe. This is what the Acceptance step means – accepting your feeling *as it is;* then you enter Direct Experience of it *as it is;* then you Witness it, *as it is;* all with no attempt to change the feeling.

At the same time, you don't want to allow yourself to be overwhelmed. When you are overwhelmed, you are identified with feelings. You have lost higher consciousness and have lapsed into lower consciousness.

Not only does detached observation of emotions and feelings from *the Witness* perspective greatly expedite their resolution, but another immensely important factor is the tranquility that accompanies it. *Witness* consciousness is always at peace with whatever is happening. You, identified with the Higher-Self *Witness*, are at peace with the world, even in the midst of turmoil. You have *transcended.* There is an inner experience of peacefulness that overrides any difficult experience and somehow makes it bearable, greatly helping your acceptance. This doesn't mean the difficult experience immediately goes away; it is still there but now, as you have shifted your sense of identity to *Witness* consciousness and the peaceful tranquility that accompanies it, you are more easily able to effectively be present with discord, so that it can ultimately resolve.

## dual awareness

An important part of emotional processing is therefore to shift your identity to *the Witness* – this is your true identity, corresponding to the Higher-Self, and the correct application of the principle of identification. As you process feelings, you are always to remain aware of yourself witnessing, which is the same as staying conscious, remembering yourself, detaching, and not allowing any difficult feeling to overwhelm you. This means you cultivate a kind of *dual awareness*. You're aware of the feeling, and also aware of yourself witnessing the feeling. Dual awareness optimizes processing. It's a skill that may take a little time to get.

# FEEL II Breath

In FEEL I, you were asked to simply breathe smoothly and easily at the start of your processing session for a few minutes. Just breathing smoothly and easily will relax you and prepare you for the work. Now, you are going to add a few simple techniques that will make the breath more effective. You will use these techniques as you apply the process in FEEL II. Do not be distracted by the breath, but as you process any feeling, try to observe the following.

The processing steps for FEEL II are the same as have been described, but as you absorb the FEEL II principles, you will find that you go to deeper levels of understanding, experience, and effectiveness.

# FEEL II Conscious Breath

### progressive fill

The most basic and essential element of esoteric breathwork is the *Progressive Fill*. Normally, we don't breathe fully into the body, which corresponds to not having complete access to our feelings. When the breath is constricted, shallow, and confined primarily to the upper chest, our feeling nature is also constricted. When you make the conscious effort to breathe into all parts of the torso, you start to reverse this deficiency.

Breathe only through the nose. On the inhale, fill from the bottom up. Let the breath go deep into the lower abdomen, expanding that area of your body, then fill the solar plexus area, then the upper chest up to the throat, being careful not to lift the shoulders. Exhale from the top down, letting the breath out smoothly.

### ratio

Make the length of the inhale the same as the exhale, with a 1:1 ratio of in-breath to out-breath. Maintain a slow, steady, rhythmical sense of timing. You may breathe in to the count of 4, and out to the count of 4, for example. Each count is about the length of a heartbeat. Maintain the sense of breathing smoothly and easily.

### letting go on the exhale

Allow yourself to consciously, deeply relax and *let-go* on the exhale. Sink into the body as the air releases. Feel yourself relaxing deeper and deeper with each exhale. Feel yourself dropping into the body. Learn to equate letting-go of the breath with letting-go of the mind. With each exhale, move deeper into the body.

# Karen

In this session, I'm acting as a facilitator for Karen. However, Karen could also be facilitating herself once she is familiar with the process. She can bring herself through all the steps, and can theoretically reach the same point of resolution, except that she would not have the energetic boost that a qualified facilitator can impart. The following is a condensed version of the session.

**Karen:** I chose a man who is emotionally unavailable. I'm numb from the waist down and I feel tremendous fear when I think about being intimate. I know I have an emotional neediness that makes me do things I later regret, like trying too hard to get people to like me, or forcing myself on people, or forcing myself on my husband when I know he's going to reject me anyway. I've had therapy and I'm aware of my patterns but they are not going away. My father was cold and sometimes violent when I was very young, and it seems the fear he instilled in me is locked deep inside and I just can't get rid of it. When I sit by myself, sometimes a tremendous sadness overtakes me when I think of how absent love is from my life. Most of the time I look normal on the outside, but inside I'm in constant anxiety.

**John:** Your excellent awareness of your patterns gives us a good place to start. You'll notice, of course, that you have conflicting emotions: There's the craving for closeness, and there's the fear of being close and the numbness in your body that makes it impossible. Something keeps drawing you into relationships with partners who lack the capacity for warmth that you want. Let's enter *Alpha* and process these feelings:

Close your eyes and look inside. Relax. Feel your body; become aware that you have a body; feel yourself in it. Feel yourself shifting from the left-brain talking and thinking mode to the right-brain feeling mode. Put the mind on the back burner and don't pay any attention to it if it starts to act up.

Let's take 2 minutes to do some conscious breathwork. Let the breath relax you and your thoughts so you feel calmer. Breathe into the full body with the progressive fill; then feel yourself letting-go of the impulse to change anything or make anything happen as you let go of the breath on the exhale. Drop deeper into the body. Feel yourself relaxing more and more. Follow my count: In, 2, 3, 4; Out, 2, 3, 4, etc...

Now that you are totally relaxed, allow any scene to come forward that represents what we have discussed.

**K**: I see myself with my husband. I'm trying to get his attention and I want him to hold me but he's watching TV.

**J**: What's the feeling behind that?

**K**: I feel rejected.

**J**: Let's welcome this feeling and invite it to come forward even more. Let it build.

**K**: It's getting stronger and now. I'm feeling the sadness I told you about – like it's just hopeless and I want to give up.

**J**: Let the sadness come forward as well. We invite these feelings, the rejection and the sadness, to come forward from the subconscious, to make themselves known and healed. The feeling of hopelessness and wanting to give up is a *reactive emotional response* and not a core feeling, so it doesn't necessarily need to be processed. Let's put it aside with the understanding that the work you are doing now will permanently heal you.

**K**: I put the hopelessness and wanting to give up aside and I'm with the rejection and sadness. I don't know if I can stand it.

**J**: Keep breathing slow and steady, with a full breath. Relax as you stay present with the feelings with no thought of changing them.

**K**: OK, I'm there.

**J**: Let's focus on these feelings, one at a time. The sadness seems to be strongest now, so let's work with that. Just stay present with the sadness. Keep breathing steadily.

[The sadness is a first-level emotion that's been stored away inside, and not a core feeling, but it still needs to be released.]

Let's take this feeling of sadness through the steps of the process. *Step 1, Awareness:* Let's assume the sadness has been building up and has become projected upon this experience, perhaps even drawing it to you. Take responsibility for the sadness and drop, to the best of your ability, any blame you may feel towards your partner.

*Step 2, Acceptance:* Look carefully inside and find any resistance you may have to the sadness. Replace the resistance with acceptance. Don't judge or push away the sadness. Relax into it.

**K**: It felt better as soon as I stopped trying to push it away.

**J**: Right. Now, *Step 3, Direct Experience:* Just stay present with the feeling. Can you find the feeling in your body?

**K**: Yes, there's a tremendous black hole in my heart. It's just a hollow emptiness – I can't describe it.

**J**: Your doing great – stay right there, and let's go to *Step 4, Witnessing:* Feel yourself stepping back from the feeling, and from the black hole, detaching from it, breaking the identification, so that you are in that altered state we call *the Witness*. Feel the peacefulness of *the Witness* as it makes it possible for you to extend unconditional presence to the feeling. Stay right here.

**K**: I'm relaxing more as I detach and watch and feel the sadness. It's starting to feel different.

[Spontaneous big tears, a sign that releasing is beginning.]

J: Just relax and stay present with the feeling. Keep breathing into it.

[We stay here for 10 minutes.]

J: Where are you now?

K: The sadness is almost gone now.

J: Good. What about the rejection? Go back to the original scene and let the rejection come up.

K: Yes, it's coming up strong. It doesn't have the sadness associated so much with it anymore. I'm looking at it detached.

J: Yes, you're doing excellent work. Let's invite the rejection to come forward now. Let it come into the Light to be healed.

K: [tears again] Yes, it's there. It hurts so bad like it goes down to the bottom of my abdomen.

J: Excellent, stay with the feeling. This is a core feeling for you. Let's invite this feeling to come forward even more and let's take it through the steps.

*Step 1, Awareness:* Recognize that this feeling has been stored in the subconscious and has been projecting itself onto your experience, attracting experiences of rejection. Take responsibility for the rejection. Drop blame. Don't blame your husband. It's your feeling, coming from your subconscious, attracting and being activated by outside people.

K: Yes, I see that.

J: Good. *Step 2, Acceptance:* Look inside and see how you have been unconsciously pushing the feeling of rejection away because it's painful and you don't want it. Reverse and replace the resistance with acceptance. Open to the feeling of rejection. Relax into it.

K: It's the same feeling I had with my father.

J: Yes, extend your acceptance to any feelings associated with your father as well. Open to the feeling. Look for the resistance and replace it with neutral acceptance – you're just acknowledging and allowing *what is* on a feeling level. You're not condoning or inviting these circumstances to continue into the future. Keep relaxing into it.

K: My husband and my father are becoming one – is that OK?

J: Yes, for now that's OK, but your focus is primarily on the feeling, not on the people. The people and the scene are only the movie that serves to bring up the feelings. Go to the feeling of rejection and put the movie aside now that it has served its purpose.

K: OK, I can do that. I'm switching to the feeling.

J: Excellent. *Step 3, Direct Experience:* Stay present, experiencing the feeling in your body, with no thought of changing it. Keep breathing into it.

K: Yes, I'm there.

J: *Step 4, Witnessing:* Step back and detach. Break the identification with the feeling. Actually feel that you are different from your feelings – you have the feelings, but you are not the feelings.

You're at a core feeling for you now – this rejection – just stay there. We are inviting the rejection to come forward even more. Stay with the feeling. Accepting, feeling it, witnessing.

[We stay here for 15 minutes. I keep coaching Karen to stay with the feeling, relax into it, feel it in the body, witness it, and keep breathing into it.]

J: How are you doing?

K: I'm doing great. The feeling of rejection is changing. I don't know what it is now – it's just a kind of pressure in my body. It extends down into my lower body also, around the navel where the numbness is.

J: Excellent.

K: The rejection seems to be almost OK now, like people are rejecting me, and I could get sad, but instead I'm just witnessing it like it doesn't matter.

J: Yes, in witness consciousness, you are at peace with whatever feelings arise. Continue to stay with it.

K: The feeling of rejection seems to be replaced by a feeling of peacefulness and even a kind of love in my heart now. It's wonderful – I'm relaxed and that hole in my heart has been filled by Light. I'm witnessing my lower body now where there's still congestion, but I'm feeling that I can't go any further today.

J: Yes, I think we've had an excellent session today, and its time to stop. Let's thank the subconscious for its wonderful cooperation.

As you may note, Karen's issues concern both the Nurturing and Heart Centers. Her basic emotional neediness and depression can be attributed to energetic congestion and deficiency on the Nurturing level, and the core level rejection would tie into the Heart. This accounts for her perception of negativity in those parts of the body.

Although it appears that Karen released much of her suppressed feeling of rejection during the session, it is likely that the feeling will need to be worked with more. Core feelings, such as this rejection, tend to come forward in bits and pieces. We released the part that came forward now, but that's not the whole. The next time the feeling of rejection comes up, however, it will be less severe, and will respond to processing even more readily. By and by, the majority of the negative feeling energy that gives rise to the experience of rejection will be significantly diminished so that it is no longer an issue.

At the start of the session, Karen is able to present a lucid description of her issue. She knows where she hurts, she knows about her feelings and her *reactive pattern:* She has an emotional neediness and sadness that compels her to *act out* at times by forcing herself on people. It can be said that she is *psychologically aware*, even though she still needs resolution.

Such an awareness is a great help to working on yourself. It calls for the ability to look honestly at yourself, and to think in terms of feelings – to see your feelings as they actually are – part of *Step 1, Awareness*. The next step might be to see how the feelings may be motivating you: I've got this feeling and its making me do _____, part of *Step 2, Acceptance*.

You may think this is simple, but it is actually not. Most of us are not aware of our real feelings. We may be aware of the emotional anger or depression that results from those feelings – but we often don't really see the feelings behind. And we don't see how they are motivating us.

For example, Karen could have been aware of only the sadness, without really seeing that it was the rejection that led to the sadness. And she could easily be deep into forcing herself on people in the unconscious effort to ease the pain of those feelings, contributing to the experience of rejection that resulted. At some point, something happens that turns on the light – she realizes that she's in the constant state of feeling rejected.

What is that something that turned on the light? It could be a movie, a book, either self-help or fiction, a talk with a friend or a therapist who is able bring her awareness to the deeper core *feeling* of rejection behind the first-level *emotion* of sadness. Or it could happen spontaneously as she started working on herself.

As you begin *Emotional Clearing* work, you may just have a vague feeling of sorts. It may be one of the common first-level emotions that we are all familiar with – anger, anxiety, sadness, depression, uneasiness, frustration, and so on, but you may not see the core feeling behind it. It is possible to begin working at that point, expecting that the core feeling will eventually become apparent.

You will be able to recognize the underlying feelings more easily if you are familiar with the cosmology of feelings as discussed a few pages back, so you can do the work on the deep level required in order to bring about lasting psychological transformation.

## how long does it take?

We all want to know how long it will take to heal ourselves. The *Emotional Clearing* format is not a superficial quick-fix, but goes to the core structure underlying recurring psychological dysfunction. The work you do here will be significant, addressing major life patterns and allowing them to realign themselves in positive ways. You are removing emotional blocks to the evolutionary expansion of consciousness, and learning how to open to unconscious higher guidance.

The work may be considered to be both short and long-term. When starting out, dramatic releases – or *catharsis* – will often occur and major life changes can follow soon after. It becomes apparent how much our suppressed feelings have been influencing our experience, limiting us and attracting negative conditions or people.

However, as we get into the work, we realize that the core patterns we are addressing have formed over long periods of time, if not lifetimes, and it would be unrealistic to expect overnight change. We must be patient with ourselves and allow time for deep regeneration. Such an attitude, in itself, reflects the idea of *acceptance* that I have been referring to throughout this book and prepares us for maximum progress. Anyone who has done any kind of deep inner work will understand the truth of this.

Does success in the work mean that negative feelings will be gone forever? To answer this, let's recap what we are trying to do. Our first objective is to clear the subconscious of suppressed negativity that has accumulated and continues to adversely affect us. As this is accomplished, however, we are still subject to the law of duality, which we will explore in detail in the next section, but which briefly means that positive and negative accompany each other. Transcending attachment to any dualistic experience then becomes the next phase of the work – we no longer desperately need the positive, and therefore are not so much at the mercy of the negative – we have transcended any particular issue, and this can be regarded as the immediate end goal. Until then, the negative will still make itself known as a normal part of life, but you will be able to handle it much more easily, using the tools you are learning here.

# Prompts

*Emotional Clearing Facilitators* use *prompts* to encourage the client to connect to subconscious material in processing mode. Here are just a few of those that may be easily self-applied. Once you are familiar with them, you can use them as needed. You just need to remember to do it. Prompts, as well as other deepening techniques which we shall discuss, such as when we speak to the subconscious, are usually applied in the *Direct Experience* stage of the process, when you are being present with feelings in *Alpha*. Use just one of these at a time:

What's happening now?
Where are you now?
What's the feeling behind that?
Relax into the feeling.
Let the feeling expand.
Stay present with the feeling.
Can you make a place for that?
*Allow* the feeling.
Can you own this experience?
Can you see how you're projecting that?
Make the intellectual assumption of owning/projecting.
Withdraw the projection.
Drop blame.
Witness it.
Detach.
Find the feeling in your body.
Breathe into it.

### see it as a movie

After you have entered *Alpha*, see the event or circumstances that gave rise to the feelings as an inner movie. Visualize the movie and let it stir up corresponding feelings so you can work on them. Then, put the movie aside and focus on the feelings:

> See it as a movie. The purpose of the movie is only to bring up feelings in you. After the feelings have come forward, put the movie aside, but stay with the feelings. Do not be drawn into the movie. Stay detached, impassive, drop blame as best as you can.

## relationships

> Bring the other person before you. Let their actions trigger your feelings. Sense deeply your relationship with them. What is the nature of that relationship?

> If you prefer, keep them outside your aura, so you are safe and protected.

## expand the feeling

> Allow the feeling to expand, while maintaining acceptance and witnessing.

> Invite this feeling to reveal more of itself.

> Allow the feeling to come forward as you contain and witness it.

> Let that discomfort expand/deepen/get bigger.

## stay present with blocking

Whenever we encounter any apparent blocking to feelings, or the sense of being unable to get to feelings, we extend unconditional presence to the blocking. Usually, in a short while, something will shift.

> Just watch and stay present with the blocking. Relax into the blocking. Gently breathe into it.

# Speaking to the Subconscious

An important skill of the *EC facilitator* is in *speaking to the subconscious*. The subconscious is the reservoir of suppressed, cut-off energies that we are in the process of bringing into the Light and integrating with the conscious self. The subconscious has acquired, however, a sense of its own self. It acts on its own behalf, intruding into our experience at various times. Since it has this sense of an independent entity, it can be addressed directly. A therapist can do this, and you can also do it for yourself. You speak to the subconscious as if it was another person, and indeed, this is not far from the truth.

This characteristic is the basis for self-hypnosis, along with the notorious *suggestibility* of the subconscious. However, we do not speak to the subconscious in an attempt to recondition, change, or influence it, which is antithetical to our philosophy of validating feelings as they are. We speak to the subconscious to have it assist us in revealing and integrating itself. We take advantage of the nature of the subconscious in the following techniques.

The first guideline in speaking to the subconscious is to talk directly to it. *Speak as if you are addressing another person.* You will not be speaking out loud; you clear your mind, pause for a second, and then deliver a mental command.

Usually, when I speak to a client's subconscious (of course I am speaking out loud), it is with a more authoritative voice than I normally use. I might raise my voice slightly. I speak as if I am commanding, not requesting. The subconscious hears the command and obeys. It responds to positive commands, or suggestions, not negative phasing. For example, in basic hypnotherapy, if you want to recondition with positive energy:

Never say: You are not tired. Don't fall asleep.
Always say: You have boundless energy. You are alert.

However, you will see that our methods of intervention with the subconscious are somewhat more creative and sophisticated. All of our forms of speaking with the subconscious are done in *Alpha*. One of the key factors in using the technique is to apply it when you already have got a feeling of some sort. You want to go further into the feeling, or to the core feelings behind it. Whatever feeling you have then serves as the *bridge* into deeper realms.

### asking for an image

The subconscious will cooperate by revealing more of itself when so instructed. Sometimes, you will feel you need a nudge to keep moving. That's when you use this technique. You might use it, for example, if you have a body feeling that is not developing, or a first-level emotion, such as despondency, but you are not getting to the core feeling behind it. In *Alpha*, inwardly speak to the subconscious, with a slightly authoritative tone:

> I'd like the subconscious to give me an image that corresponds to:
> - that pressure in my Heart
> - that emptiness in my Navel
> - that sense of despondency
> - etc.

When you get the image, stay with it no matter what it is or how irrelevant it may seem. Allow it to bring up new feelings. Don't be judgmental. The connections will be revealed in time. Assume something new is coming through – that's why it may not make immediate sense. This is one of my personal favorite techniques. It has led to important turning points, many times triggering a crucial past-life recall or present-life childhood experience. There is something about an image that can be even more potent than a verbal description. You can use this technique more than once in any session. If you are not able to bring up an image, it's a good indication that there's undeveloped right-brain intuitive capacity that you will have to allow for, but don't try too hard – let the subconscious do the work.

With one client, she was able to sense in *Alpha* a dark ball in the pit of her stomach that she normally was not aware of. I asked her to allow the dark ball to come forward even more, to stay focused on it, and then I asked the subconscious to give us an image that corresponded to the dark ball. She immediately found herself draped across a horse, trotting through an open field. She could not make sense of this since it did not relate to her issue. I urged her to go back into the image and see it as if it was happening now. It took several minutes for the scene to develop. She was being taken captive after a bloody battle in the Middle Ages in Europe. It led to a rape scene and more brutalizing. After we processed this experience, she reported a major reversal of her symptoms of sexual disinterest.

### asking for a feeling

If you have got only a first-level emotion, or body feeling, you can ask the subconscious to reveal the associated core feeling. As before, allow the first-level emotion to expand, quiet the mind, pause for a second, and then:

> I'd like the subconscious to show me the core feeling behind my_____,

### inducing a regression

Let the feelings/emotions build up *strong*, clear your mind, pause, and then:

> Let the subconscious take me back to a time when I first had these feelings.

The feelings serve as the bridge to the past. Don't hesitate to allow them to become strong and vivid. You can also specify if you want to go to a childhood or past-life event.

### creative visualization

We again address the subconscious, this time more in line with traditional post-hypnotic suggestion, inviting positive experiences of health and abundance by visualizing them. However, it's critical to understand that creative visualizations do not work if there is substantial opposing negativity suppressed in the body-mind. No matter how much you visualize success, if you have suppressed failure stored away, that's what gets activated when you visualize success. Negative feelings in the subconscious cannot be reconditioned by positive visions, they must be released before the visualizations will have any effect. But then, if you have released the negativity, would you need the positive visualizations? Actually, you don't. Things naturally fall into place when negativity is released. You don't need to knock yourself out with visualizing what you (your ego) think you need. But there may be a time when you feel you have done the work and released most of your baggage relative to any department of life, and you want to try to fine-tune your results. That's when visualizing might be of some use, but not before.

> Visualize what you want to bring into your life. See it as if you have already attained it.
>
> **food:** See yourself in a new relationship with food – happy and content – eating healthy, moderately, and wisely.
>
> **career:** See yourself in the exact position you want. Feel yourself executing your job with skill and success. See and feel yourself successful and fulfilled.
>
> **intimate relationships:** Visualize yourself in the exact relationship you want. Let the image go deep into the subconscious so it is drawn to you. Repeat to yourself: "Soul of my soul, come to me."
>
> **peak performance:** See yourself competing and winning.

Again, all of these visualizations have the potential to stimulate negative feelings that have been preventing success. If you are aware of this tendency, it can become a technique that you use in the work. As the negative feelings come into view, they are processed and released, so that they no longer prevent attainment of goals.

## thanking

Just as we gave instructions, we take time at the end of a session to thank the subconscious if it has been cooperative in uncovering negative energies. We build a harmonious relationship with it and within ourselves.

> It's been a productive session today, so I'd like to thank the subconscious for cooperating.

> I would like the subconscious to understand that in addition to the attention given to it today, I will be giving it ample opportunity to express itself in the near future. There is no need for it to make itself known through projection. It will attract only harmony and abundance.

### dreamwork

The subconscious reveals itself through dreams as well as the projection mechanism. Working with dreams is central in Jungian therapy. Dreams are likely to become more intense and significant as you embark upon *Emotional Clearing* practice. While we don't emphasize dreamwork, if you have any interest, working with them can be quite helpful. Get into the habit of writing down dreams immediately upon awakening to build recall ability.

But then, don't fall into the trap of thinking you must decipher "what it means." What's important about dreams are the feelings. Use the dream experience as if it was an incident, processing the feelings evoked just as you would any event; don't struggle for intellectual meaning.

# Depression

Depression is the psychic condition of being listless, tired, disinterested, with chronic negative feelings such as sadness, anger, anxiety, loneliness, remorse, neediness, not having any direction or purpose in life, feeling lost.

It's primarily the build-up of suppressed feelings that results in chronic depressed and manic-depressive conditions. Depression is not a disease or illness we catch, even in its most severe forms. It is not genetically acquired. Depression is the result of ignorance and mismanagement of experience. We fall into a pattern of suppressing feelings instead of allowing them to release, which results in addictive tendencies, depletion of energy, and the condition we call depression.

If you are experiencing significant depression, you need to enter upon a dedicated program, either by yourself or with help, of releasing these suppressed feelings. Many feelings – basic first-level feelings such as anxiety, anger, sadness, jealousy, sexual compulsiveness – are likely to be already conscious, waiting to be properly engaged so they can clear. If you work with them, you will be led to deeper core feelings and patterns that will ultimately result in complete healing and balance.

If you are conscious only of the depression and not of any negative feelings in particular, then you are in a *repressed* condition – without awareness – and working to uncover and release the feelings is even more urgent. The repressed feelings attract adversity, failure, accident, and ultimately result in breakdown of the physical body.

Don't react to depression by trying to escape or compensate through other activities. Don't blame circumstances, events, or other people for your depression. It is possible to lose perspective and project depression onto unrelated areas of life, thinking that you are depressed because of this or that condition without understanding the real cause. Instead, process the depression.

Processing the experience of depression, even though it is largely the result of suppression and can be regarded as a first-level emotion and not a core feeling in itself, may proceed exactly as with any feeling. Recognize that depression is the condition of energetic depletion. Feel it, witness it, as an energetic experience. Detach and break your identification with it. Use the powerful tools of breathwork and bodywork to build up your energy field. Activate healing energy, enter *Alpha*, and especially breathe into the feelings of depression. Allow the healing energies of the universe to come in as you accept and watch. As you engage the feeling of depression, surrender entirely to the sensation. Allow the depression *to be*. Doing only this can bring tremendous relief, because you are no longer straining to avoid.

Ceasing resistance to the depression will change your entire energy flow. As you sit with depression, the feelings behind it eventually will come into awareness to be processed. These can be any kind of feelings; no one particular type of feeling is behind depression. Do not think you are getting worse when this happens. Recognize that the subconscious is being revealed to be healed. Trust that you are being guided and protected.

*Depression is the condition of energy depletion.*

Suppressing feelings requires large amounts of psychic energy. This contributes substantially to the condition of energetic depletion that we call depression. When you work with feelings of depression, you will sense a recharging taking place. You will draw energy to yourself to replenish your exhausted reserves. When the experience of depression itself is integrated, it becomes the natural complement to the expenditure of psychic energies. Depression becomes the time to recharge, to heal. It can be joyous and restful, once surrendered to. Physical imbalances that may correspond to the energy depletion also will come into alignment.

Mild depression will arise from normal cycles of living. Since we are active beings, a certain amount of depression is inevitable; it is the dualistic complement to activity. If you can accept and open to depression, you will recharge your energy reserves instead of suppressing the depression with rejecting attitudes, such as becoming depressed about the depression.

Depression can be suppressed and stored in the energy body; the depletion becomes larger and is unable to satisfactorily recharge. If you have a pattern of avoiding depression, you probably have a good deal of suppressed depression. You will have to work with it in a reasonable manner. Do not react to your depression; do not become motivated by it. Acceptance will eventually bring you to the point where you experience depression as the natural recharging of energies.

*Chemical substances act as suppressants.*

Modern medical science has attributed chronic depression to abnormal brain chemistry. Pharmacological intervention then seeks to restore normal brain chemistry balance. However, science is somewhat at a loss to account for what threw the brain chemistry out of whack in the first place.

It is not altered brain chemistry that has caused the depression; *the altered brain chemistry is the result of the depression.* Trying to affect brain chemistry with medication is trying to muscle your way to health while ignoring the root cause of the problem, which occurs on a non-materialistic, psychic, inner, feeling level. The drug intervention approach is based on fighting. We aggressively attack the "bad" chemistry, forcing it to conform to more desirable profiles, instead of healing the basic inner imbalance that has given rise to physical imbalances.

All chemical substances used to modify or *mood-alter* feelings, including depression, do not serve to actually resolve the feelings but only to temporarily suppress the feelings from conscious awareness. This includes natural substances such as St. John's Wort as well as prescription drugs. Unfortunately, that it may be of "natural" origin does not change the way any mood-altering substance works: by suppressing feelings. If we regularly turn to substances as the means to control feelings, we are only digging ourselves deeper into the dark hole of suppression.

I view the medical establishment's reliance on pharmacology as the primary strategy for handling mood disorders as materialistic ignorance of the highest degree. Whether it's lithium, Prozac, illegal drugs, alcohol, caffeine, nicotine, sugar, St. John's Wort, or any of the newest, latest designer drugs, all chemically induced mood changes take us out of our feelings. Integration becomes impossible. We enter a no-man's land of self-rejection, cut off from our soul and the eventuality of real healing. The popularity of mood-altering substance use today is a compelling comment on both the poverty of the world's emotional state and the utter lack of comprehension about how to handle it.

However, in spite of my blanket condemnation of substance usage, at times it may be called for. If conditions are so severe that it is impossible to function, judicious use of substances may be justified when coupled with other forms of holistic psychological work – meditation, breathwork, bodywork, emotional processing, therapy, or support groups. And I am not so prudish as to not recognize that occasional recreational substance-induced mind-altering may be helpful in decrystallizing ego formations and cracking open the door to higher consciousness – hey, I grew up in the seventies, in which I fully participated, if you catch my drift. But you should recognize that progress with inner work is limited when substances are regularly used. If you are regularly using any form of substance to *mood-alter,* your priority should be to get off of it.

*Release yourself from the illness and "syndrome" trap.*

The medical establishment is fond of labeling depression an illness. I wish to make clear that, in my opinion, implying that depression is an illness is a disservice as well as an impediment to resolution. Illness is usually interpreted to mean something that has been "caught;" it is beyond the individual's control, and the "cure" must be affected by outside intervention. Even though the motive behind the labeling of the patient's condition as illness may be benevolent – trying to assuage feelings a patient may have of being "bad" – the subtle shift of responsibility away from self and into a blaming or victim mode (it's the illness, not me) undermines the most basic healing orientation, that of taking full responsibility for oneself and one's condition.

The medical establishment currently is encouraging this distortion of responsibility by identifying and blaming a multitude of other "syndromes" for behavior or experience. I understand the need for a label to identify types of behavior, but what is implied is, again, that an illness is present. Instead, we need to understand that behavioral acting out is a form of defense from underlying feelings, especially in the case of obsessive-compulsive syndrome and other similar ones, and that painful inner experience such as depression and even disease is the result of unconscious mismanagement of personal psychic energies.

Other modern-day emotional-dysfunctional syndromes, such as *ADD (Attention Deficit Disorder) or ADHD (Attention Deficit Hyperactivity Disorder)*, and *OCD (Obsessive-Compulsive Disorder)* are similarly founded as depression. The problem can always be traced to a build-up of negative subconscious energies resulting from mismanagement of feelings, and abnormal brain chemistry understood to be the result and not the cause. Prescription medication may be necessary for temporary control of these energies, but it must be understood that other measures must be employed to release the negative subconscious in order to restore normal brain chemistry without drugs in the long run.

*ADD/ADHD* personalities – which regrettably would appear to include a large percentage of the population today – are challenging, because they lack the basic tools of concentration required for the work, and in fact, may not be candidates for the type of inner work we are exploring here. However, we must all start where we are. Difficulty in concentration is only a result of mismanagement of feelings, bombardment from the subconscious, and ignorance about how to proceed. Working with a therapist who can energetically transmit constructive qualities is probably essential in severe cases.

# Regression

As you process feelings, they may bring up memories of the recent or remote past that you have forgotten. It's common for childhood experiences that contain the same feelings you are working with now in relation to current events to flash in front of you during an *Alpha-State* processing session. If a regression spontaneously occurs, allow yourself to go back to the childhood events. *See yourself as if you are that child now; as if you are experiencing those events in the present moment.* Allow the feelings to come up, and stay with them as you apply the process to them: Own, accept, experience, and witness them. Note how unresolved feelings from past events have been carried forward into the present and still influence you. If you have painful childhood memories, you need to proceed slowly but you can still do this work on your own, without a therapist, if you are so inclined.

Don't think you are particularly warped if it seems that childhood feelings from even 50 years ago are still strong, unresolved, and influencing you. That's the nature of the subconscious. Time is not a factor. Suppressed feelings do not diminish over time; on the contrary, they tend to increase as we keep resuppressing the original and similar feelings.

> Watch the child. Send your support and love to the child as it encounters this experience. Allow the child to feel what is happening, and to understand that it's OK to have these feelings.

> Go back and become the child. Experience the event as if it is happening now. Take the event through all the processing steps from the child's perspective.

> To induce a regression: Let the subconscious take you back to a time when you first had these feelings.

> If the feeling is too frightening, go to a safe place that you create inside. Once you are there, you are safe to feel the feeling. Are you

in that safe place? Then let the feeling come up. Watch it from your safe place.

When that event occurred, a part of you fragmented. Make the intention to call back that split-off part now. Imagine that part returning to you, as a long-lost child returning to a parent. Invite your personal spirit guides to find these parts, wherever they are, and bring them back to you.

*Fragmentation* is another way of looking at the suppressed condition. When trauma occurs, a literal part of the psychic self dislocates, along with corresponding emotions. The fragment is an energetic part that is split-off from the main conscious awareness. The fragment can be hidden in a number of places on the psychic plane, including becoming attached to other beings, incarnate or discarnate. As we invite the subconscious to come forward, and we process those feelings, we automatically retrieve the split-off fragments. However, it can be helpful at times to directly invite fragments to rejoin.

If it appears that childhood or parental experiences are of importance to you, don't hesitate to engage them. Most of my client work sooner or later touches on parental issues. But the most important aspect of parental work is getting past the sense of blame. It's easy to fall into the trap of blaming your childhood for the way you are now, which leads to a brick wall.

Classic psychology, in its trail-blazing attempts to decipher the human psyche, presumed that we are "blank slates" primarily molded by random childhood experience – this would be another major wrong turn inadvertently taken. We now know about "past lives" and the influence they have upon us in our current life. Can it not be said then that those past lives are the true "cause" of our current psychological make-up? I would tend to lean in this direction. I see childhood events serving only to *crystallize* character and as not the primary cause. We come into this life with subconscious suppressed energies, and we attract circumstances including parents that will act upon us accordingly. If you happen to be familiar with the fascinating science of Astrology, you know that character is concisely mapped by the birth chart. How then, could it have been originally formed by childhood events?

Similarly, I don't believe that dysfunction is genetically passed down from parent to child. That would be another form of blame. It may be true that persons of similar disposition are attracted to each other, but to think you've got some particular mental/emotional affliction because a parent "gave it to you" is avoiding responsibility, and you go nowhere.

Even though we regard childhood experiences as the catalyst for character and not the primary cause, working on this level can be instrumental in releasing negative feelings. Childhood regression can be moving and effective. However – all that being said – I don't want to give you the impression that you *must* go back to childhood to get clear.

Suppressed feelings from the past are projected onto current experience, and if you work on yourself *now*, you are working on those feelings from the past. We always start with focusing on present experience because these feelings are generally more accessible than the remote past, even though there may still be incomplete recognition of the core feelings behind any issue when starting to work on it. In clearing any issue, therefore, it may not be necessary to go back into the past. While regression to either childhood or past lives may be helpful, I have found that it occurs spontaneously, when needed. There is no urgency to pursue it aggressively or to think it imperative for healing. When it comes up, we use it as a movie to elicit feelings. Whether the recall is accurate, whether it "really" happened is irrelevant. The important thing is that it has emotional significance for you.

The key insight here is that trauma from the past, whether it's a childhood event or a past life, is carried forward to present experience. If you work on yourself now, on the feelings that come up in your present life, you are working on the "past." Those feelings and emotions you are faced with now are the same as those that became suppressed sometime in the past, and have stayed with you. They have been brought into this life and are attracting your experience to you. If you work on yourself now, therefore, you are clearing the past. Regression is only necessary when it spontaneously occurs. Trust that you will be given what you need.

# Trauma

Trauma is the involuntary shutting-down to severe feelings. The mind clamps down, keeping painful feelings from conscious awareness, in an effort to protect. There is often a sense of *disassociation*, of going numb, blank, sometimes feeling out of the body. The feelings are not allowed to complete their cycle and so become trapped in the subconscious, from where they project themselves, just as with any trapped feeling, and cause the emotional disruption known as *post-traumatic stress disorder (PTSD)*. Trauma, therefore, is only a more drastic version of the usual suppression syndrome we have discussed. Trauma and *PTSD*, no matter how severe, absolutely may be addressed with the method you are learning here.

Trauma can occur anytime, although childhood trauma has always been emphasized in traditional psychology. Any highly stressful experience, at any age, can result in trauma. Obvious potentially traumatic events would include assaults and other violent experiences. But occurrences less dramatic can also be traumatic: When your spouse did not support you; when you were ridiculed; when you lost money. Don't be afraid to go into a traumatic memory just as you would any event, but remember to go slowly if it's an extreme experience.

When I first started counseling, I had doubts. Would I really be able to handle serious cases, which real psychotherapists had presumably prepared for with years of training? I thought/hoped that maybe the people wanting to see me would be only mildly distressed and I would not be too dramatically tested. But of course, right from the beginning, I was presented with the most challenging of cases. Anything you can name – there it was, asking for help. Many of these people were disillusioned with mainstream psychotherapy, and eager to try feeling-based work instead of talk-therapy.

So I went with it. I kept telling myself to just apply the principles, no matter how extreme the situation. And it seemed to work. Whatever the seriousness, tragedy, pain, and horror of your experience, I am confident, after more than 20 years of counseling, that the approach you are studying here can help. Moreover, I would like to think this work is ahead of its time, that at some point a feeling-based methodology of inner healing will find its way into the mainstream.

But let's get to the seriousness of trauma. Trauma cases can be brutal, and it's reasonable to question if processing principles can apply. They can. But they may have to be more gently applied. For example, what about taking responsibility for war atrocities, violence, or childhood sexual abuse, as well as less physically harmful but equally traumatic experiences such as financial ruin, treachery, desertion, humiliation, etc.? In the face of such horrors, intellectualizing about taking responsibility can seem tactless, insensitive or even cruel; yet, if we apply the principles, if we have faith in the principles, we may be able to accept and eventually release our deep pain because the blame principle still applies. If we are deep into blame, including unconscious blame, healing is prevented.

The principle for taking responsibility: We have attracted extreme experiences because of suppressed negative energies contained inside. The feelings have built up to the point of explosively manifesting. If there is no apparent cause to which such extreme suppressed energies can be attributed, the only possible explanation has to come from a metaphysical origin: Subconscious energies from previous existences are brought into the present life and attract corresponding experiences.

Acknowledge that these feelings are coming from the suppressed subconscious, and are only being *activated* by the event.

In some way that we do not fully understand, the energy trapped inside has brought this event to you.

The purpose of the experience is to make you conscious of trapped negative energy so it can be healed and released.

Put aside any blame that may be present and focus on the feeling behind it.

Allow yourself to take responsibility, even if only in theory, even if only for this session.

When you take responsibility, you EMPOWER yourself – you stop being the victim.

Recognize that this is a Karmic experience, coming from your subconscious past, being reflected by the present.

We don't know for certain why this difficult experience has come to you. It may be part of your Karma, which can have two meanings: It can mean that negativity from the past is being cleared in large amounts, or it can mean that certain souls take on difficult experiences to strengthen them.

What are the feelings in trauma cases? Being hurt, experiencing the physical and emotional pain of being attacked, the threat of death, severe loss, breach of trust when you were a child, acute heartbreak, and so on. Serious trauma usually occurs in the lower feeling centers – Survival, Power, Sex – or with Heart issues.

In highly severe trauma cases, an alternate personality can be created that splits itself off from the prime identity, resulting in the fascinating phenomenon previously known as *Multiple Personality Disorder*, now known for no good reason except to use confusing, pretentious language as *Dissociative Identity Disorder (DID)*. In theory, therapy would consist of contacting each of the personalities and releasing trapped feelings. If you think you might have DID, it might be best handled with a therapist. You would be guided into experiencing each personality and carefully letting the feelings be activated.

# Cindy

I'd like to tell you in detail about some of the clients with whom I've worked to try to give you an appreciation of what the process is like in depth; but even as I contemplate it, I know it is not going to be fully possible. Each client brings with them a complex world – their memory, experience, and suppressed darkness. Then there are the dynamics between myself and the client, sometimes including what is termed transference and its eventual companion, counter-transference. The overtones are deep and mysterious. Where does the individual soul end and the collective subconscious begin? I sometimes feel as if we are bumping up against the collective subconscious as we go deep into ourselves. Fear becomes collective fear; rage becomes collective rage. Yes, we can focus on that feeling, yes, it will respond. But can there be an end to it? Can we really make a difference? I only mention this useless notion to try to convey some sense of the ineffable that always accompanies deep work for me. You need to be *transcendent*. I think I've learned to be philosophical; detached; tolerant of darkness; awestruck; accepting; slightly whimsical.

Cindy was a 41-year-old woman when we started working together. We logged 54 sessions. She had issues with her husband, feeling lonely with him, even though he was emotionally and financially supportive. She would eat compulsively, no particular food. She was overweight and guilty about that. She believed she was a *Multiple*, and although we never went too deeply in that direction, she sometimes spoke of *lost time* and other *Multiple* characteristics. From my point of view, I felt as if she was caught in a revolving-door cyclone of dark energy that she could not break free of. Events and personalities were attracted to her, acted on her, all because of the darkness within.

Her main issue was childhood sexual abuse, and continuing *PTSD*. Her history was extreme and shocking. Both her father and mother had sexually abused her, starting from a young age. Her parents belonged to what we would now call a pedophile group, in which she had been passed around. She reports that her first severe abuse was when she was vaginally penetrated at the age of 6 with a coke bottle, at a meeting of the group. Her father often displayed rage and disapproval, except for praising her when she performed sexual acts for him, and she grew to crave the approval. At 13, she became pregnant by her father and had an abortion. This became an additional trauma, as she felt torn from the child.

Her mother was no less brutal. Cindy recalls one event where she was playing by herself in her bedroom after school, around 10 years old. Her mother came home from work and barged into the bedroom and forced her to perform oral sex on her. "I can still taste her," she reports. In the course of our dialogue, numerous other elements came into the picture: Other dark characters, witchcraft-like cursings, and occurrences that would suggest a satanic undercurrent in rural Missouri, where she grew up.

How to approach this? There's always a sense of trepidation with horrendous cases such as this. Can the process really work? Can the client really apply the steps, especially the *acceptance* step? Again, the starting point is always to observe the principles. In all of our sessions, we began by talking for a while about current events or a particular memory that had been revived, and then we entered the *Alpha-State* mode. In *Alpha*, we would go into the feelings behind what was just discussed.

I always think in terms of the Centers of Consciousness when approaching a major issue, which I find helps to clarify it. Sexual abuse for both genders I would place as a second center issue, the Power center, the archetypal feminine sexual center, where *receptiveness* is one of the key psychological qualities. The sexual aspect of receptiveness has two potential, dualistic possibilities: It can be a voluntary, loving act of taking in; or the negative experience of being violently controlled, subdued, enslaved, and invaded. These are the negative core feelings to take through the process. They would be accompanied by first-level emotions of rage, fear, disgust, and hate.

Cindy had psychotherapy counseling, but felt she had never moved to a feeling level, which is why she was attracted to work with me. She also had an interest and background in metaphysical healing. She was psychically sensitive and had explored past lives, and had discovered much negativity there, where she "did bad things." I think she was able to see or sense the continuity of her experience, how it carried over from previous times and had manifested in this life. Her acceptance of it seemed to be a spiritual, intuitive acquiescence and not primarily a logical, left-brain deduction. Although of course we did not have any scientific evidence on the authenticity of the past-life influence, her acknowledgement of it did seem to fit in with and contribute to her healing mind-set.

So our work proceeded. We applied the steps, we went slowly through all the memories. We brought up feelings and relaxed into them. As we did, other forgotten memories would surface. We owned and witnessed those feelings, processing them, sometimes with emergency sessions. There was a lot of childhood regression – going back and becoming the child. With each memory, feelings would be activated. These were both the first-level emotions and core feelings mentioned. As we took them through the process, they gradually dissipated. This is the essence of the process in action: The processing of emotions/feelings activated by traumatic memory results in the release of those emotions/feelings trapped in the subconscious, which served to attract those experiences in the first place.

If you are struggling with the idea that suppressed violent negative energies within are responsible for attracting such extreme experiences, I would ask you to give it time. This kind of realization comes with increasing awareness. But in the meantime, remember that you only have to extend acceptance to the feelings, not to the events connected to them. Perhaps you will be in agreement with the logic that feelings resisted in the past must be accepted now in order to release trauma. But, I believe you will find, if you accept feelings, that you will have accepted the event in a certain way as well. This does not mean you condone, permit, or invite any harmful event to continue.

After 2 months of weekly sessions with me and working on her own, Cindy reported "feeling good for longer periods." It was a gradual uphill ascent after that.

# Ben

I worked with Ben for two years. It didn't take all that time to straighten out his issues, but he got to appreciate the support that counseling provided and so stayed with it. I had realized early on that "masculine nurturing" was what he craved in order to compensate for a psychological deficiency associated with an absent/abusive fathering experience, and I was willing to go along with his tacit request as long as we were able to make headway with processing as our primary focus. Being a psychological surrogate – providing what was missing in childhood – is how much of traditional therapy has been conceived. I've never felt this was a viable solution to emotional dysfunction. It's too simplistic. I've always felt it was just another form of trying to recondition subconscious negativity instead of directly releasing it, avoiding responsibility, and I've usually not been comfortable trying to fill that role for a client. In my opinion, the inner blocks that have apparently resulted in any kind of psychological underdevelopment will in the long run prevent the client from fully taking in the positive attention offered, and dependence and transference issues are bound to occur. Nevertheless, I could manage it in limited amounts if it were not the main strategy.

Ben's main concerns centered around his wife and career. They both related back to childhood trauma. Let's start with the childhood, since that's how Ben began his story. But allow me to interpose that although childhood experience can seem to be responsible for character development, the way I would suggest you look at it is that we come into this life with our subconscious intact; it draws childhood experiences to us and crystallizes the character accordingly, not the other way around.

Ben had a difficult time with his father. Although an educated man, his father was quite backward about emotional/psychological matters and tyrannized his son with "beltings" and generally harsh, cold, angry, dismissive behavior. Ben grew up with an intense fear of the physical abuse, which has carried over into his current life and attached itself to other issues.

Did Ben project these events? Yes, we would consider that this fathering experience was drawn to him because of suppressed negativity brought into this life, even though we did not have specific insights into what that negativity was or where it originally came from. Why does this matter? It's an important element in encouraging the ego to shift out of blame; it's what a higher perspective confirms; it enables Ben to get past being a victim; to take responsibility and release the past.

Fear had infiltrated many aspects of his life, but especially with regard to money. Ben had constant anxiety about money, and on occasion had acted in such a way as to lose money in business deals. He had the insight at one point that he unconsciously viewed money as a means to counter fear, but it was never able to work out that way, and he was never able to get to the point of feeling financially secure.

Along with fear, another key core feeling had developed in his childhood. This was the sense of not being good enough, of not being respected, of being inadequate, of never being listened to, all of which could be said to have been associated with the absence of fatherly approval, if not active disapproval and maltreatment.

Then there were the current relations with his family. Ben felt his wife was often unapproachable, cold, critical, overly logical and didn't give him the affectionate support and attention he would like. He felt his mother was clinging, manipulating, and using him for emotional support. His father had died when Ben was 21 and was no longer an active factor. This was our starting point.

In terms of the Feeling Centers, there was intense fear in the Survival Center and intense inadequacy in the Significance Center. We eventually deduced that the coldness he experienced with his wife was a carry-over from those same feelings associated with his father. This was another stage of projection: how he perceived his wife, and the probability that he had attracted a woman to begin with who activated the same feelings as his father. When we discovered this, Ben was amazed that the hunger for approval generated by a cold, abusive father could be transferred to a woman, but there it was, plain as day. I have often noticed this in other clients as well; i.e., that negative qualities supposedly generated by a parent can be projected upon and attract an opposite-sex partner with the same potentials to re-stimulate those feelings. Of course, it can happen with a partner of the same sex as the parent as well. The following is a typical session:

**Ben:** Something happened last week with Lisa [his wife] that really got me going. I had a bad day and was trying to tell her about it with the hope she might understand and be a sympathetic ear, but instead she got annoyed with me and ignored what I was saying. I asked her what was wrong and she blurted out that I needed to learn how to take care of myself and not expect her to solve my problems. It didn't go any further – I thought it could get nasty and didn't want to go there, but it affected me for a few days. I felt completely alone and rejected, like she made me feel that I really couldn't handle my own problems and was dependent on her.

**John:** Let's enter *Alpha* and take this through the process.

[John leads Ben through a 5-minute *Alpha* induction]

Let's go back to the incident. See yourself in that setting, as if it's a movie, and let the feelings come up. Let me know when you've got some feelings.

**B:** I'm feeling disappointed, angry, and hurt.

**J:** Good. Let's stay right there. Put the movie aside, and focus on the feelings behind it. Let's take those feelings through the process: *Step 1, Awareness:* These are first-level emotions coming up in response to the event. We're going to allow them to release just by extending unconditional presence to them.

*Step 2, Acceptance:* Find the resistance you have to the emotions – any part of you that makes them wrong. Drop the resistance, replace it with a sense of being OK with the emotions. You're no longer resisting and pushing them away. How are you doing?

**B:** I'm relaxing more into the emotions. I can see that I've been compounding them by getting upset by them. When I relax into them, they don't seem so bad.

**J:** Let's move to *Step 3, Direct Experience:* Keep feeling the emotions. Try to find them in your body. Breathe into them.

**B:** There's a big pressure in my Solar Plexus, like it's clenched up.

**J:** Good – focus there as we move to *Step 4, Witnessing:* Consciously step back and detach from the emotions. Keep breathing into the emotions and the Solar Plexus.

[We stay here for 10 minutes]

I'd like the subconscious to show us the core feelings behind these emotions of disappointment, anger, and being hurt.

**B:** There's the feeling of not being good enough, like I'm a total fuck-up.

**J:** That sounds like an authentic core feeling. Let's welcome it and invite it to reveal more of itself. Can you find the feeling in your body?

**B:** Yes, its in that same place, the Solar Plexus. It feels like a tightening and a pressure at the same time – like a knot.

**J:** Breathe into that place as you stay present with both the body sensation and the core feeling of not being good enough. Let's take it through the steps:

*Step 1, Awareness:* Recognize that this core feeling has been trapped within and has only been activated by the event, and has possibly even created the event. Take responsibility and try to pull back on any blame you may feel towards Lisa.

*Step 2, Acceptance:* Look for any resistance to the feeling and replace it with a sense of being OK with it.

*Step 3, Direct Experience:* Shift to a feeling level and open to the feeling in your body, in the Solar Plexus.

*Step 4, Witnessing:* Step back and detach.

[A few minutes pass by]

Where are you now?

**B:** I'm totally detached from the feeling and I'm just watching it in my Solar Plexus. It's like a big throbbing knot of energy.

**J:** Great. Stay right there. Keep breathing into it. Let the feeling expand.

[We stay at that point for 10 minutes.]

What's happening now?

**B:** The pulsing feeling is lessening, and I'm starting to lose my concentration a little.

**J:** Take a few full body breaths to wake up, and then let's deepen our experience.

I'd like the subconscious to give us an image that corresponds to this feeling of not being good enough.

When you're ready, tell me what you see.

**B:** I'm with my family, my parents and two sisters. I'm 13 years old. We're going into a crowded restaurant to eat. There's only one table available. They all jump into the seats, but there's no place for me. My father says jokingly, well I guess Ben is not going to be able to have dinner with us. Everyone laughs. I stand there for a few minutes until a waiter brings over another chair.

**J:** How are you feeling?

**B:** I'm humiliated, shamed, I feel terrible, like I'm just no good and don't deserve to eat like everyone else.

**J:** This is a genuine traumatic core-level experience. Let's treat it seriously and take it through the process:

*Step 1, Awareness:* Let's recognize that this experience represents an emergence of the suppressed subconscious. These feelings have been held inside, and are drawing this experience to you. If you didn't have any suppressed feelings, you would not have reacted as drastically. Try to find the blame and put it aside. Move into *owning* the experience.

**B:** When you mention blame, I can see that the blame has been so bad that I've almost not been aware of it. But now I can see it. I'll try to drop it.

**J:** Excellent. *Step 2, Acceptance:* Look for the knee-jerk action of the mind that pushes the feeling of being no good away. Reverse the rejection of the feeling with a sense of neutral Acceptance. Relax into the feeling.

**B:** OK.

**J:** *Step 3, Direct Experience:* Stay with the feeling of being no good. Find it in your body. Move to a feeling level, and stop any thoughts about the feelings – just be present with them.

**B:** It's in my Solar Plexus again. It's starting up, pulsing and throbbing.

**J:** Stay with it and move to *Step 4, Witnessing:* Detach and watch with a sense of *choiceless awareness.*

[We stay here for 10 minutes.]

What's happening now?

**B:** The feelings seem to be easing up.

**J:** Excellent. I think we've had enough for today. Let's thank the subconscious for cooperating. Close the door to the subconscious now, so that you will not be confronted with any other suppressed feelings until your next processing session, with me or on your own. When you're ready, slowly come back to normal consciousness and open your eyes.

In my work with Ben, we went far and wide into his psychic-emotional-feeling life, touching upon complicated, interwoven facets of present and past experience. As time went by, we both could see that major shifts in his subconscious landscape were occurring.

As a side note, however, I would caution you against thinking that these case studies somehow represent extraordinarily disturbed individuals. On the contrary, from my experience in the field, I would say that the clients with whom I usually worked, with perhaps a few exceptions, represent the normal kind of psychological conditions that pervade modern life. I would say the outstanding characteristic of people who work on themselves is an above-average intelligence and sensitivity, distinguishing them from "civilians" who are blundering about in FEEL 0. This work is not easy to comprehend or easy to do. I have the greatest respect for those who are able to embark on the journey.

After you have gained some proficiency with the concepts presented in FEEL II, and when you feel a natural curiosity to deepen your experience, you may be ready for the next level. FEEL III takes the two-dimensional, intellectual, psychological understanding with which we have been engaged and expands it into a living, pulsating, three or four-dimensional transcendental cosmology that will shift your consciousness radically – if you are ready. To be ready, you need to have your right-brain active.

# Feeling-Emotional Enlightenment Level III
# Transcendental

*Getting out of the mind. Altered-state work. Opening the Heart. Energetic Foundations. Working with energy currents. Advanced energetics. Witnessing is the key. Higher/Lower-self*

## energetic foundations

You can dramatically turn your life around if you understand and apply the principles of only FEEL I. Just validating and opening to your feelings as they are will place you in the vanguard of the human evolutionary movement.

But then, your enlightenment potential makes a major jump when you step up to FEEL II. Understanding the psychology of suppression, projection, self-rejection and acceptance, the types of feelings, along with more advanced breath techniques and basic witnessing skills adds another spectacular dimension of intellectual adroitness and effectiveness to inner work.

FEEL III comes into play as you do the work. Your capacity, ability, and intuition develop. You start to naturally see and sense more than just the obvious. You move out onto another dimension of inner space, and your potential for feeling-emotional enlightenment and fulfillment undergoes yet another quantum leap. You find that, although you may have begun this work with the immediate aim of getting your feelings in order, you are now glimpsing other, higher vistas, and your goals become modified. You now feel the need for a personal practice that will not only continue to cultivate your right-brain feeling self, but will also enable you to activate higher consciousness potentials. As your FEEL practice goes to deeper and deeper levels, it becomes the *basis* for a unique self-realization and consciousness-expansion program.

In FEEL III, we become *proactive*. We are not content to passively wait for negative feelings to be triggered by projection and interactions in the world. We enter upon a dedicated *Emotional Clearing* practice, designed to bring the subconscious to light and to release it, propelling us to permanent heights of well-being. We find, to our delight, that disruptive unconscious projection is greatly lessened; we spontaneously become more balanced and rational; life becomes much less of a struggle; we are *unconditionally* happy.

FEEL III *Transcendental* is for those who hear the call to higher consciousness and are eager to apply themselves to this end within an ever-deepening feeling-based paradigm. Everything we have discussed in FEEL I and II of course still applies, but now you will be *blending* feeling-emotional work with what has been known as the spiritual arts, metaphysics, and Eastern philosophies. We will talk about the "energies" of the universe, your Higher-Self, reincarnation, Karma, and chakras as if they are as obvious as the pavement under your feet. Hopefully, we will be looking at these topics with which you are probably already familiar from a newer, higher perspective, relating them to our concern with emotional well-being.

I will be not attempting to prove or justify the reality of any of the concepts we will cover here – some of which I believe you will find challenging, even if you consider yourself to be a veteran of the New Age path – since that would take a lot of effort and would probably not be all that fruitful. Let's just assume that if you're compatible, you'll find this section interesting and helpful. If you're not, it's not my job to try to persuade you, and you can still have great success with FEEL II, which is centered around intellectual psychological concepts.

In the FEEL III *Transcendental* consciousness shift, we enter *the moment*, going beyond the mind. In this timeless place there is no past or future, only *what is NOW*. We go beyond acceptance or rejection, to a place of *choiceless awareness*. As we come into the moment, shifting to *the Witness*, feelings and emotions are perceived as *energies*. We watch these energies as they play in the body, clearing and balancing themselves under the guidance of a higher intelligence. We enable both emotional and physical healing.

With FEEL III *Transcendental, we are going beyond the mind.* Let's start with some hardcore philosophy:

## consciousness shift 7: forget about happiness

When you are locked in the mind, you think the purpose or goal of life is happiness. From a metaphysical point of view, this is where you start to run into trouble. If you are obsessed with everything going right, with your ego-based preoccupations, with stamping out any appearance of the negative, with the demand that you must be "happy" all the time, you are setting yourself up for chronic unhappiness.

*The end purpose or goal of life is not happiness, but the acquisition of wisdom through experience. The sooner you get this, the happier you will be.*

Look at it this way: What percentage of your total time are you on the Earth? And what is your purpose here?

If there is any truth to the reincarnation concept, you are on the Earth anywhere from 10 to 25% of your total time. If you are of advanced consciousness – which I think would probably apply to you if you are reading this book – you would be spending more time on the higher planes between incarnations than the average person, perhaps as much as 5000 years Earth time unless you wanted to reappear for a special occasion. The rest of the time you are on the inner invisible planes of existence – the higher planes – where you have your being when you are not sporting around on the three-dimensional Earth plane.

These "higher" planes are generally completely exhilarating, reportedly far surpassing Earth in quality of life, although of course there is a place for the reaping of negativity begun on Earth. The majority of souls involved in human evolution are usually existing on the inner planes, although in current times we are experiencing an unprecedented surge of incarnation that undoubtedly has important ramifications.

Everyone makes a trip to Earth sooner or later because it's only here that you can have certain types of experience that are essential to your consciousness evolution. In order to do this, you need to be exposed to stimulating influences that you normally would not seek out. These experiences in the material world may not primarily be happy ones – in fact, we know they're not; that's the basic existential "dilemma" of life. But after you go through them, you are changed, usually for the better, unless you fail to make the most of the experience.

To make the most of these experiences, and the small percentage of your total time spent on Earth, you must first not be disappointed when the road gets rough. You must be glad that you are now being confronted with the chance to advance yourself. If you resist the experiences, you do not make optimal use of them. If you accept, and even better, process the experiences, you do. So relax and forget about happiness; work on evolution. Make the most of your Earth-time.

Look at it from yet another point of view: The ultimate purpose of life is to evolve. Evolution primarily means evolution of consciousness, not of the body. A key aspect of evolution is to drop the personal ego. The personal ego is that part of you that wants to be happy. You are self-oriented, driven by ego and self-interest. What if you forgot about yourself, and found some other basis to make decisions? This is what some spiritual disciplines advocate. Forget about yourself, and about being happy – work for others, they say. Then, you will be happy. This is a kind of kindergarten approach to spirituality, but there can be some value to it.

The ego can still get involved when you work for the happiness of others. First, obviously, you're doing it in order to benefit yourself. Then, you naturally want to succeed in your new endeavor. You switch from being concerned about yourself to being concerned about others, but you are still *attached* to the results of your work. Being attached to the results of your work is seen as a major obstacle to liberation, and the primary cause of existential dissatisfaction and bondage. Advanced Eastern philosophical thought emphasizes the cultivation of action without attachment to results as the means to personal freedom.

It's not so easy to put the ego aside, but that's the name of the game. The mind is ego-based. That's one of the reasons I keep saying you must go beyond the mind in conscious evolutionary work, which includes FEEL work.

# The Duality Trap

An important metaphysical concept regarding the mind is that of *duality*. In order to go beyond the mind, we must fully understand the concept of duality and how it keeps us trapped.

The unenlightened *wisdom body* believes it possible to possess pleasure, excitement, satisfaction, and happiness infinitely and indefinitely, and eliminate all traces of the negative. Many times we think this is the goal of life, and if we don't reach it, we have failed. Many self-improvement advocates today, in encouraging you to work hard for personal happiness, perpetuate this false belief. Indeed, it has become the basis for the materialistic American dream, still widely bought into. But yet, there is a place for this level of experience as we evolve.

Duality is how the mind perceives. The mind can only perceive in terms of dualistic, complementary, positive and negative qualities. When the mind is turned towards the material world, it experiences opposites such as hot and cold, dark and light, up and down, even life and death.

However, duality applies not only to the material world, where it is most apparent, but to the inner world of feelings: Sadness and happiness, pleasure and pain, love and hate, are all subject to the law of duality, especially when we are *attached* to the objects associated with those feelings, such as intimate relationship or career, and especially when we perceive feelings through the mind. This means that any important experience is bound to have strong positive/negative swings. If we ignorantly disvalidate and suppress the negative when it arises, it builds in the subconscious and we never get free of its troublesome influence.

The principle of duality also implies that there must be a kind of balance between positive and negative. Thus, day and night are approximately balanced. But what about pleasure and pain? Are they to be balanced also, so that we are condemned to a constant cruel cycle of ups and downs, never to obtain any permanent amount of security, health, or love?

If you look at your life, and the lives of other people, I believe you will have to admit that this is the way things are. This is what you struggle against. You believe your purpose is to conquer the negative and attain a continuous state of the positive. But the sobering truth is that the more you go after and attain the positive, the more the negative will manifest in your life because they go together. They must balance.

This syndrome is especially difficult when we are coming at life from an aggressive, ego-based, lower-self consciousness – identified with the mind and with the feelings. Then, duality operates full force. When we start to raise our consciousness to a higher level, we realize we are not the mind, nor our feelings, although these are vitally important parts of ourselves that need to be aligned correctly for us to function optimally.

As we shift our identity beyond the mind and feelings, we start to experience stability, even in the face of turmoil. This is the way out, the way past the ceaseless entanglement of pleasure and pain: Raise consciousness, stop identifying with lower-self ego-based compulsive desires or drives, lift your vibration and start to identify with the higher, *transcendent* self.

What about the basic New Age value system of light over dark? This is where you will have to do some real stretching, especially if you consider yourself to be a lightworker. Because of the principle of duality, positive and negative, light and dark must balance in the manifest universe. If you create more light, darkness is immediately created in order to balance. If you are struggling to allow only light inside, the darkness will seep into your subconscious to balance.

In today's unbelievably complex world (2020), we see darkness making itself overtly known. Part of the reason for this is to stimulate lightsiders into fighting back. Trying to create more light and fighting back only strengthens the dark. And in fact, the again sobering and unbelievable truth is that on the Earth plane as we know it, many if not most of the agencies of light are created by, strongly influenced by, or aligned with *dark forces*. This includes ancient and recent religions and all types of prominent New Age spiritual leaders, channellers, holistic healing modalities, groups, YouTubers and websites you will find. Information about this is now coming out in unprecedented ways, mostly on the internet.

The "dark forces" to which I am referring have been known throughout the history of mysticism. There has always been the realization that light and dark coexist in balance; this is a foundational principle of the manifest universe. I do indeed believe that dark forces are rampant in the world today as they have been at all historical times, and that we can come under their influence if we are careless as we go about our lives.

A principal aim of the dark forces is to perpetuate the condition of polarity – another term for duality. When things are polarized, we have extreme groups of light and dark, good and evil, positive and negative, political factions, and other identity groups fervently opposing each other. The temptation being offered is for you to identify with a side – either side. When you identify with either side, you are lost to higher consciousness; your evolutionary potential comes to a standstill or regresses; you are tricked into playing the game, and distracted from focusing on how to withdraw from the game. This is what the dark is trying to achieve.

This is a complex subject that I can only hint at here. If you are provoked by my brief remarks, you can research it on your own, and I would most earnestly encourage you to do so. Understanding what's going on in the world today is essential to avoid being trapped in it. But if this is getting too confusing and complicated for you, here is an immediate strategy you can apply to this basic quandary of dualistic human existence:

Accept pain. Witness it.

If you can only accept and stop fighting pain, you start to solve the dualistic dilemma. You dispel the power that dualities have over you and you start to integrate them; you release suppressed pain, and you disentangle yourself from ego-mind attachments; you release the negative and no longer need the positive so desperately.

If the discussion of duality has had significance for you, you will stop efforting, trying to make things happen, because all effort will only bring more of the positive/negative dichotomy. Also you will

STOP BLAMING because you now see how the positive and negative go together. And if you have been mildly shocked by reading just now about duality, recognize that the shock has jolted you, in a small way, *beyond your mind*. Going beyond the mind is the way out. Feel where you are right now, more detached.

Recognize that if you feel like giving up when faced with the futility of duality, it's because of the unenlightened lower-self mind. It's the lower-self that pushes for self-interest, and generates most powerfully the positive/negative dualistic experience, and then gets overwhelmed, depressed, and despondent.

The lower-self still naively thinks that happiness depends on an absence of negative feelings and a preponderance of positive feelings. The lower-self does not yet understand the dualistic nature of feeling; that we each have the complete spectrum of positive and negative within, and that true *unconditional* happiness is the result of accepting, integrating, and transcending all aspects, not the pursuit and attainment of only what appears to be "positive" or desirable to our limited ego-based consciousness.

If you are in the habit of unconsciously suppressing your negative feelings, you allow the negative to take over your life. By not allowing the negative, not recognizing it, not seeing it with neutral acceptance, it never clears itself when it arises, and instead accumulates in the subconscious.

But then, there is a bright side to all of this. You have chosen to incarnate in this time and place to experience exactly what is going on. You have accepted the challenge, with the understanding that it will be brutal at times, but that once you graduate, you will have accomplished something great – something, as far as I understand, that is regarded with awe by beings outside the Earth sphere. You will be an Earth graduate, admired and respected, on your way to an incomprehensibly glorious new kind of existence.

# Opening the Heart

As we get into New Age consciousness pursuits, usually we are presented with the goal of opening the Heart – to become more Heart-centered, to make love our central mode of consciousness, to heal the world and ourselves through love. If we have low or no activity in the Heart, we are certainly missing one of the most important human qualities, and activating or opening the Heart is essential. But the aspiration of attaining a permanent dominant condition of blissful love can be a trap for the unsophisticated spiritual seeker - alluring and intoxicating, unrealistically setting us up for failure, disappointment, and self-condemnation. Let's start this discussion by looking at some of the pitfalls that can be encountered when we embark upon opening the Heart.

We experience duality in each of the Centers of Consciousness, or *chakras*, as we will now refer to them. Fear in the first chakra will be balanced by the feeling of safety, and we will find ourselves oscillating between both poles. If we think we are oppressed in the second chakra, we may be drawn into fighting for our rights, and can easily become irrationally rebellious, but even if we win, new circumstances will again arise that *appear* to oppress or enslave us. The same type of dichotomy exists with the Heart chakra. The Heart is similar to all other chakras in that it is strongly dualistic, especially on the ego-based lower-self level, where most of us operate. That means that love and loss, or love and fear, or love and hate, however you prefer to think of it, will be dualistic complements, always accompanying each other according to the laws of duality discussed.

I have no doubt you have experienced the dualistic nature of the Heart in your own life. You hunger for love, you are drawn to love like a moth to the flame, your life has no meaning unless you find love, and yet you always crash. You find yourself highly *ambivalent* in relationship. You may even think you are demented; how could a sane person be going through the intense swings of love and hate that I feel? The more compulsive, the more intense, the more this love means to you, the more *attached* you are, the stronger will be your swings. This heartbreaking syndrome can even be observed in current affairs, where leaders in all areas but perhaps most especially in the spiritual arts who have been loved by their followers are turned against for the flimsiest of reasons – reasons often unconsciously projected from their own collective subconscious and exaggerated if not outright fabricated. Sometimes we may love someone or something intensely, and we project our hatred onto another apparently unrelated person or thing. We don't see that our love and hate go together.

Some people have tried to contend that love is not dualistic, but I do not agree. I consider this wishful, unenlightened, idealistic, perhaps even immature thinking. The love we normally experience is of the lower-self, and I would say is quite dualistic. It is well-known in the humanistic psychological community that as you open the Heart, you increase the capacity for love, but at the same time you increase the capacity for the pain of the Heart – loss, grief, loneliness, and perhaps even hate, if we want to be brutally honest.

It may be possible to experience a non-dualistic Higher-Self form of love, but I don't believe it can be attained by deliberate, direct cultivation. If it exists, it will come about as we transcend lower-self consciousness, including the lower-self Heart. Kindliness and compassion will then be genuine and not forced and hypocritical. Simply making a mental effort to cultivate love, whether it's for a personal love partner or love for humanity, will be superficial and transitory and is bound to have unsatisfactory, unstable results. There will be suppression of the negative, ultimately resulting in a tragic backlash.

In the meantime, we are bombarded by enticements and false goals of love as being the answer and the endpoint of our evolution. God may be love, but that love is most probably not what you think of when you think of love. We make the mistake of *anthropomorphizing* God on an emotional level.

So what are we to do? The opening of the Heart is of course a desirable and essential part of our evolution, but if we are intent upon trying to cultivate only positive Heart qualities through a willful act *of the mind,* we are bound to fail. Genuine growth of the Heart, and transcendence of lower-self Heart-based ambivalence, occurs through the integration of the negative – what I have been talking about throughout this book.

When the negative appears, don't buy into it, reject it or condemn yourself for having it. Recognize it is just the appearance of the complementary pole to your love. Don't be motivated by the negativity. Take it through the steps of the process. Allow it to release. When you accept and open to yourself as you are, on a feeling level, when you stay present with the pain in the Heart, when you stop trying to be something you are not, when you choicelessly *witness* without extending it into the world, you achieve real growth.

Throughout this book I have been continually referring to the importance of activating the right-brain capacity for feeling, as opposed to the left-brain mode of analytical thinking. This is how I prefer to approach Heart-centered concerns. The right-brain corresponds to the Heart. As you activate self-acceptance and the capacity for feeling, you move into the authentic Heart, unhindered by preconceptions, prejudices, and projections of the ego-based mind.

In the end, the problem has come about because we confuse lower-self love with Higher-Self love. Most of us here on Earth are embedded in the lower-self, where love is strongly dualistic. When authentic spiritual mystics speak of love, they are referring to Higher-Self love, which we cannot know or understand because we do not, at this point in our evolutionary growth, possess Higher-Self consciousness, except possibly for occasional glimpses. We try to emulate Higher-Self love but we merely imitate without grasping the true essence. Higher-Self love is *not an emotion*. It is a *state of being*, a major consciousness shift, related to the transcendental witness of which I have spoken, and the *Crown* chakra.

I do not believe the opening of the Heart chakra, while important, is the endpoint of personal growth, or meant to be the focal point of our evolved being, as so many New Age advocates preach. As we will discuss, the *Third Eye* represents a higher, more evolved, transcendent consciousness that supersedes the Heart while including it, and which leads to activation of the Crown chakra, the seat of authentic Higher-Self transcendent love. I would suggest shifting your priorities to self-acceptance and the awakening of the right-brain self-love feeling capacity, the Third Eye, and eventually the Crown – this is my path. The Heart will open on its own, as you do the work, and as you learn how to activate love from within.

## self-acceptance / self-love
## consciousness shift 8: activate love from within

Let's take the concept of *Acceptance*, which we discussed in FEEL II, to a deeper, more mystical level. In the *Emotional Clearing* book, I started with an introduction called "*The Art of Loving Yourself*" because for me this is a highly significant topic. So many of us in this world know how to make a living, but we don't know how to live, and we don't know how to love ourselves. Loving yourself, or self-love, means that your love comes from within, is generated from within, and not because you possess any particular object or person that may please you immensely.

The idea of loving yourself is a tremendously potent concept, but often we think that loving ourselves just means being good to ourselves, or being extra nice to ourselves. It's very easy to confuse loving yourself with pampering yourself, or yielding to ego-based "needs" - going after what you think you need. It can be an excuse for selfishness. Or, it can be taken to a pseudo-emotional level where we think that we have to generate kind feelings about ourselves or others, but I tend to believe that any results obtained from such a practice will be mind-based and not soul-based, and will not reach into the deep levels of our being.

For me, loving yourself is the same as accepting yourself; and accepting yourself, for me, is most relevant when taken to a feeling-emotional level; and accepting yourself on that level means, to me, finally, to say, that it's ok that I'm angry; it's ok that I'm afraid; it's ok that I'm sad; it's ok that I feel insignificant, that I have these sexual compulsions. It means accepting and opening to all these feelings that we usually have been conditioned to resist, to turn away from, to escape from. The act of opening to them, and learning that it can be done safely, doesn't mean that you're opening yourself to misery; on the contrary, it means opening yourself to a tremendous experience of integration. When I say "integration," I mean reconnecting with yourself. Psychology talks about split-off parts and how one of the goals is to bring these parts back into integration, in order to achieve a whole, or *holistic* person. In order to do this, we need to reclaim, to welcome back what we perceive as painful parts of ourselves, and to do it in such a way as makes it manageable and not overwhelming. On the contrary, it becomes a beautiful experience when you start accepting a feeling about yourself that you were previously unconsciously rejecting or condemning yourself for.

Many people don't realize they are rejecting themselves, and stuffing these feelings in a corner deep inside themselves. That's part of what becomes apparent as you start working on yourself along these lines - you start becoming aware of the amount of feeling that is really there, and how you are mistreating yourself.

The complete opposite of avoidance and selfishness is *self-acceptance*, which eventually becomes *self-love*. Authentic self-love begins with self-acceptance. Self-acceptance is how you get to self-love. The spiritual principle, said in simple language, is to just *accept yourself*. In so doing, you create the foundation for spiritual fulfillment. If you reject and do not accept yourself, even in the name of goodness, or for spiritual reasons, you will never be able to change your life for the better. The foundation for all transformation and change is self-love - not selfishness - but self-love, which is very different. Selfishness leads you completely in the opposite direction. It takes you further from your true self and true self-esteem, which is essential for transformation. Real change can come only through self-love, beginning with self-acceptance.

As you apply the *Acceptance* step in the *Emotional Clearing Process*, especially over time, stay alert to how it automatically generates the feeling of authentic self-love in you. Relaxing the mind, dropping resistance, and genuinely opening to your feelings as they are will bring about the authentic self-love / self-esteem experience. You apply this in your processing work, allowing the feeling of self-love, self-compassion, and tenderness for yourself to melt any negative energies it encounters, in conjunction with the all-important *Direct Experience* and *Witnessing* steps.

Does this self-love pertain to the Heart chakra, and will it be subject to dualistic swings, or will we be accessing a type of higher, non-dualistic love? I'm impressed that you have asked the question - it shows that you are thinking, but I'm not going to give you my opinion - you'll have to see for yourself.

### attachment / aversion

*Attachment* is a phenomenon of the mind that creates pain and strongly evokes the dualistic experience. From the point of view of Buddhist philosophies, the mind-state of *attachment* and its accompanying mind-state *aversion* are the principal sources of pain. Freeing yourself from the attachment/aversion syndrome is seen as a central liberating goal. It is a key step to going beyond the mind.

In today's world, attachment is a major obstacle on the road to enlightenment or just simple contentment. Being so busy, so enmeshed in day-to-day material pursuits, we don't even realize that we are often compulsively fixated on goals that have much less value than we assign to them. Or else we find ourselves, perhaps through no fault of our own, with pressing needs that must be fulfilled, but still the same blind drive impels us forward in a frenzy of activity, frantically *doing* with no time to pursue higher goals of self-realization. We have no clue about our level of *unconscious attachment*.

As mentioned, we come here to have certain experiences, and these experiences attract us and keep us attached to them, even when they are painful, because that's what our Higher-Self has planned for us. So there is a purpose and benefit from attachment; it supplies us with the experiences we need so we can eventually gain wisdom and spontaneously liberate ourselves from attachment. At the same time, attachment stirs up subconscious negative feelings that are crying for release.

Attachment/aversion occurs when we become fixated on obtaining or keeping the positive side of any dualistic experience, and on avoiding the negative side. Since the positive and negative must always balance each other, according to the principle of duality, I hope you can see that when you fall into the attachment/aversion trap you are setting yourself up for continual frustration and pain.

We become attached to people who fill a certain need, to material objects such as a car or house, for example, or to non-material things such as recognition, power, or status. Attachment to material objects is considered to be a lower, less enlightened form of the syndrome. Attachment to other people is often thought of as love but this is in reality a type of dependency that must be overcome before we can make any significant progress on the spiritual path, although when we are starting out, we often first become involved in dependent, lower-self Heart-based relationships that do serve to stimulate the Heart into action. As we advance, however, we realize that these addictive, dependent relationships no longer serve us and must be out-grown.

*Pain occurs when the mind becomes attached.*

The first kind of pain we feel with attachment is *fear*. Attachment itself immediately generates fear of losing the object of attachment, whether a person or possession. The fear builds over time, usually getting suppressed into the subconscious, until eventually it surfaces in the form of some kind of crises, often involving resentment of the attached object or person, since we unconsciously assume they are the reason for our fear.

The second kind of pain we experience with attachment is the negative pole of the dualistic experience. We become attached because we feel incomplete, weak, or unhappy. The object to which we attach seems to fill our need, at least for the moment. But soon, the negative pole makes itself felt. It is the opposite of the reason we are attracted to the person or possession. We resent the intrusion of the negative, we rebel against it, but the more we push it away, the more it makes itself known. The negative pole usually is tied as well to an accumulation of suppressed negativity in the subconscious.

For example, you feel secure and warm when you are with a loved one, but then it seems as if there are too many times when they don't seem to be there for you when you need them. You experience these times as unbearably lonely and painful, and they seem to roughly balance out the beautiful times – this is the suppressed subconscious making itself known.

You are attached to your partner, expecting them to compensate for the inner pain. This is not love, but a *dependency* that interferes with love. The harsh truth is that most of our intimate relationships are based on mutual dependencies, which of course generate the intense, ambivalent, attachment/aversion experience. This is true of any intense relationship, including parent/child, business or work partnerships and relations, and even our relationship with our pets, which for many of us has tragically taken the place of human relationships.

What is the way out? It would be wonderful if you could simply see a dependent attachment for what it is and then, as a result of this insight, just drop it. However, very few of us have the capacity to manage our emotional selves to the extent that we can do away with dependent attachments through an act of will. A more practical strategy is to process the experience: First bring *awareness* to the syndrome, because it has probably been unconscious; then apply *acceptance* to it, stopping blame, taking responsibility for the pain; then choicelessly *being present* with the pain, *witnessing* it, feeling it as an energy in your body.

*Processing the pain of attachment takes you out of the attachment.*

To continue our example, when your partner is absent or appears to have abandoned you, that is when the negative side of your attachment/aversion is coming up: loneliness, abandonment, heartbreak. You make the most of the experience by taking it through the process. You free yourself from accumulated suppressed negativity. This is one of the key ways to use pain for your benefit. Break the attachment by processing the pain that occurs when you are denied the object of your attachment.

On a higher level, the purpose of any dependent attachment is to reveal and release the pain that accompanies it, which has been accumulating in the subconscious. If you understand this, you will approach relationships and possessions with an entirely new, enlightened frame of mind. Actually, this can be regarded as the first step of enlightenment. Then, you allow yourself to enjoy relationships and possessions as much as possible, and when the inevitable, painful, negative side surfaces you view it as the opportunity to do significant work on yourself, releasing those feelings through the process you are learning here.

*Addiction* is an advanced form of attachment. Attachment and addiction are rampant in the world. They result in what we think are our "needs." However, as we start to get clear, it becomes obvious that most of our needs are neurotic dependencies. They may be appropriate for our current level of consciousness, but if we are to move forward with our personal and collective evolution, these dependencies must / will be eventually outgrown.

# Integrating Polarities

consciousness shift 9

Bringing dualistic opposites together was one of the central tenets of Jung's philosophy. In modern times, however, it unfortunately has been largely neglected as mainstream psychology has degenerated from humanistic to materialistic, left-brain, mind-based, cognitive strategies. But we recognize that it is one of the goals of authentic inner work.

When we bring opposites together, we *transcend* them and the issue they represent. It becomes a non-issue, and this is one way to look at the goal of inner work. Until then, you are trapped, caught in the loop of dualistic experience. You reject the negative and cling to the positive. Making a place for both negative and positive, dark and light, *without going to either extreme*, is a central key in personal liberation.

How do we do this? By taking it to a feeling level. Take any personal issue. Identify the dualistic feeling components that have been driving you. What do you seek and what are you trying to fix/avoid/fight? What do you love and what do you hate? Usually, you will feel a fierce aversion to negative feelings and the objects they are projected upon, and a fierce desire for positive feelings and the objects they are projected upon, which you assume will make the negative better.

Go beyond both the aversion and the desire, so you are perceiving the feelings without the interference of the mind. Hold the dualistic positive and negative feelings simultaneously in awareness as you process them in *Alpha*. They will start to meld into each other. See them merging. Recognize that both sides go together, that they are dependent on each other, that they are not the enemies they may appear; they are two sides of the same coin.

*Your goal is to no longer resent the negative, and no longer be driven to obtain the positive.*

When you are starting to work on an issue, you will generally be focused on painful negative suppressed feelings. You may not be aware of how you are caught in a dualistic loop. You may not see how you are chasing the positive in order to avoid the negative. But eventually, you will want to understand the dualistic nature of any serious issue. Bringing the opposites together often occurs after you have been working with a serious issue for a while – it could be regarded as being part of the final stage of integration.

Let's look again at the examples from FEEL 0, revising our attitude towards the basic dualistic experience and making an effort to identify dualistic components. We will discuss each example from an Impersonal Dualistic level; a Personal Healing level; and in keeping with our FEEL III emphasis, a Transcendental level:

**the issue:** Your spouse or romantic partner is not satisfying you emotionally or sexually any longer. Or, you are alone and lonely.

## the solution:
### impersonal dualistic level

You are working on the Heart level. Recognize that emotional closeness and alienation go hand in hand. Accept both. Whenever the negative hits, don't bombard your partner with demands and threats. Go inside, and bring the opposites together. Sit with the alienation you now feel, and also recall the closeness you have felt. As you maintain awareness of both, choicelessly feeling and experiencing them both, you are bringing them together, integrating them, and transcending the dualistic level.

### personal healing level

At the same time, recognize that there is probably something in you that has attracted this experience. It's possible you have emotional Heart-based issues. There may have been unresolved abandonment or abuse of love relationships in the past that resulted in suppressed negative feelings, which now manifest as acute loneliness that a relationship just cannot make better. Take responsibility for the feelings, and move the experience through the process.

## transcendental benefits

As you work with integrating the negative, you are also developing the inner strengths of independence, self-reliance, self-activated individuality and genuine self-love. You are moving beyond emotional dependency. You use this opportunity to blossom into a higher level of consciousness and growth that you could never have anticipated or realized if you did not have these opportunities. Love becomes non-dependent and of a higher order. You recognize that it's not only your own personal loneliness that you are working with, but the collective, existential loneliness we all feel. By integrating it with the above steps, you have transcended onto a new level of emotional well-being and enlightenment.

. . . . . . . . . . . . . . . . . . . . . . . .

**the issue:** Your career is more a source of pain than fulfillment. You're not successful, you feel unrecognized and a failure.

## the solution:

### impersonal dualistic level

You are working on Significance issues, which is number 5 on our list of the Centers of Consciousness. The related negative feelings are inadequacy, worthlessness, disapproval, failure. You have now been enlightened that these negative feelings are part of the package; that you cannot experience only success and recognition. You stay conscious of them both as you sit, no longer resenting the appearance of the negative. Through your enlightened acceptance, the negative feelings take their place and soon are no longer a source of distress, as you begin to transcend instead of being stuck at this particular experience loop.

### personal healing level

You also realize, however, that it is very likely that there is more than only dualism at play here. Your personal history of conflict with your father suggests an unfulfilled, compulsive need for approval and guidance, which now unconsciously drives you and at the same time sabotages your career efforts. Recognizing that the situation on the job is the opportunity to permanently heal yourself on this level, you apply the process, releasing the suppressed feelings of inadequacy and failure that the job triggers.

### transcendental benefits

As you work on the Significance level, you develop strength you never could have foreseen. You greatly reduce the compulsive need for recognition. You switch from needing and seeking outer approval to being content with just knowing you have made a significant contribution to the forward evolution of humanity. Eventually, you find yourself with a priceless maturity and wisdom that has resulted from the outgrowing of the lower-self ego.

...........................

**the issue:** Your children are not behaving.

**the solution:**

### impersonal dualistic level

Issues with children are complex, and we don't want to trivialize them, but let's focus on one of the main dynamics often involved, and let's apply the idea of dualism slightly differently. We know that children are dependent upon parents, but are we fully aware of the extent to which parents are usually dependent upon their children? Let this represent the dualistic pattern in this case. We need to fully acknowledge this dynamic – that you are as dependent on your kids, if not more so, than your kids are on you. How is this dependency actualized? Energetically. Whenever you are dependent, you are siphoning psychic life-force energy from another. When you depend on your kids for your fulfillment, you are siphoning their energy. Children may not completely understand what is happening, but they feel it, and automatically react with resentment.

### personal healing level

The situation of siphoning energy is something that we fall into without realizing it. It may be that it's just a natural potential quagmire that must be avoided. However, it's always possible that personal energetic dispositions may strongly encourage the tendency. We are now talking about Consciousness Center 4, Nurturing. If you have Nurturing deficiencies, you will have pronounced emotional neediness and emptiness. You will tend to unconsciously look for others from whom you can energetically fortify yourself. Understanding this, you bite the bullet, admitting that you have tendencies of this nature and that you may inadvertently be using your kids as targets. And of course, you can easily fall into the energy-siphoning trap with other adults. You need to exercise extreme self-awareness and restrain from behavior that results in energetic siphoning, and fall back upon your own resources, processing the pain of the deficiencies you experience. Processing the emptiness, the hunger, the absence of support, will bring you through it. It's a Karmic debt that must be paid. However, processing makes facing it much easier, and you can actually take steps to access this energy that you lack directly from cosmic sources, which we will discuss soon in the advanced Induction.

### transcendental benefits

As with the other examples, working on yourself will eventually give you skills and self-reliance that would never otherwise have come your way. You use your weakness as a starting point, recognizing that healing it is one of the major purposes of this incarnation. You learn how to non-dependently love.

. . . . . . . . . . . . . . . . . . . . . . .

**the issue:** You have serious money worries. You are broke, in debt, and unemployed.

### the solution:
#### impersonal dualistic level

You are challenged with a major Survival Level issue. Survival issues are *fear-based*. Fear is the most basic of the negative core feelings with which we contend. It permeates all areas of life and can intertwine with all the other negative core feelings. The dark forces at play in the world today use fear as their major tool to keep you trapped on a low level of consciousness, which benefits their twisted agenda. Fear is broadcast 24/7 on all media: news, TV, film, music, corporate internet. Events in the world, including political tensions, war, and the economic climate, are orchestrated primarily to incite fear. If you allow yourself to be overrun by fear vibrations, you become a cooperative victim.

The complementary polarity to fear is also broadcast into the world, to trap you as you frantically look for a way out. The polarity to fear is security, well-being, mass entertainment, love and religion, including many New Age sects. If you buy into the trap, you become compulsively attached to these counter-values. You think possessing them will eradicate the fear, but you don't see that you are just being manipulated into another experiential dualistic loop, where each side depends on the other for its existence, the purpose of which is to keep you at a low level of consciousness.

To start breaking the loop, become aware of the basic dualistic, light-dark, Survival Level quandary being presented to you. See it as the trap that it is, and stop buying into it.

### personal healing level

As always, you must assume, if you are having major Survival issues, that your personal history contains significant suppression of fear. It has built up to the point where it is affecting you more severely than it might affect others, attracting adverse conditions. What's more, you may have had an active albeit unconscious hand in precipitating those conditions. You may have made unwise financial decisions or you may have been careless at work – this is how the subconscious interferes and self-sabotages in order to make itself known. In the extreme you may be highly fear-motivated, grasping and acting solely out of self-interest, which all works against you. But even if these descriptions don't apply to you, it's still the suppressed subconscious negativity that has brought these difficult circumstances to you.

Shake yourself out of victim consciousness, take responsibility, and apply the powerful techniques that you have been exposed to in this book.

### transcendental benefits

Fear is the trademark of the lower-self personal ego. Isolated and alone, the ego and fear define each other. In our evolutionary journey beyond the personal ego, we will naturally leave fear behind. However, we are now being given the opportunity to make spectacular leaps in our evolution by being confronted with the extremely difficult conditions in today's world. It could be said that this is a primary reason we have incarnated at this time. Fear, which has been hidden in the background, is now being thrust upon us and brought to our attention in possibly unprecedented ways. If we take advantage of the opportunity, we maximize our growth. The dark forces – which are very real, active and organized – are acting only for their own benefit. The irony is that while so doing, they have created this magnificent opportunity for those who are aware enough to take advantage of it.

. . . . . . . . . . . . . . . . . . . . . . .

**the issue:** Your health is a major worry. You have chronic illness; you have ongoing pain; you are in constant fear of getting/being seriously sick.

**the solution:**
impersonal dualistic level

Once again, you are faced with a Survival Level issue. Let's look at it from a different angle than the previous example. If you are *excessively identified with the body*, you will experience any threat to your physical existence as highly unsettling. You will be preoccupied with the body, somewhat hypochondriac, easily alarmed with the body's natural up and down cycles. You don't see that you are not aware of the dualistic aspect of all things physical – that their existence goes along with their non-existence. To cling to only one aspect of the dualistic manifestation/non-manifestation syndrome is to be in ignorance of the true nature of the world.

However, today there is an abundance of literature and testimony concerning the other side of life that I personally find reassuring. It documents that existence continues after death and that you are not only this physical body – you are an immortal soul temporarily occupying a physical body in order to have experiences and to evolve in ways you otherwise could not. When genuinely grasped, this realization does much to assuage the terror of death and the frantic fear that arises because of body identification.

personal healing level

At the same time, illness is a reality. Let's reframe illness to be the manifestation in the body of negativity held within. If we don't release the negativity, it seeps from the psychic levels to the physical, and we get sick. Therefore, a primary strategy with illness is to clear inner negativity, which becomes known to us as emotions and feelings.

### transcendental benefits

As we increase body awareness, we paradoxically tend to identify less and less with the body. We feel we are a consciousness that is momentarily occupying a physical body but we are not the body. At the same time, our increased body awareness becomes a highly potent doorway to inner exploration and evolution, going beyond the level of physical healing. We recognize that all the various types of psychological dysfunction that we are addressing in this book are indeed reflected in the body. Working with the body then becomes a wonderful means for transcendental work, when viewed with this objective in mind. Yoga, breathwork, acupuncture, bodywork, Reiki, and so on, all impact the psychic-emotional-psychological being through the physical. It could be said that having a physical body with which to engage in this type of work is another reason we incarnate.

### consciousness shift 10: coming into the moment

An important concept for you to understand as you move into transcendent, energetic experience is that of *coming into the moment*, or being in the *NOW*. This metaphysical state is generally regarded as one of the goals of consciousness work. Relative to our endeavors, it is where feelings can best be experienced and resolved. But what does it mean to be in the moment? Where are we if we are not in the moment?

To not be in the moment means we are in *the mind*. Mind activity is characterized by a sense of being *time-based*: looking forward to the future, or thinking about the past, or generally being in the left-brain mode of planning, thinking, analyzing, desiring, anticipating, worrying, and doing. To come into the moment then means to stop the mind; to go beyond it into a timeless state of non-thinking, non-striving, non-doing.

So if I were to say to you: *get out of your mind*, you might now have some idea of what I'm talking about, although the average person in the mall would think I was deranged. But getting out of your mind is crucial. It's a primary skill that must be cultivated. Try it right now:

Stop all mental activity. Drop the mind.

I hope you are able to sense a shift. It's the same as *the Witness* consciousness we have discussed. You feel different, more present, more alert, as if you are waking up. Previously you were enmeshed in mental activity and identifications; now, you have disidentified from those preoccupations and have shifted to a higher plane of consciousness.

As we drop the mind, we make it possible to more deeply enter the *Direct Experience* of feelings, because it is primarily mental activity which gets in the way. The mind and the feeling capacity are different functions of the human operating system. Stopping the mind does not stop feelings. The mind can be thought of as the door through which feelings enter awareness or are blocked, according to whether the mind is passive or active, open or closed, allowing or blocking, in the moment or not.

When you are in the moment, your perspective changes. Being no longer time-based, there is no past or future, there is only *NOW*. Astoundingly, the question of acceptance or rejection of inner experience, of which we have spoken, becomes irrelevant. There is no sense of acceptance or rejection, because those are functions of the judgmental, analytical mind, which is now dropped and transcended. There is only *what is*. There is no question of turning away from *what is*, there is only the reality of it. In our work, *what is* equates to our feeling experience. It is there, it just *IS*. We are fully, choicelessly present with it. We enter the transcendental state of *choiceless awareness*.

In this heightened state of choiceless awareness, beyond the mind, our perception of feelings changes dramatically. Since we usually perceive through the mind, our feelings take on a certain kind of mental coloration. When the mind is dropped, this coloration disappears and what we previously thought of as feelings and emotions simply becomes energetic currents that course through our body.

As you start to sense your feelings from this new perspective, you become aware of the extent to which the mind has been distorting your experience. You have thought of feelings as being either "good" or "bad." With the mind transcended, there is no longer this unconscious dualistic compartmentalizing. There is no longer good and bad; there just *IS*. And *what is* takes the form of *energetic currents*. There may be pressure, contraction, movement, congestion. There may be colors, vibrations, layers, densities, fluidity or stagnation and blockage. You simply witness it all – choicelessly, joyously.

You feel as if you more deeply understand your intuitive, empathic identification with the stream running through the forest that we talked about at the start of this book; that you are indeed a stream of energy cascading through the banks of time. You have free-flowing movement; you have eddies, whirlpools and snags. Previously you thought of these conditions as pleasurable or painful. Now, you see that it is all good. Is all part of the flow. You have transcended pleasure/pain, light/dark, attachment/aversion. You are on the verge of dropping the personal ego and merging with cosmic consciousness.

All of our previous discussion concerning witnessing will of course apply to your FEEL III process as you shift from a mental to an energetic perspective.

# The M-Word

I know you are allergic to the m-word. I know you wince and frown when you hear it. I could pamper you and avoid using it by substituting less provocative, bland, wimpy phrases such as "sit quietly" or "go within" or "enter *Alpha*." But there is a trend towards being frank and honest in society, and just as the f-word is now unreservedly used by almost everyone, I am going to be the first to crash through the modern politically incorrect oppressive glass ceiling social injustice taboo on the m-word and stick it in your face.

M-e-d-i-t-a-t-i-o-n is not a new thing. Back in the sixties and seventies it was in vogue, and everyone was excited about it and trying it. Before that, it was of course popular for thousands of years among spiritual-consciousness seekers in the East. Nowadays, I'm not sure who would be interested – there's been a breathtakingly, heartstoppingly discernable drop in mass consciousness over the past 50 years, shifting away from higher pursuits to lower materialistic self-interests. Nevertheless, I'm going to give you the skinny about meditation, including crucial points you probably will not readily find elsewhere if you were ever to get serious about meditation training.

*Meditation is the practice of coming into the moment and dropping the mind.*

What we call meditation is a prerequisite to effective inner healing, consciousness advancement, and personal evolution work. It's like going to the gym if you want to build your body. It's basic. It's how you develop the capacity for the *Alpha* state. It's a time when you "sit quietly," look inside and perform certain tasks. You:

1. Enter an Altered *Alpha-State*
2. Experience Peace of Mind
3. Clear the Subconscious
4. Sit in Samadhi
5. Establish Psychic Protection

6. Activate Healing Energies
7. Perform Metaphysical Tasks
8. Clear Karma

I want you to understand, therefore, that as part of your FEEL III ninja clearing the subconscious and elevating your evolutionary vibration program, you are going to dedicate yourself to a regular, daily, meditation practice. In short order, you will learn to enjoy this practice so much that you will switch all your addictive attachments to it. You will go to the breath instead of food, TV, internet, or cell phone. You will go to the Third Eye instead of another person for support. You will self-induce *Alpha* instead of drugs, excitement, or sleep.

## MEDITATION BENEFIT 1: altered *Alpha* state

I know I just compared meditation to going to the gym. This is not exactly correct. Meditation, once you get it, is fun, not work. You don't grunt and sweat when you do it. It's the best part of my day. I don't know how I could function without it, I don't know how other people function without it, and the logical conclusion about this would be that they don't, given the absolutely insane state of the world.

When you "go within," the first thing that happens is that your brainwaves slow down to the *Alpha* range or lower, to the *Theta* range. This corresponds to a *deep relaxation* of body and mind. *Deep Relaxation* shifts you out of left-brain, ego-based activity into the *right-brain*, which is inherently feeling-oriented and associated with the body. The right-brain *Alpha* state is essential for emotional healing. Just going there, even if you don't make a point of processing feelings, has significant value. With the mind on hold, no longer interfering with energy currents in the body, automatic adjustment occurs. A higher intelligence appears to take over and guide the energetic flow; healing energies are spontaneously evoked; creative ideas appear; inspiration strikes.

## MEDITATION BENEFIT 2: peace of mind

*Going beyond the mind = peace of mind.*

## MEDITATION BENEFIT 3: clear the subconscious

Does the idea of clearing the subconscious resonate with you? I hope so, because that would be an indication of your aptitude for this work. When I first heard this phrase I was shocked and transfixed: *Jesus yes show me thank God are you kidding I can't wait to learn how to do this.* When you sit to meditate, even if you are not doing it perfectly, even if your mind is wandering much of the time, one of the first things you will notice is that feelings will start to pop up from both the recent and remote past. This is the subconscious mind clearing itself. Generally, you have no say in what feelings will emerge. If you try to control and dictate what your feeling experience should be, even and perhaps especially if you are trying to force "positive" feelings upon yourself such as love and peace, you only clamp down harder on the suppressed subconscious and it stays trapped.

Instead, you must find a neutral place of *choiceless* non-expectation and non-control. From this neutral place, you *surrender* to what comes forth. Make the assumption that there is a higher intelligence that guides the process, giving you just what you need. If you recognize and do not disvalidate these feelings as they appear, thinking you are having a "bad" meditation, and instead take them through the process you are learning here, you are clearing the subconscious.

Clearing the subconscious is one of the most valuable benefits of meditation; however, it is rare to see it discussed or taught in spiritual circles. Across the street from my home in New York City there is a Tibetan Buddhist center that I often drop in on. It's one of the most popular in the city with around 300 people attending the weekly public meeting. I once asked the leader in the question session after the group meditation what to do when painful feelings came up as I was meditating. I tried to explain that it seemed to me that these feelings were emerging from the subconscious, and this was the opportunity to release them if they were handled correctly. I was shocked and disappointed to get the stock response of "don't be distracted – go back to your breath." She didn't appear to know what I was talking about.

Meditation can be the primary mode where the negative subconscious reveals itself in order to be healed. This is where we can optimally perform energetic clearing. As you sit to meditate, you will address feelings and issues that are being *projected* now in your life, and you will spontaneously be presented with feelings from the past that are suppressed and need to come forward. Usually, there will be a correspondence between the two.

### MEDITATION BENEFIT 4: Samadhi

You have probably vaguely heard of *Samadhi*, and thought of it as something very hard to obtain, that you would never be able to experience, and that it wasn't for you. Let's reframe it:

*Samadhi is the condition of sitting quietly with the mind dropped.*

Because we are so completely immersed in the mind, we are unable to conceptualize what it would be like to be out of the mind. That's why you practice meditation. The primary goal of meditation is to come into the moment and still the mind. Meditation is not pondering some subject deeply, whatever it is. That would keep you in the mind. Your goal is to get out of the mind. Similarly, prayer, without getting into a discussion of its value, generally but perhaps not always, takes place on a mind level; you are intensely asking for something, but it's still the ego-based mind.

Since it's not easy to get out of the mind, students have been traditionally taught to begin their practice by focusing attention on one particular object in order to still the mind. Buddhists focus on the breath; other traditions use other points of focus, such as an inner one-word sound, or an inner or outer image or a part of the body. It doesn't matter so much what the point of focus is. As you try to stay with it, your mind drifts, and you keep coming back again and again to your focus point, building your capacity for concentration.

Eventually, you gain the ability to stay on the focus point and then jump to no focus point. The mind has stopped, you are not focusing on anything but you are super-aware. This is Samadhi: awareness without an object. There are various levels to the Samadhi experience, but Samadhi Level I is not all that impossible to attain. You may be able to do it right away, now that you've been informed about it, or maybe it will take you a few weeks/months/years to get there.

Why bother with this? Because in Samadhi, you are contacting higher energies; you're having concrete meshing with your Higher-Self; you're deeply into an *Alpha-State* awareness that is innately healing; you're accelerating your personal evolution; you rejuvenate and refresh; you set the stage for clearing the subconscious; you consciously come into the moment and experience dramatic *non-doing*; you activate witnessing.

## MEDITATION BENEFIT 5: psychic protection

Although most people don't realize it, we live in a psychic soup. Our five-sense perceptions reveal to us only a fraction of the total world that exists all around us. Those who are able to sense the hidden beyond the visible are designated as psychics, clairvoyants, mystics, artists, or lunatics.

But you and I, with our unusual sensitivity, know that such a world exists and that it fiercely determines our three-dimensional Earth plane experience. It is said that everything that manifests on the Earth first appears on the higher Astral and Mental planes. This is the world to which we ascend when we "die."

On these planes, there are multiple energetic swirls and entities. They have identities and intelligence and go about their business. Some of their concerns are directed toward Earth plane inhabitants. The study of these inner planes is totally fascinating, and you can find much information if you are so inclined. For our immediate purposes, it is enough to know that these energies exist and can become a substantial disruptive influence. When you start doing serious *Emotional Clearing* work, you need ample and reliable protection so that you open only to your own suppressed energies and not to some other psychic influence.

One of the basic ways we are adversely influenced by inner plane forces is that they become attracted to energies which are similar to their own, especially, it seems, to negative energies. If you have anger stored away, for example, you will attract corresponding inner plane energies – foreign to yourself – that will amp up your basic storehouse of pain and make you act out in ways you might not ordinarily do, such as becoming hurtful, dishonest, or lazy. If you have addictive habits, you attract entities who have the same tendencies but cannot satisfy them in their present location, so they seek to attach to you to appease their cravings. In sexual addiction or abuse cases, this is virtually always the case.

There are entities – and this is a huge topic – that simply seek to siphon off your life force for their sustenance. You are, in essence, their food supply. They thrive particularly on negative energies such as fear, anger, pain, and lustful raw sexual energies devoid of love, and that is basically why the world is kept in the condition it is. Then we have, in our modern world, the vicious onslaught of invisible electronic Wi-Fi and microwaves, completing the soup recipe. And, as if all this wasn't enough, as we enter the path of conscious evolution, we encounter energies that deliberately try to derail us.

I am bluntly describing the reality in which we live in order to impress upon you the importance of protection. But I don't want to leave you with a disheartening picture of our world. The critical thing to keep in mind is that, as mentioned, we are here only for a short time, and that we all chose this experience voluntarily as a means to accelerate our evolution. Use these obstacles to make yourself stronger and wiser – that is their higher metaphysical purpose.

When you are in the state of Denial and Disvalidation of your feelings, you are most vulnerable to these entities. To protect yourself, you basically need to raise your vibration. Your vibration is the core frequency to which you resonate. If your vibration is low, you are attracted to and you attract coarse energies. If your vibration is high and refined, the negative energies are not as attracted to you, but can still seek you out to attack you.

Some will tell you that to avoid attracting negativity, you should keep your thoughts high. There may be some minimal value in such advice, but this is again attempting to fix yourself with the mind. It's not primarily your thoughts that attract negativity to you, it's the suppressed negative energy in the subconscious that attracts outside negativity. The inner suppressed negativity *determines* your thoughts as well as your moods, and simply trying to change superficial thoughts will not modify the suppressed negativity. The inner suppressed negativity becomes known to us as feelings and emotions, and that's why we focus on them in our work. As you release the negative subconscious, you substantially raise your vibration.

We can also work with inner visualizations to raise our vibration and this becomes our first line of psychic self-defense as we work on ourselves. Throughout esoteric literature, it is advised that you visualize light surrounding yourself on an inner, psychic level to form a protective shell that will repel negativity. There is some variation among different schools about the type of light to be invoked to form the protective shell, but that's of secondary importance. What's important is your intention. You make the intention to protect yourself and visualize light surrounding you.

You can perform this exercise quickly and routinely, and it will be effective, or you can linger with it during an *Alpha* meditation and get into it. With new clients, I will sometimes suggest we spend 5 or 10 minutes concentrating on building their protective shell because I'm sensing it is weak. I will ask them to take their time sensing the shell, and to carefully look with their inner vision at the shell from all points: in front, in back, from the top, from the bottom, from the left and the right. You may think this type of sensitivity would be beyond the capacity of the average person, but when they are in *Alpha*, and perhaps with the benefit of my energy supporting them, they are often surprisingly perceptive and will describe things such as seeing a hole in the back of the shell, for example, or feeling a draft. We then focus on repairing that tear in the protection, just by visualizing it being repaired. You can do this on your own. In meditation, don't be afraid to take time to build the safety of the protective shell, or *aura*.

For most of my life, I have simply used the image recommended by most psychics of light coming in from above on the inhale, and then going out on the exhale to create the protective shell. The light coming in does more than just that, however; it energizes you and can itself raise your vibration. It is one of the healing energies of the universe, and connecting to it puts you in touch with an essential resource. Assuming you will get some kind of meditation practice underway, you will invoke the protective shield each time.

### MEDITATION BENEFIT 6: activate healing energies

In the meditative *Alpha* state, you are able to activate your innate, natural healing energies. You may think of these energies as coming from inside you, or you may see them originating from a Universal source outside yourself with which you connect. Either way works. In practice, you can use both approaches together. After closing your eyes and becoming silent within, you visualize a powerful image of each energy source. As you connect, you self-generate a corresponding inner energetic experience.

We work with three Universal healing energies. It is desirable to have them activated *before* you enter the all-important phase of processing feelings. The *Light* and the *Earth* represent the dualistic energetic foundations of the material world. They compliment and balance each other, but are very different kinds of energy and give rise to different experiences. The *Witness* represents the transcendence of the dualistic world, and we regard it as the third force that helps maintain equilibrium of the first two. You might note the similarity of this threesome of forces with most religious cosmologies, which usually are based on a trinity of principles.

> **the Light:** The Light is the shamanic symbol for the archetypal masculine Yang energizing principle, corresponding to the left-brain. Its qualities are strength, power, vitality, protection, thinking, reasoning, doing.

> **the Earth:** The Earth is the shamanic symbol for the archetypal feminine Yin grounding principle, corresponding to the right-brain. Its qualities are nurturing, warmth, softness, receptivity, intuition, creativity, unconditional love, feeling in general, and groundedness.

> **the Witness:** The Witness is the transcendental integrating principle, serving to lift us onto the higher non-religious spiritual planes. The Light and the Earth, while vital to our well-being, can be said to still be aspects of the lower-self. Our ultimate intention is to raise our vibration and sense of identity to the Higher-Self. Becoming active on the witnessing level is how this is done.

Our primary means for activating healing energies is *inner visualization*. Visualizing means to both *see* and *feel*. For example, if I ask you to visualize the Light entering your body, try to see an inner picture. Your eyes are closed, you are *seeing* inwardly, much as if you were dreaming or imagining the picture. Then, you add inner *feeling*. Feeling occurs on a different level from seeing, but can be perceived simultaneously. Just as you feel the physicality of your body, you feel the energy of the Light – powerful, vibrant, protective. The feeling may start in your imagination, but soon will become "real," expanding your capacity for inner sensitivity.

In the following pages you will find a detailed *induction* for invoking the healing energies. I would recommend that you take time to become fully familiar with them. Get to the point where they become living energies you can draw on whenever needed.

Just activating the healing energies and allowing them to work on you is a tremendously rejuvenating experience in itself. The healing energies are intelligent and know where to go to do the most good. Even if you don't need to or are not in the mood to engage with feelings, you can sit with the healing energies for the full duration of a meditation session and have a thoroughly beneficial inner experience. If you feel you might be lacking in either of them, you could spend more time with that particular one.

For example, if you are a man and feel an absence of the feminine in your life, you could work with invoking the Earth. If you are a woman feeling an absence of the masculine, you work with invoking the Light. This will cultivate the missing or weak qualities within and make you less compulsive and dependent on outside sources. Of course, you might also feel a deficiency of masculine energies if you are a man, and of feminine qualities if you are a woman, so you would proceed accordingly.

## androgyny

I would like to emphasize that the masculine and feminine principles are *archetypes;* meaning they are imprinted as ideal forms in the collective subconscious that we are instinctively drawn to manifest as best we can. An objective in self-realization higher consciousness work has always been to harmoniously activate both of these principles in ourselves, known as *androgyny*. If we are primarily active in only one of them, we are lopsided. We tend to seek out in intimate relationship someone who is themselves lopsided in the opposite direction, who balances our one-sidedness so we can feel whole. This is no doubt a type of energy siphoning and dependency which intrinsically adds stress to any intimate relationship.

I would suggest you try to evaluate exactly where you are on the archetypal Light-Earth scale. If you think you are lopsided, see if making an effort to cultivate the complementary qualities adds to your sense of wholeness and well-being. You can start by working with the Light and Earth, as discussed.

As we develop an androgynous sense of our energetic self, this does not mean that the Light and Earth, positive and negative, masculine and feminine within us become diluted with each other and result in a non-descript neutered mishmash of wimpiness, sentimentality, and ineffectiveness. Each remains strong, separate but integrated, working in harmony with the other. We call forth each at different times, according to what is needed. A man is still a man, only he has cultivated his feminine side so he can experience a wider scope of individuality, creativity, and growth, but the masculine is still strong and dominates his personality. Likewise, a woman is still a woman even as she cultivates and draws upon masculine traits when needed. Note that in the classic Yin-Yang symbol, the two do not combine to form a single gray entity; they remain black and white, integrated but separate:

### MEDITATION BENEFIT 7: metaphysical tasks

Meditation is not all about just blissing out. It's where you perform various metaphysical tasks that benefit yourself and others:

**Healing physical-psychic congestion.** As you focus inside, you start to become more sensitive to energetic currents in the physical-psychic continuum, as we have discussed.

You start to sense the chakras. You start to sense congestion, blocks, energetic knots. These are usually first felt as sensations in the physical body. You can unwind these imbalances by applying the same processing principles to them as you do to feelings and emotions:

Bring passive, accepting, direct experience to these energy points. Breath into them by visualizing the breath going there. *Feel and witness them.* Visualize the two healing energies coming in. We will go into more detail later.

**Contacting higher levels of intuitive knowledge.** This happens automatically as you bring the mind to rest. There's a huge unconscious part of you called the Higher-Self that will start sending you advice and information about your concerns as well as creative ideas. All you have to do is quiet your ego-based mind – the mind we have been talking about – and those insights will come. You don't even have to make a point of asking questions – your Higher-Self knows what you need.

**Advanced practitioners can go out of body.** *Astral travel* is a huge step up in consciousness expansion and you can have amazing astral plane experiences. This is not all that common or easy to attain but has been written about by many authors. What might be relevant for you is to realize that many of your dreams take place in the astral world, where you meet with others including friends, lovers, and teachers. When you start seriously meditating, it's likely you will have more active, interesting dreams as well as possible spontaneous astral excursions. This is what happened to me when I first started out, and I still regard them as a gift to let me know I was going in the right direction and to forever impress upon me the reality of the inner planes. These astral experiences may range from lucid dreams to experiences where you completely wake up out of body during sleep to some fantastic adventure. For me, they have always been a reflection of the suppressed subconscious, but that doesn't mean they can be easily interpreted even though they are always mesmerizing. Because they were so meaningful for me I have compiled an assortment of my bizarre astral experiences into a book called *Moon Walking,* published years ago, and now available on the emclear.com site as a freebie if you're curious.

**Magical invocations.** Meditative capacity enables you to engage in white or black magic activities. I am definitely not recommending black magic. I'm only mentioning it to round out your understanding of the meditative arts. Black magic is always highly self-oriented and always ultimately brings bad Karma back to the practitioner and chaos into the world. You wouldn't want to be associated with that, would you? But do you realize that you are engaging in a mild form of black magic if you sit and practice the *Law of Attraction?* By visualizing what *you* want, for *your* benefit, what *your* ego thinks will make *you* happy instead of trusting that your Higher-Self is providing you with exactly what you need at this moment to make the most out of your Earth experience, you are allowing yourself to be motivated by the same principles that black magicians do when they call up assistance from the lower astral planes to fulfill self-oriented whims. I've had a few clients who have hurt themselves by strenuously applying self-oriented visualization techniques.

## MEDITATION BENEFIT 8: clear karma

For us, this is one of the most important benefits of establishing an ongoing meditation practice. Karma is usually explained with simplistic statements such as you get back what you give out, usually from a previous life. There may be some truth to this, but I believe that Karma has a deeper foundation. I believe it can be equated with the suppressed subconscious of which we have been speaking. The suppressed subconscious certainly accompanies us as we enter this physical body at birth. In no way are we born with a clean slate, as "experts" have suggested. Just observing how individualistically and distinctly children develop differing character traits in the same family is enough to convince me.

In our discussion of projection in FEEL II, I tried to emphasize that in advanced forms of projection, suppressed feeling energy goes out into the world and attracts corresponding events in order to make us conscious of itself and to clear itself – not to punish us or to pay-back for our "transgressions." This is how I understand Karma. Suppressed feeling energy is what draws events to us; feelings are where the power is.

This is a hugely empowering concept, for if you recognize and take responsibility for attracting events because of the suppressed feeling energy within, you also make it possible to change those events through clearing the energy. And this is exactly what happens in practice. As you clear suppressed energies, you find that situations change automatically and miraculously. There is no need to fight them; indeed, if you fight, you are only fighting yourself, because what you are fighting is your projection, and you can never win.

Clearing Karma has always been understood to be important on the path of Eastern spiritual practice. The ancient yogis say that the ordinary person, who has no interests beyond the material plane, goes through life the victim of Karma, experiencing all kinds of pain, kicking and screaming all the way, fighting as best as possible. At the end of the life, some progress has been made, some Karma has been experienced and exhausted, some growth has occurred. Of course, new Karma has been incurred out of ignorance. The person then comes back to continue this process, and this is what we normally call "life." By and by, growth occurs.

The yogis also say, however, that if you can simply be aware that what is happening to you is the result of your Karma, and if you can accept these experiences in a way that doesn't imply becoming a doormat, you will make much faster progress in clearing your Karma, and you will lead a happier life as well.

But then, the yogis also say that if you want to make especially fast progress clearing Karma, you should engage in *Raja Yoga*, the practice of meditation. Now think about this – how does sitting on your butt, doing something we call meditation relate to being out in the world, having all these painful experiences in order to exhaust your Karma. How can I possibly clear Karma just by going inside myself when Karma means the need to have certain experiences?

I didn't understand this for a long time in my personal practice. When I first learned to meditate, I was doing what could be called *suppressive meditation*. If a "bad" feeling came up, I thought I was having a "bad" meditation. I pushed it away or tried to replace it with a positive feeling – I had no way to release it. I eventually realized that if I work with my feelings in certain ways in meditation, I will clear those feelings and make it unnecessary to attract events into my life in order to bring up the feelings – I will clear my Karma. This was a major turning point for me and can be for you also if you resonate with what I've been saying. This is what this work is all about.

I think there's general agreement among humanistic therapists today that releasing trapped feelings is the essence of therapy. There are other purposes, of course, such as recognizing and validating needs, strengthening the ego-self when necessary, building boundaries, understanding relationship dynamics, getting the support of the therapist, etc. But once we understand and agree that the primary purpose is to release feelings, it becomes apparent how we could do what could be called *self-therapy*. And when we see that life is bringing up our suppressed feelings to be released, we have a new and radical view of life. It's no longer: Why is this happening to me? Why can't things go right? What did I do to deserve this, or even, what did I do in some past life to deserve this? Instead, it's thank you. Thank you for showing me what I need to work on, thank you for bringing up these feelings in me, thank you for the free therapy. I'm going to use these circumstances for growth.

It's not that you are being punished. It's just that you didn't release the feelings. The feelings have built up and are attracting events and people to you. These are all opportunities for growth through releasing the feelings. This is one of the reasons for life on the material plane, if not the main reason. Clearing feelings is all that's necessary, you don't have to reprogram yourself for success or goals. If you release trapped unworthiness, self-esteem is there. If you release resentment and isolation, love is there. It's just a question of releasing the feelings.

## how to meditate

From our discussion, you should have a good idea of what you are trying to accomplish with a meditation practice. Your first goal is to still the mind, relax, unwind, rejuvenate. Then, as feelings come up, you are going to take them through the steps of the process to clear them.

In basic meditation, you choose a focus point and keep your attention on it. I would probably recommend the basic Buddhist technique of focusing on the breath if you are a beginner. The advantage, as I see it, is that it starts to tie you into body awareness, which is important for advanced processing work.

Sit quietly, with eyes closed. Stop thinking and watch the breath. This means to sense the physical body as it breathes, with the mind on hold. Usually, it is taught that you do not employ any sophisticated breathing techniques; you are to just breathe normally. However, I have found this to not be entirely necessary. After you have become somewhat comfortable with trying to stay focused on the normal breath, you can breathe with any of the techniques covered in this book. This adds additional interest and physiological benefits. You just don't want to be preoccupied with controlling your breath – that's the mind. You want to be focused on the physical sensation of breathing, with the mind dropped.

As you concentrate, your mind is bound to drift. You start to think about what happened yesterday, or money, or lunch. If you are a complete beginner, you should probably go back to the breath because in the beginning you are trying to learn how to concentrate on a single point. Don't get discouraged when the mind refuses to settle down. Learning to still the mind takes a long time. In fact, I often tell even advanced meditators to put the mind on the back burner and focus on the feeling. The implication is that the mind has not stopped churning itself to death, but we just do not pay attention to it. We keep our attention on the feeling, which is now the focus point. The mind will eventually – or maybe not – come under control on its own schedule. We don't need it to be completely subdued to be able to do our work.

> Do not fight the mind, trying to force it to be quiet. Just stay on
> your focus point. Fighting the mind keeps you in the mind.

Soon, as you practice basic meditation you will need to exercise discrimination about what is coming up that takes you away from your focus point. Is it just the mind spinning its wheels, or is there something of significance emerging from the subconscious that needs to be validated? If it has a strong emotional component, it is usually coming from the subconscious and needs to be validated and taken through the process. This is your opportunity to clear the subconscious – don't turn away.

### sitting

There's a reason why the ancient yogis sat on the floor, cross-legged, with no back support, and it's not because they didn't have furniture. It's important to keep the spine straight. This allows the energies to move freely up and down the spine. If you are hunched over, you constrict energetic movement. It is said that an erect posture easily absorbs cosmic energy from above and Earth energy from below. If you are lying down, you don't get this benefit. When your legs are crossed, less blood goes into the lower body, and it instead goes up into the brain, stimulating it. It will therefore serve you if you build the capacity for sitting, on a firm cushion, on the floor, in the same place, every day at the same time, twice a day, for 15 minutes minimum each time. If you just can't handle the floor, sit on the edge of a hard chair without leaning back for as long as you can, then lean back. When I was starting out, I would sit on the floor in front of a wall, and then lean back when I had to.

### yoga

Traditional Hatha Yoga postures before meditation can do a lot to get your body unwound and make it easier to sit without the usual aches. You can also go to Yoga after sitting for a while, when you just can't sit any longer because of body aches. Stretch out with 10 minutes of relaxing, meditative Yoga, then go back to sitting if you wish to continue.

If Yoga is performed as a relaxing meditation, it can be quite helpful in releasing suppressed feelings. The negative feeling energy gets stored in the body, and gentle stretching produces the release. Meditative postures – not power Yoga – also stretch, bend, flex and stimulate the chakras into self-clearing. Trapped feelings will jump into awareness and will need to be taken through the process.

My own practice is between 11 pm to 12 am five days a week, plus 20 minutes every morning, as a minimum. In the morning, I'm focused on breathwork, building up energy for the day, going through any interesting dreams, and waking up. I use breathwork to wake up instead of caffeine, of which I have been free for many decades now, except for whatever is in a cup of decaf green tea. In the evening, I start with 20 minutes of meditative, non-power Yoga, then breathwork for 10 minutes, then meditation for 30 minutes, which includes any emotional clearing that may be necessary, sensing and clearing chakras, contacting the Higher-Self, and receiving ideas and inspiration, much of which takes form in creative projects such as the one you are now reading.

## buddhism / yoga

If you have been an explorer on the consciousness path, you have probably noticed that there are basically two major traditional routes. Each of these paths offers valuable tools for the inner journey and I would recommend combining them in your personal practice, as I do.

My first love was Yoga, which I see as an unsurpassed methodology for higher consciousness, when approached from a *traditional* point of view. Yoga advocates not only body postures, which go far to heal all levels of your being, but includes the sophisticated mystical science of pranayama – the use of the breath to achieve higher states of consciousness.

Buddhism perhaps emphasizes meditation more than Yoga, even though it does not teach the invaluable pranayama breath techniques, Hatha Yoga postures, or the chakra system. Buddhist philosophy is quite interesting as well. Do not hesitate to draw from each of these schools to create your own practice – they are not incompatible. That is what I have done and what I have been talking about all through this book.

anxiety

If you are new to meditation, or even if you are not, it's common to experience anxiety as you sit to practice. You may close your eyes and think "what am I supposed to do?" or "this is a waste of time," or just feel restless. Recognize that you are learning a new skill that takes time to develop. Low-level anxiety is usually present in the background with most of us. You are just becoming aware of it when you try to sit quietly. Treat the anxiety as a feeling coming up. Don't be intimidated by it or subverted from your work. You can use it as a focus point, and take it through the process:

**Step 1 Relaxation:** Breath smoothly and easily, relaxing as much as possible.

**Step 2 Awareness:** Recognize that the anxiety is always present. Don't blame the meditation.

**Step 3 Acceptance:** Revise your attitude towards the anxiety. Allow yourself to relax into it, without trying to change it. Accept it. Understand that you can do meaningful work on yourself whether the anxiety is present or not.

**Step 4 Direct Experience:** Just stay present with it, feeling it in your body.

**Step 5 Witnessing:** Detach and break identification with the anxiety.

There's another side to the anxiety issue, which I hesitate to discuss because it's not yet entirely clear how much of a factor it actually is, but I'm starting to question if the all-pervasive electronic Wi-Fi microwave atmosphere is contributing to difficulty in meditation. As I've mentioned, the tragic cell-phone addiction omnipresent around us indicates a mentality in constant need of external stimulation. This tendency greatly lessens the interest or ability to still the mind and look within. It seems possible that Wi-Fi contamination directly contributes to this mental unrest, which manifests as the cell-phone addiction. To whatever extent this is true, it must just be treated as another obstacle on the path.

# The Chakras

The "Centers of Consciousness" discussed in FEEL II correspond to the chakras. The chakras are energy centers in the psychic body. They are not found in the physical body, but they have a correspondence to and are felt as if in the physical body. They are to be regarded as mini "brains." Each chakra relates to certain well-defined human needs, drives, and core feelings. When I work with clients, we often talk chakras. A client will report they had solar plexus issues come up during the week, for example, meaning they were faced with feelings of inadequacy and not being good enough.

Identifying the chakra(s) that correspond to your core feelings adds another dimension to your practice. You can start to work directly with the chakra through energetic techniques, bringing healing and balance to them. The most basic way of working with any chakra is to make it your meditation focus point. Visualize it, sense it, feel it, and breathe into it while experiencing and witnessing its corresponding emotions and feelings in *Alpha*. You can also bring in the Yang/Yin healing energies of the Light above and/or Earth below directly to the chakra, depending on what your intuition tells you it needs. Just stay present with passive awareness, without wanting to change anything. Keep allowing the body sensation of the chakra to increase along with the feeling you are addressing. I routinely instruct clients in *Alpha* to focus on the chakras appropriate to their issues as part of our work.

> Find the chakra that's related to this feeling. Send the breath to it.
> Sense a gentle expansion and contraction in sync with the breath.
> Visualize, sense, feel.

As you focus inside, you will start to sense blocked places or places where there may be darkness. It's normal to find things such as a black blob surrounding the Heart, or emptiness over the Navel, or to feel constriction, tightness, weakness, and pressure in the Solar Plexus, and so on. Or to not feel anything – to be numb. Having no consciousness in certain parts of the body corresponds to suppression of feelings. If you can't locate sensations in any chakra point, don't be discouraged. Just stay choicelessly present with all these manifestations, following the process protocol and they will eventually come into balance.

## The Chakras

| | | |
|---|---|---|
| 1. Survival | Base of spine | Masculine / Light |
| 2. Power | Perineum | Feminine / Earth |
| 3. Sensation | Pubic Bone | Masculine / Light |
| 4. Nurturing | Navel | Feminine / Earth |
| 5. Significance | Solar Plexus | Masculine / Light |
| 6. Heart | Mid Chest | Feminine / Earth |
| 7. Expression | Throat | Masculine / Light |
| 8. Creative | Back of head | Feminine / Earth |
| 9. Intuitive | Third Eye | Neutral |
| 10. Spiritual | Crown | Neutral |

The chakra points we use are not the usual seven-point system described in traditional esoteric literature; the chakras we use are derived from *Taoist Yoga*, but I have assigned the psychological characteristics to them. I have found this system to hold up well in practice, and to rectify the shortcomings I experienced with the seven-point system when I was starting out. My assumption is that in the traditional system, closely located centers are consolidated into one, or that "minor" chakras have not been taken into account.

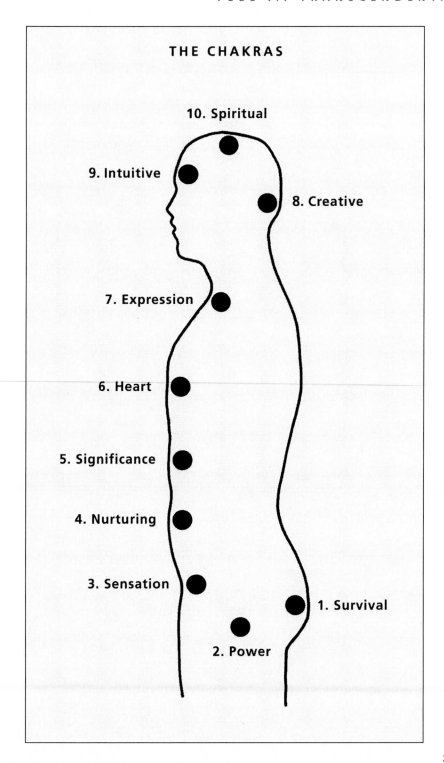

THE CHAKRAS

10. Spiritual

9. Intuitive

8. Creative

7. Expression

6. Heart

5. Significance

4. Nurturing

3. Sensation

1. Survival

2. Power

One of the foundational goals in Taoist Yoga is to activate the *Microcosmic Orbit*. There is an energy circuit in the psychic body that begins at the base of the spine, goes up the back through the hollow in the spine to the top of the head, and then down the front of the body to rejoin the base of the spine. Placing the tongue on the roof of the mouth completes the circuit. When the microcosmic orbit is activated, we become fully potentialized. Until then, we remain undeveloped works in progress.

In order to activate the microcosmic orbit, you cultivate a meditation practice where you spend time focused on each of the chakras, one at a time until you can sense them all. You may spend weeks or months concentrating on one specific chakra, working through the emotional issues connected to it. When you feel you have cleared out that center, you move on to another one. If any chakra is blocked, congested or inactive, it prevents the free flow of energy. When they are all cleared, the energy will start to flow. This is a long-range project – it may require months of daily practice to fully clear out a particular center, and years to do them all, but that's another reason why you have a lifetime at your disposal. Start by working with the centers that are relevant to you.

### bring in the light or the earth

An interesting subtlety concerning the chakras is that they each can be described as being either masculine or feminine in nature, except that the higher ones are generally considered neutral. This is true regardless of your gender. The lower chakras will tend to crave the corresponding masculine or feminine, light or earth energy as part of their healing and balancing process. When you are working with any particular chakra, therefore, make a point of bringing in the healing energy it resonates to by visualizing and feeling the light or earth going to it as you breathe into it. Usually, there will be a sense of dramatic relaxation in the chakra that occurs as it is nourished with its proper energy. It will become apparent how you have been carrying this tension with you, which corresponds to the blocking we have been discussing. If you are working with an upper, neutral chakra, it may need either the light or earth or both together.

For example, if you are working with first chakra Survival issues, you would bring in the protective Light. With fourth chakra Nurturing issues, bring in the soothing Earth, etc. However, always go with what your intuition tells you, for example if your Survival center seems to prefer the Earth, that's fine.

Always remember that stimulating a chakra by any means, whether it's bringing in the healing energy, or feeling into it, or breathing into it will tend to release the negativity that is being held in the chakra. Don't be discouraged when this happens, but use it as a therapeutic technique to dislodge the negativity so it can be taken through the steps of the process.

## validating the body

As you get into sensing your chakra energy centers, you naturally start to connect more with your physical body. Becoming more sensitive to the physical body is quite helpful in the quest for emotional healing. Suppressed psychic-emotional energetic negativity gets stored in the physical body. The chakras, although they are based in the psychic body, feel as if they are in the physical body. Both core feelings and first-level emotions therefore appear to be taking place in the body.

*For practical purposes, we assume that feelings occur in the body. Focusing into the body is a key strategy.*

Suppressed negativity can accumulate in any particular part of the body as well as in a chakra. In fact, most of the suppressed negativity corresponding to any chakra will get stored in the body, and not directly in the chakra. Working with clients has led me to hypothesize that around 20% might accumulate in the chakra itself, and 80% in any part of the body, although the first choice of a storage location is usually close to the chakra. For example, suppressed third chakra Sensation center anger would typically manifest as lower back pain, but it could also accumulate elsewhere. I once had a client who felt that his anger was being stored in his calves, and they were actually swollen. In general, there will always be some kind of body correlation to significant emotional suppression. There are schools of psychotherapy that specialize in reading the body in order to determine psychological traits.

As negativity builds in the body, it directly contributes to health issues. Some would say that all physical body ailments are caused by the accumulation of emotional-energetic negativity. If we are attacked by a virus or some kind of bacterial or environmental infection, we have become *susceptible* to it because of the negativity we hold within. If we suffer injury such as a broken leg or car crash, it is because negativity has built up to the point where it attempts to release through explosive expression. If we experience heart trouble, it is because Heart chakra issues are unresolved and there is energetic congestion in the chest.

If you have any physical health condition, it's safe to assume that in order to bring about a complete healing, the emotional-feeling residue behind it must be released. Include the body in your work by becoming aware of sensations in the body and validating and processing them along with emotional feelings, especially if they are recurrent. You may have thought that body aches and pains were simply the body randomly malfunctioning; this is usually not the case.

## body scan

As you sit in *Alpha*, scan the body to see if anything is jumping out in the form of a body sensation. Often, feelings emerging from the subconscious will first make themselves known as physical body sensations, but don't think that you *must* find something in the body. *If you find something, it can become your object of focus.* It will usually correspond to a current issue, but it could also refer to chronically suppressed negativity.

For example, if you are currently contending with feelings of not being good enough, a sensation of tension, pressure, or contraction may most likely be sensed in the solar plexus, but could be anywhere in the body. It could be a pain in the shoulders, or the knee, or the top of your head. Stay present with the physical feeling and it will likely tie into other events or emotional feelings.

You can do a body scan right after the induction, or breathwork meditation, or anytime during the session. If you process the body sensation just as you would an emotional feeling, you will start to release negativity even if you are not yet aware of the emotional component. Taking the body sensation through the process will release negativity and eventually reveal the emotion if it has not yet come forward.

I always feel it's better to eventually get to an emotional feeling, but if body sensations, including any kind of aches or pains, chronic or not, are dominating your meditative experience, it's not a problem. Let them become your focus point and take them through the process. Stay with them for as long as necessary – minutes, days, or months. Body sensations are a completely valid pathway to subconscious holdings. Eventually you will be led to the corresponding emotional feelings, and then you can include them in your process. Go with whatever is most dominant – body or emotional sensations, they both lead to clearing suppressed psychic negativity.

### vipassana

*Vipassana* meditation is one of the few Eastern spiritual practices I know of that emphasizes clearing the subconscious. In Vipassana, suppressed energetic knots are referred to as *samskaras*. The practice consists of sitting quietly and passively observing the body sensations that come up. From S. N. Goenka, the founder:

> "The observation of physical sensations without reaction during Vipassana meditation produces a remarkable effect. It causes the old stored-up past conditionings such as anger, hatred, ill-will, passion, etc. to come to the surface of the mind and manifest as sensations. Observation of these sensations without any reaction causes them to pass away, layer after layer. Your mind is then free of many of these old conditionings and can deal with life experiences without the color of past experiences."

I found another quite interesting statement by Goenka on the internet some years ago. In it, he says that when he was devising the Vipasanna system, he knew that the most effective way of releasing the samskaras was to extend passive awareness to *feelings and emotions* which spontaneously came up during meditation, but he felt that was too difficult for the average person, so he built his system around body sensations, which he felt everyone could manage. He assumed, or perhaps knew from deep inner experience, that emerging body sensations correspond to emotional feelings.

The social climate when and where he introduced Vipassana was different from today. There may not have been the potential capacity and eruditeness necessary to engage in feelings work that exists now. But if you are only aware of body sensations, this may be the place for you to start, and you will still be doing valuable inner work.

Does every body sensation correspond to an inner holding? Probably not – you can get back pain from sitting too long, or indigestion if you eat the wrong foods. You could make a case that these are all related to psychic negativity, but we don't want to get too carried away. We try to exercise discretion, and if it intuitively seems like a body feeling is just accidental, we don't follow up on it. If, however, a subtle body sensation comes into view soon after you sit and enter *Alpha*, that would seem to be an authentic case of body correspondence to an inner energetic knot.

I tend to feel that our work has gone to the next level beyond Vipassana; that while connecting to body sensations is a valid approach to inner work, engaging with feelings directly will still be the most expeditious means of clearing inner negativity, especially when combined with the sophisticated tools we are employing, such as breathwork; the Third Eye; transcending the mind and experiencing feelings as energies in the altered *Alpha-State*; our knowledge and use of the chakra system; the five-step process, and our psychological foundations. Vipassana 10-day retreats, however, still provide an intensive format for the brave to release the negative subconscious. You can easily apply *Emotional Clearing* processing principles as you participate without any conflict.

# The Third Eye

## consciousness shift 11

We have thoroughly discussed the importance of witnessing in FEEL II. All these principles apply to FEEL III of course, but now we are going to take witnessing to the next level. You will use the *Third Eye* technique to induce witnessing consciousness, both in the *induction* at the start of a processing session, *before* contacting the suppressed negative subconscious, and during processing when feelings are coming up strong.

The Third Eye technique is an ancient semi-secret Yogic practice. It consists of stimulating the *Ajna* chakra, located between and above the eyes on the forehead, by focusing the closed physical eyes on it. As you are sitting in meditation with eyes closed, look up into the Third Eye. Hold for 15 – 60 seconds, but you can hold longer if you want. You do this at the start of a session and 2 to 4 times during the session, whenever important feelings are emerging. At first you may find you are unable to stay with a feeling when you look up in the Third Eye. This is normal, but after a short while you will develop the capacity for *dual awareness* – doing both at the same time.

In addition to inducing witnessing consciousness, another benefit of the Third Eye technique is that it produces what is known as *bilateral brain stimulation*, which leads to left-right brain integration. Integrating left- and right-brain allows trapped emotions to resolve themselves, because in many ways the lack of emotional integration is paralleled by the lack of left-right brain integration. Feelings are considered unintegrated when they have been denied, resisted, disvalidated, suppressed, and relegated to the subconscious.

But the Third Eye represents more than just bilateral brain stimulation. The Third Eye connects to the pineal gland in the center of the head, which is considered to be the doorway to higher consciousness including witness consciousness, entering the transcendental *NOW*, higher intuitive knowledge, and directly accessing the Higher-Self. A consistent practice of focusing on the Third Eye will therefore give you the tangible, concrete experience of shifting into higher, intuitive, altered states of consciousness. They will no longer be just an intellectual conceptualization. You will feel as if you are stepping out onto another more spacious and expansive plane of being. You are waking up as perhaps never before. You effortlessly come into the moment, detaching and disidentifying from lower-self body, mind, and emotions, shifting your sense of identity to the Higher-Self. We have been talking about higher consciousness all through this book; this is how you can start to have the *personal experience* of it, if you are ready.

Regularly shifting into higher consciousness leads to the transcendence of the ego, one of the goals of Eastern spiritual practice. When you're in that witnessing place, detached from the lower-self, you naturally become less self-centered and self-involved. You've got the perspective to see things as they are, rather than distorted through your projections. You start to understand what it means to drop the ego, and how you are steadily moving in that direction.

How long does it take to have this experience? If you are one of the few who has an ongoing meditation practice, perhaps where you focus on the breath, you will probably get immediate results. If you are new to this work but sensitive to higher frequencies, it might take only a few days or weeks to start feeling something. At first, the sensation can be faint, and you may not be sure if you are really feeling something or just imagining. Stay with whatever you sense, and it will grow.

As with serious inner work in general, the Third Eye technique works best if you are not approaching it as a quick-fix. A dedicated practice that includes Yoga, meditation, breathwork, proper diet and lifestyle, philosophy, and a genuine desire to heal and evolve is the platform upon which you will succeed.

Note that *fluoride* in the water supply attacks the pineal gland, calcifying and disabling it, drastically interfering with Third Eye function. Distilled water is said to decalcify it. I now drink only distilled water, with occasional mineral supplements, since distilling the water removes essential minerals. I have my own small distiller, which works quite well.

## third eye technique

> Sit quietly, close the eyes and turn them upward, straining slightly. Look into the blackness at the Third Eye center in the forehead. Hold for 15-60 seconds or longer. Keep a relaxed breath.
>
> Allow yourself to shift to another, more spacious state of consciousness. Feel as if you are stepping out into space, as if your boundaries have expanded.
>
> Activate Witness consciousness: Step back, detach from lower-self body, emotions, and thoughts. Witness them choicelessly, impassively, joyously.
>
> It's OK if your eyelids flutter and tend to open slightly.

Monitor where you are throughout the session in regard to *the Witness*. You should always feel that you are in *the Witness*, detached from lower-body feelings. If you slip down into identification with the feelings or start getting overwhelmed, reactivate *the Witness* by looking up into the Third Eye and maintaining a steady breath.

Aside from using the Third Eye when processing feelings, you can expand your focus on it to develop its unique qualities as part of your meditation, as you might with any chakra. The easiest way to do this is just to extend the Third Eye step during the *Emotional Clearing Induction*. You can spend anywhere from 10 to 20 minutes or longer on the Third Eye. If you have any issues to process, you can then shift to them, or they may jump out when you are on the Third Eye, and you go to processing them at that point. If no emotional issues are coming forth, the Third Eye meditation is a valid, fulfilling experience in itself, empowering you to achieve your key goal of consciousness-shifting. When you focus on the Third Eye, if you are at all psychically sensitive, you will feel yourself shifting out of ordinary awareness to another plane, out of the mind. You may become dizzy or disoriented if it is overdone. Or, you may not experience anything at first if you have not developed basic sensitivity.

The Third Eye meditation is not widely taught in spiritual circles, even though it is one of the most powerful routes to higher dimensions. This is probably because not all schools are aware of it to begin with, and if they are, it will be regarded as an advanced technique. There is some validity to this, because if you are significantly suppressed in the lower centers, you probably will not be able to sustain the Third Eye focus, and any results you do get will tend to be unstable and ungrounded. In any event, now you know about it, and it is there when you are ready. It's one of the keys to my personal practice. Just proceed with caution.

When you are doing the Third Eye meditation correctly, you will feel a throbbing in the Third Eye as well as in the lower back of the head, the *medulla oblongata,* which is the other chakra point that connects to the Third Eye. The Creative chakra in the back of the head rules creativity and inventiveness in general. When the Creative chakra is working harmoniously with the intuitive functions of the Third Eye, it naturally leads to high creative expression and activation of higher humanistic potentials. Eventually, the two of them working in harmony lead to activation of the Crown chakra, which is the next step up to cosmic awareness and directly connecting with the Higher-Self. These three chakras form a higher trinity of energies that come into play as you evolve.

## emdr

You may be familiar with the mainstream therapy, EMDR *(Eye Movement Desensitization and Reprocessing).* EMDR utilizes the technique of moving the eyes from side to side in order to resolve traumatic memories. The client visualizes the traumatic scene, allows feelings to come up, and then engages the eye movement. Francine Shapiro, the originator of the technique, says in her book that she accidentally discovered it and does not understand why it works. However, you may notice that it is similar to our Third Eye practice. Moving the eyes from side to side produces "bilateral stimulation," meaning the hemispheres of the brain are stimulated and brought into harmony.

The Yogic technique of activating the Third Eye while holding a feeling in awareness works the same way, serving to integrate any suppressed feeling, not only trauma, and could perhaps even be considered to be a more efficacious manner of bilateral stimulation because of its ancient and reputable origin. In Yogic physiology, the Third Eye is regarded as the connecting point between left and right brain. EMDR therapy is available only from licensed therapists, but there is no reason you can't produce bilateral stimulation on your own with the Third Eye technique.

# Level III Breath

Why does the breath have so much influence over feelings and emotions? The chakra/energy centers in your body are directly connected with your emotions because it is the blocks in these centers that create the emotions in the first place. As discussed, when a core feeling encounters resistance – the same as a block in a chakra energy center – a first-level emotion results.

The most important chakras from the standpoint of our work are in the torso. As *energy* centers, they need to be nourished, and that's one of the functions of the breath. But, since there are usually blocks in some of the centers, depending on your personal make-up, the energy, or *prana*, that you take in with the breath often cannot fully reach these centers. They remain chronically undernourished and constricted, and result in chronic negative emotions. Therefore, if you consciously make an effort to send the breath to these congested centers by breathing fully into the torso, you will find that your inner experience will change spontaneously.

At the same time, it's possible you will encounter difficulty in breathing into the full body, because of your history of energetic congestion. Don't be discouraged. Stay with it, gently building your capacity and you will eventually get results.

### calming

If a strong emotion is coming up, and you sit and calmly breathe into the full torso with the Progressive Fill, you will often find that the emotion will soon dispel and no longer needs to be processed, although with emotions that have built-up, processing will most likely still be necessary. In general, however, conscious breath will soothe disturbing emotions. You don't bury emotions as they arise, you allow them to naturally complete.

The interesting thing about this is that the breath does not seem to alter core feelings behind emotions. The breath quiets emotions and makes it easier for you to contact core feelings, where the critical processing work is to be done. As you process core feelings, the breath still nourishes the energy centers so that feelings, which are also connected to specific energy centers, can be held in awareness and taken through the process.

## dislodging the subconscious

A regular breath practice has the effect of stimulating the chakras and dislodging subconscious energies so they come into awareness. Once they come into awareness, they must be taken through the steps of the process to completely clear. Working with the breath with this intention is one of the key *proactive* FEEL III practices for revealing and healing the subconscious.

## mobilizing

The breath has another vital function of providing psychic energy to mobilize *Witness consciousness*, which is one of the most important elements required for processing.

We are again going to take your practice to a new level in FEEL III by emphasizing breathwork in your meditation routine. You will be consciously using the breath as a primary tool for dislodging and integrating the suppressed subconscious. In theory, as you allow suppressed energies to surface in your meditation, you reduce the need for them to make themselves known to you through projection, and your external life starts to spontaneously come into balance.

Breathwork can be the foundation of the regular personal enlightenment meditation practice that you begin in FEEL III. Spending only 15 minutes twice a day, or more if you can, will have far-reaching psychological effects. It's likely you will feel immediately better – breath relaxes. Some difficult emotions may diminish, and you will start to get in touch with core feelings. You will be more energized, less depressed or apathetic, more capable of applying processing techniques.

What I am teaching here is based on the traditional Yogic science of *Pranayama*. If you want to explore further, more detailed books by other authors are available. FEEL III breath techniques include previous techniques as well as new ones.

# FEEL III Conscious Breath

### breathe only through the nose

While there may be a few exceptions in advanced breath practices, classical Yoga emphasizes that in basic breathwork both the in and out breath must be taken through the nose.

### tongue position

Place your tongue on the roof of your mouth, bending it back as far as you comfortably can, without straining. Try to keep it there as long as possible, throughout the whole session if you can. This completes an energy circuit up the back and down the front of the body. Get in the habit of keeping the tongue in position whenever you sit to meditate or process.

### progressive fill

On the inhale, fill from the bottom up. Let the breath go deep into the lower abdomen, expanding that area of your body, then fill the solar plexus area, then the upper chest up to the throat, being careful not to lift the shoulders. Exhale from the top down, letting the breath out smoothly. As you breathe, watch for any places where the body seems to tremble, or be tense, or constricted, or hard to fill. These places represent blocks in the energy centers. As you keep working with the breath, these blocks will be gradually lessened and corresponding feelings will jump into awareness for processing.

### ratio

Maintain a slow, steady, rhythmical pattern, breathing smoothly and easily. The 1:1 ratio previously mentioned is adequate to induce *Alpha,* but as you become more proficient with the breath, you should shift to a 1:2 ratio, with the out-breath twice as long as the in-breath. Each count is about the length of a heart-beat. For example, you may use a 4:8 count.

### letting go on the exhale

Allow yourself to consciously and deeply relax and to *let-go* on the exhale. Letting-go in this case means dropping the mind and sinking into the body. Relax and sink into the body as the air releases. Feel yourself relaxing deeper and deeper with each exhale.

### connected breath

In the connected breath, there's no subtle sense of pausing between inhale and exhale; each flows gently into the other. The torso is relaxed and there is no tensing, especially on the exhale. It's as if breathing becomes one movement instead of an alternating in-out.

### orbiting

Feel as if there's a circular motion of breath energy, rising from the bottom of your torso, up your back, to the top of your head as you inhale; and down your front to the bottom again as you exhale. This is most effective and delightful when tied into the Connected Breath.

### chakra breathing

If you have identified congestion in a particular chakra, you can make that your object of focus as you breathe. You breathe into it, sending the prana of the breath into that center, stimulating it into releasing its negativity into awareness, at which point it must be taken through the process.

### sound

In the classical *Ujiya* breath, an audible physical sound is made from air passing through the partially constricted glottis that results from the tongue position. This sound adds to the mystery of the breath, and I would recommend it.
IN BREATH: A deep "ahh" sound.
OUT BREATH: A hissing "eee" sound.

**alternate nostril breathing:** This is one of the most traditional yogic breaths. Since in our work we are primarily concerned with bringing the left- and right-brains into balanced functioning, this breath can be very helpful. At times in your practice you may want to emphasize it, for example twice daily for a few months. It should be performed simultaneously with any of the other elements, such as the progressive fill, ratio, connected breath, orbiting, etc. As you breathe into one nostril, it stimulates the opposite side brain; e.g., breathing into the left nostril simulates the right-brain. By alternating left and right nostril, another form of bilateral brain stimulation is achieved, which will help to integrate feelings. Use the fingers to block off one nostril; breathe into the other open nostril, and then block it off, breathe out and in through the other nostril, then shift, etc. Doing this for 5 - 10 minutes can relax you and bring the brain hemispheres into harmony.

**holding:** Another important advanced aspect of yogic breathwork is holding between inhale and exhale, which packs prana into the body. Maintain the 1:2 ratio, but hold as long as you can for up to 4. Your ratio of in/hold/out is therefore 1:4:2. You will have to build up your capacity for holding for this length of time. Most Yoga authorities do not advocate holding after the out breath.

**pacing:** In advanced pranayama, the breath is slowed down so that each count of a 1:2 ratio will be equal to 2 heartbeats. Maintaining a slow count for 20 minutes takes the breath experience to another meditative level. The very slow out-breath seems to be more like holding than breathing. This is one of the keys of advanced Yoga, for packing prana into the body, energizing chakras, achieving radiant health, extending life span and entering altered states.

As congestion due to resistance and blocking of feelings has accumulated in your energy centers, it has shaped your posture. You tend to cave into any affected area. Correcting your posture as you sit is the first step in opening up blockage. Sit up straight without becoming unnaturally rigid, on a firm cushion on the floor with legs crossed or on the edge of a hard chair without leaning back. Don't forget to close your eyes. There's something about the simple act of closing the eyes that gets you going in the direction of *Alpha-State* relaxation and inner awareness. If talk-therapy psychologists would just tell their clients from time to time "Close your eyes and feel that feeling" it would make a huge difference in the effectiveness of their work.

The most important component of the conscious breath is the Progressive Fill, which was introduced in FEEL II. Master this first, and then when you feel you might be ready, include other elements, one at a time. You might practice for a few weeks with only the Progressive Fill and Tongue Position, and then add the Ratio, for example. Your eventual goal is to combine them all in practice but not to become obsessive about it or distracted from feelings. At times, when you feel like it, you may include certain elements such as the Circular Breath, or Alternate Nostril Breath, and leave out others. You don't have to have all the elements engaged to benefit. Just do what feels good and learn to enjoy and have a relaxing experience.

The breath by itself can be a satisfactory route to *Alpha*. It provides psychic energy for spontaneous healing, for revealing the subconscious, for integration and release of negativity, and for *Witnessing*. However, as with any genuine spiritual-consciousness practice, it may take time to see the results of your work on a deep level. If you learn to *enjoy* the practice, you do it without thought of gain, and it changes you steadily. Over the weeks and months, you become a different person than you would have been with no dedicated practice.

You will observe the elements of the breath when starting the *Alpha* session, or when practicing breathwork by itself for relaxation and rejuvenation, or when intentionally employing the breath to stimulate suppressed negativity into awareness. During a processing session, when difficult feelings come up, you will use the breath somewhat differently, by "breathing into" the experience. While it is still best to observe the above protocol, you do not want to be distracted by being concerned if you are breathing correctly. You just breathe, and if you have been practicing the breath at other times, you will naturally include those components.

### breathing into

Often, I will advise you to "breathe into it." What does this mean, and how do you do it?

You can breathe into any physical body point or sensation, any chakra, any first-level emotional or core feeling, or any psychic sensation. It basically means to step up your breath slightly as you stay focused on the point of concern. Pranic energy brought in with the breath goes to your focus point, and guided by the innate intelligence of the prana, healing and balance occur.

For example, in working with a chakra, once you have identified the chakra that corresponds to a feeling coming up, or if you spontaneously feel sensation or constriction in a certain chakra, or any part of the body, breathe into it, gently expanding and contracting the area if possible.

> See if you can find the chakra that's related to the feeling. Breathe into that chakra, sending the breath to it. Sense a gentle expansion and contraction in that part of the body in sync with the breath.

*Breathing into* is as much a psychic exercise as a physical one. In my professional trainings I take the group through a drill in order to deepen awareness about the breath. You may find it interesting and worthwhile to try:

> Breathe into the solar plexus. Feel the physical body expand and contract. Decrease the breath so it is very shallow. You will still feel the body expanding and contracting slightly. Now stop the breath, but maintain the *mental impulse* to breathe in and out. You can still feel a sense of expansion and contraction. What you are sensing is the *psychic body* moving with your thought impulse. Now breathe into your elbow. Sense the same kind of psychic energy expanding and contracting there.

In other words, as you are breathing into any point, it's primarily a *psychic* expansion/contraction that you tie into, even though the physical body may or may not be moving.

## breathwork meditation

You will have more success with processing and releasing negative feelings if you maintain a regular practice. If you keep processing in reserve only for emergencies, you will not be developing the skills that allow it to flow easily when circumstances arise. A regular practice goes a long way to actively release the suppressed subconscious and your personal Karma. Doing lasting work on yourself – and that's really what we all need – takes some degree of commitment. As mentioned, I would recommend that you establish a regular daily practice, with optional Yoga at the beginning and perhaps another shorter breath boost at some other time during the day. Here's an ideal basic practice flow:

1. Yoga postures (optional):    15 minutes

2. Emotional Clearing Induction: 2 -5 minutes

3. Breathwork:    10 minutes

4. Processing Meditation:    10 minutes minimum

### 1. yoga

Whenever possible, it's helpful to begin with traditional Hatha Yoga postures to relax and start releasing the subconscious. Maybe you can find time for this a few times a week. You do this on your own, at home, at the beginning of your session.

### 2. Emotional Clearing Induction

Always begin any meditation, breathwork, or processing session with the *Emotional Clearing Induction* that we will discuss next. We devote 2 minutes to the breath at the start of the induction, but that's just to get you relaxed and prepared for the activation of the strengthening/grounding/witnessing energies. With this done, in *Alpha*, you are ready to give full attention to the heavy-duty 10-minute breathwork meditation phase intended to stimulate the chakras and dislodge suppressed negativity.

### 3. breathwork

In this phase, we combine breathwork and meditation. You will start with the basic Buddhist meditation of using the normal breath as your focus point, coming back to it again and again as the mind wanders. You are building concentration. After a few days or weeks, when you feel ready, introduce the Progressive Fill. Then, after a few more days or weeks, add the other FEEL III breath elements one by one until eventually they become second nature, but always include the Progressive Fill, Tongue Position, and Ratio. You are still focusing on the breath, but be sure you are not preoccupied with doing the breath correctly – that's going to keep you in the mind. You are meditating and stilling the mind so that subconscious releasing can occur, precipitated by both the energetics of the breath and the single-pointed stillness of the mind.

Stay in the breathwork meditation for at least 10 minutes, but if at any point a strong recent or remote memory, body *samskara* or emotional feeling flashes into awareness, go with it. That's the breath working, shaking up the subconscious. Shift to focusing on the feeling, keeping 15% of your attention still on the breath, and take it through the process. If no feelings come up, don't be discouraged. It doesn't happen every time, but you are always building your skills and rejuvenating yourself.

### 4. processing meditation

After 10 minutes of conscious breath you will put aside your primary focus on the breath and shift into a processing mode. Usually a body sensation or feeling/emotional issue will have made itself known. Regard this as the emergence of the negative subconscious. Don't hesitate to stay focused on it as you apply the steps of the process.

Sometimes, however, you may not have a pressing issue to work with. That's when you can shift to any of several options that become your focus point. Focusing on these other points will direct prana to them and can result in spontaneous adjustment as well as related feelings being released into consciousness for processing. With any of the focus points, however, the main objective is just to give the mind a single point to concentrate on, as you still the mind. Don't start thinking about any of these points, just focus there. Here are some optional focus points:

- Any chakra that's important for you.

- Third Eye Extended Meditation.

- Light or Earth Extended Meditation.

- Body awareness in general (*Vipassana* technique).

- Go back to any element of the breath.

There are times during your meditation when you may want a big, deep breath, but there will be other times when a quiet, gentle, shallow breath will be more appropriate. Pay attention to what you intuitively feel is right concerning the speed and depth of the breath. Usually you will start with a deep breath for the breathwork phase but as the meditation proceeds, the breath will become quiet and shallow. The shallow breath can coincide with heightened awareness and even sublime inner realizations. I have found that what's most important is not the depth of breath, but the smooth, even pacing, observing the ratio, the connected breath, and letting go on the exhale. When the breath is quiet and shallow, you still observe any/all of the elements of the breath: Progressive Fill, Ratio, etc.

Don't forget – the above is flexible. Do what you feel is right for you – what you need. I don't want to confuse you with too many options but I also want to alert you to all the possibilities, so you can employ them as you see fit, perhaps years down the road. These are all different tools for you to use as appropriate. Make up your own routine according to what you need – you can't go wrong as long as you are entering the basic *Alpha* mode and opening to feelings as they are.

I'd advise you to get into the habit of a daily breathwork practice, for all the reasons mentioned. Always precede it with the induction. If you have a pressing specific issue you want to take through the process, you may not want to spend time with the extended breathwork, and you might want to go right to the issue. On the other hand, it can be productive at times to *not* go right away to any current issue. Sit in the silence, engage the conscious breath, wait for something to come up, use the body scan. In this way, the subconscious is given an opportunity to spontaneously present material that will tie into the issues, often in an unexpected and creative way.

I have suggested a minimum of 10 minutes processing whatever has emerged for you in your daily breathwork meditation practice, but if serious issues are coming up, you will obviously want to spend more time in processing mode, ranging from 15 to 30 minutes.

When you are ready to conclude the meditation, you will wind down with a formal exit. Observing exit protocol is important because you have psychically opened yourself up and you need to close your psychic door before going out into the world. I have described the exit at the end of the next section.

### mini-retreat

Something I do a few times a month is to take a half day, usually on a weekend morning, and indulge myself in a 4-hour session. This always impresses me with what the practice can do in terms of unwinding me into a non-doing *Alpha State*.

The first step in a mini-retreat is to find a quiet place where you will not be disturbed by anything. If you do not live alone, this in itself can be challenging.

The essence of the session is to keep rotating between various segments. You start out with 30 minutes of Yoga, followed by 20 minutes of breathwork, followed by sitting meditation with processing, Third Eye, or chakra focus, etc., until your body starts to ache, and then you go back to Yoga postures, which then feel absolutely like heaven. Then, more breath, meditation, etc. Each rotation through the segments brings you into a deeper experience.

### guided meditation

As you prepare yourself for a meditation practice, you may come across offerings on the internet or elsewhere for pre-recorded "guided meditations." I feel it necessary to comment on this. If you are new to meditation, you may believe that using pre-recorded guidance is normal and valid, but in reality, it is not.

Let me give you some history about this. I began my consciousness-raising journey in 1968, if you can believe it. I learned yoga, breathwork, and several forms of meditation. At that time, just as in the thousands of years prior, using any kind of pre-recorded guidance was unheard of - it was just not available, nor was it considered desirable. Meditation, as I have explained, is the act of going inward and dropping the mind. Any kind of verbal prompting keeps you on a mental, mind level.

The first "meditation" tapes to appear on the market in the seventies were largely produced by hypnotherapists. They were mostly concerned with, firstly, inducing relaxation; and secondly, with attempting to recondition the subconscious, which as I have explained, will not be successful with regards to suppressed emotions.

Nowadays, we see the same type of strategy being propagated. Sentimental music, a tranquil voice telling you to imagine blissful, peaceful scenes - this is not meditation, although, just as with any of the bailing techniques mentioned at the start of this book, perhaps it could be helpful for some. Meditation starts with relaxation, but relaxation is not the same as meditation.

The heavy-duty Buddhist meditation schools never recommend using any audio prompting to help you achieve meditative states. You sit quietly, learning to be alone with yourself. Of course, there are exceptions. Binaural beat stimulation can be helpful to induce *Alpha* as a training device. I have an offering on my website for an audio program, but these are generic therapy sessions designed to jump-start your inner work. You are not to become dependent on them or any form of audio assistance, or think you cannot meditate without it.

I find it quite horrible that people may try to take up a meditation practice, but then turn on their smart phones, put the ear pods in, and think they are "meditating." This coincides with the general addiction to electronic devices and spiritual decadence of the day where yoga is no longer real yoga; psychotherapy is no longer real therapy; meditation is no longer real meditation; and most New Age advocates are ignorantly telling you to ignore your dark side. Don't fall for the trap.

# the Emotional Clearing Induction

Your FEEL III practice, whether you are sitting for a regular breathwork meditation such as we have just discussed, or have an immediate issue to take through the process, always begins with the formal *Emotional Clearing Induction,* which powerfully prepares you for inner release work. It provides psychic protection and energizing, connection to the healing energies, awakening of the Third Eye, and generates a profound *Alpha-State* relaxation. I always use the induction with all clients.

How will you know when you are in *Alpha*? *Alpha* is deep relaxation. This should be your first clue. You should feel more relaxed and detached, meaning not so identified with lower-self body, thoughts, feelings. Paradoxically, you can still enter *Alpha* when difficult feelings are present. This is because you separate consciousness into dual components, which we call the lower and Higher-Self. The lower-self is comprised of the body, the thoughts, and the feelings. The Higher-Self transcends all of these and corresponds to *the Witness.* You can shift your conscious identity – the feeling of you – into the peaceful *Alpha-State Witness* in spite of turmoil in the lower-self although, granted, it may sometimes be more challenging. But remember, in meditation we expect to be in a relaxed place as distressing feelings come up for clearing. We even deliberately trigger those feelings while maintaining a relaxed higher perspective.

The induction can be short (a few minutes) if you want to get to an immediate event, or the induction can be more extended and leisurely and become a meditation in itself if you don't have any particularly pressing issue to look at. You could spend time with any of the healing energies, or on the Third Eye, whatever appeals to you. The induction is based on esoteric energetic principles that not everyone will be ready for. That's why I have kept it in reserve until now, along with not wanting to make the process too complicated or challenging for beginners. The short, perfunctory inductions used in previous FEEL levels were adequate for introductory work, but as you start to get seriously proactive about releasing the subconscious, a more elaborate induction is desirable.

The *Emotional Clearing Induction* takes the form of a *script*. In the beginning, if you are recalling the script from memory, you will generally stay close to what's written. As you become skilled in the induction and get a feel for each step, you can be flexible and creative with it. You may want to alter it for each session so it doesn't become mechanical – changing the length or the language you use – all according to what you need to get into *Alpha* or to have an extended or abbreviated experience of any one of the steps.

Of all the steps of the induction, witnessing is the most important. *Emotional Clearing* is most successful when there is a strong element of witnessing present when engaging any negative feeling. Processing can be thought of as a balancing act between the *transcendent* Higher-Self Witness (Third Eye chakra) and the feeling in the lower body. There must an awareness of both. Identification, entanglement, and overwhelm can occur if there is just awareness of the feeling. Witnessing may be thought of as a key element that enables the process. Keep this in mind as you bring yourself through the induction and throughout the process. Make sure you get a sense of *the Witness* during the induction, as much as you are capable of, and then during the process keep sensing if you are witnessing the lower-self feelings as they come up. Go back up to the Third Eye whenever you need to reactivate *the Witness*.

The following instructions are concise. I would like to encourage you to observe each and every line of the instructions carefully and literally. For example, when I say "Feel yourself energized and protected by the Light" I want you to look within and make an effort to *FEEL* the Light energizing and protecting you.

# FEEL III Emotional Clearing Induction

## 1. Deep Relaxation Body Connection

Sit comfortably. Close your eyes and focus inwardly on the body. Feel your body. Relax into it.  Feel yourself in it. Feel its heaviness, its earthiness. Allow a strong sense of *being in the body* to develop. Be conscious that you are starting to shift out of the left-brain thinking mind into the right-brain feeling body, the doorway to the emotions. Relax even deeper.

Drop all sense of striving. Drop all intention to achieve anything or make anything happen, even here in this session. Allow everything to be just as it is. Come more and more into the moment, the place where healing occurs. Experience the complete peacefulness of the moment, where there is no sense of looking forward or back, just *being*, without needing to be anything other than what you are right now. Allow the experience of *non-doing* to develop. Relax, and deeply absorb the peacefulness of non-doing.

Duration: 2 minutes

## 2. Breath Deepening

Shift your attention to the breath. Breathe smoothly and easily, observing whatever elements of the FEEL III breath you are comfortable with. Relax.

In order to deepen the effectiveness of the breath, you're going to breathe with a count. You'll breathe in to the count of 4, and out to the count of 4. Start now with a full exhale, contracting your abdomen, pushing out the air, and then, begin: In, 2, 3, 4, Out, 2, 3, 4.....

Maintain a smooth count for 2 minutes minimum.

Now breathe normally. Let your breath find its own natural pace. Feel yourself sinking deeper and deeper into the body, relaxing and letting-go even more.

Keep 15% of your attention on the breath throughout the remainder of the session, breathing smoothly and easily without being preoccupied with it. Again drop all sense of striving and just relax.

# 3. Aura Strengthening – the Light

Visualize your aura. See it as a sphere all around you, perhaps eight feet in diameter, with charged electrical particles inside.

As you inhale, visualize – *see and feel* – a beam of Light shining down from above, entering the top of your head, and going to your solar plexus, where it forms a brilliant energy ball about one foot in diameter. See and feel the energy as dazzling, powerful, strong, energetic, protective, joyful.

As you exhale, visualize the energy ball expanding outward to fill the entire space inside your aura, pushing out any negativity it may encounter. See it extending to the edge of your aura, where it forms a protective shell. See and feel the shell as being strong and impenetrable. Visualize vibrations outside the shell being deflected as they try to pass through.

Feel yourself energized and surrounded by strong, vibrant positive energy. Feel yourself safe from all forms of outside negativity.

Duration: 1 minute.

• • • • • • • • • • • • • • • • • • • • • • • • • • • • • • • • • • • • • • • •

You can see the Light coming from any spiritual source that resonates with you. I prefer to see it coming from my *Higher Self*. Assume that as you bring in the Light from your source, you are strengthening the connection with it, so that you can easily access its benefic influence and guidance in meditations, or times of need.

Some psychic authorites whom I respect have advocated using Gold Light for protection instead of white light - I think there's probably something to it.

# 4. Grounding – the Earth

Visualize a link from the center of the Earth up to the base of your spine.

As you inhale, visualize blue-green Earth energy being drawn up along the link, touching your first chakra, and then filling up your entire body.

Experience the energy as soothing, warm, nurturing, unconditionally loving.

As you exhale, visualize the blue-green color absorbing negativity, turning to a reddish-black, and being drawn back down to the center of the Earth, where it is neutralized and dissolved.

Allow a feeling of *groundedness* to develop.

Duration: 1 minute.

............................................

As you connect with the unconditional love energy of the Earth, allow it to start to move to the Heart, and to awaken a sense of love from within and self-compassion. Apply these qualities to the feelings you are working with when you move to the processing *Acceptance* step.

## 5. Activating The Witness

Keeping your eyes closed, look up into the Third Eye point on the forehead, just above the eyebrows. Gently strain the eyes as you look up. Look into the blackness with the physical eyes.

Feel yourself shifting into Higher-Self *Witness Consciousness,* as if you are stepping out onto a higher plane. Allow your perspective to shift. Become more aware of yourself. Feel yourself awake and focused.

Step back and detach from lower-self body, emotions, and thoughts. Watch these parts of yourself as if you are looking from the outside. Allow yourself to feel centered more and more in the Third Eye.

Feel yourself approaching your Higher Spiritual Self, however you conceive of it. We are inviting this spiritual force along with your personal spiritual guides to be with you now and always, and to guide this session for your highest good.

Hold for 1 minute minimum.

Lower your eyes.

# FEEL III Emotional Clearing Process

You've now entered a deeply relaxed *Alpha-State* and have prepared for inner work. You can proceed to the regular breathwork meditation practice, or you can bypass the breathwork phase and go right into a processing mode if strong feelings are coming up, or if you have an issue ready to look at. The *Emotional Clearing Process* for FEEL III has become modified because of our advanced understanding of the principles:

The induction you have just experienced has taken the place of *Step 1. Deep Relaxation.*

In *Step 3. Acceptance*, you will apply the sense of self-compassion and self-love to the negative feelings.

In *Step 4. Direct Experience*, where you were staying present before with a feeling, you now make the jump to experiencing the feeling as an *energy* in the body. You still sense the basic psychological-emotional nature of the feeling, such as fear, helplessness, anger, emptiness, inadequacy, loneliness, heartbreak, etc., but your perception of it has been modified because you have developed the capacity for being in the moment and sensing the energetics of the body.

In *Step 5. Witnessing*, You will use the Third Eye focus from time to time during the processing session itself, just as you did in the induction, to restimulate Witness consciousness and facilitate left-right brain integration and integration of negative feelings.

You will use the FEEL III breath techniques as you are maintaining a steady breath throughout processing, being careful to not be distracted by needing to do the breath "correctly." Use any of the techniques that you are comfortable with or feel that you need, but always include the progressive fill. You don't have to use them all at the same time.

# 1. Emotional Clearing Induction – BODY plane

Feel yourself to be in a deep *Alpha-state.*

# 2. Awareness – INTELLECTUAL plane

Open the door to the subconscious.

Bring the event or circumstance before you. See yourself in that setting. Let the experience take place in your mind.

Allow your true feelings to be activated.

Recognize or assume that you are projecting.

Drop blame; take responsibility; *own* your experience.

Scan for any body sensations.

· · · · · · · · · · · · · · · · · · · · · · · · · · · · · · · · · · · · · · · · · ·

When working with clients, I will often ask them to do a body scan right after feelings first come up. If strong body sensations are present, we will focus on them for at least a few minutes, taking them through the process along with or prior to focusing on emotional feelings. Strong body sensations will often precede recognition of and tie into deeper emotional feelings. The body scan can be done at any point, during the *Direct Experience* step as well.

# 3. Acceptance – MENTAL plane

Find your inner resistance to the feelings.

Replace the resistance with acceptance.

Apply the sense of self-compassion and self-love.

· · · · · · · · · · · · · · · · · · · · · · · · · · · · · · · · · · · · ·

Recognize that in your advanced state of being *in the moment,* you have transcended the mental dualistic acceptance/rejection syndrome. You have started to open the Heart through your self-acceptance. You are in a place of pure choiceless awareness, simply staying present with *what is* on a feeling level. You allow the self-compassion and self-love of the Heart to melt any negativity.

# 4. Direct Experience – FEELING plane

Stay present with the emotional / body feeling.

Experience it primarily as an *energy* in your body.

Open completely to it. Let it run through your body as it will, unobstructed. Come into *the moment* with this energy.

Maintain a smooth, steady breath.

Let the feeling develop.

· · · · · · · · · · · · · · · · · · · · · · · · · · · · · · · · · · · · ·

Go to the energy level. Come fully into the moment, the place beyond time, where there's no past or future, just you, now, with your experience. Sense the feeling as an energy in your body. Drop the mind. Feel yourself to be here and now, present with the feeling. As you move into the moment, your perception of the feeling shifts from being a 'feeling' that you experience through the mind to being an energetic sensation that you experience directly, bypassing the mind.

## 5. Witnessing–TRANSCENDENTAL plane

**Step back and detach. Witness the feeling.**

**Look up into the Third Eye to re-stimulate Witness consciousness.**

......................................................

Cultivate the *dual awareness* of staying present with the feeling and looking up into the Third Eye simultaneously.

Go up to the Third Eye for 15 to 60 seconds or longer, two to four times in every processing session, whenever a feeling is coming up strong.

After you have spent enough time processing your issue (from 10 to 30 minutes):

# 6. End Processing

Start winding down now, and get ready to come back to normal consciousness. Let any strong feelings that may be present pass away.

If you feel as if you had a productive session, thank the subconscious for its cooperation.

Close the door to the subconscious, just by willing it to be.

Once more, visualize the connection to the center of the Earth, and allow any lingering negativity to be drawn to the Earth to be neutralized and dissolved.

Bring in the Light from overhead one last time. Feel the Light as powerful and joyful. Let it fill any dark or empty place inside. Feel the Light raising your vibration to a strong, high level.

Send the Light out to form a protective shield all around you that will stay with you during normal everyday activities.

Count yourself up from 1 to 5. When you reach 5, come back to normal consciousness and open your eyes.

. . . . . . . . . . . . . . . . . . . . . . . . . . . . . . . . . . . . . . . . . . . . . . . . .

Always make a point of ending the breathwork meditation or processing session with a formal exit, even if your mind has drifted back into a normal mode. You've been opening to negative energies, but now you want to make a point of closing the door to them and re-establishing protection that will stay with you so you aren't susceptible to negativity from the environment. Contacting the Light and Earth and invoking protection again can be especially important if you've been dealing with severe, dark energies in your session.

### resistance and defense / blocking

As you do the work, you may occasionally come to a place where you feel blocked. You can't get a feeling, you feel stuck, nothing is happening. This is different from blocks in the chakras which give rise to emotions in the first place. It is due to conscious or unconscious resistance of the mind. The mind always wants to defend itself from pain, and so you get stuck.

The way around this is through acceptance. Acknowledging and accepting that there is blocking, letting it be, allows the mind to relax, and for the blocking to self-dispel.

> Let's just sit here for a minute. Let's be OK with the blocking. That's where we are right now, and that's what we accept.
>
> Can you find that blocking in your body? Just stay with it, choicelessly watching.

### strong emotions

1. Protect yourself.

2. Support what is happening.

Do not be thrown off balance when strong emotion comes up. After protecting yourself from any kind of injury, assume that involuntary convulsions, uncontrolled crying, unrestrained shouting, hysteria, and so on, are signs of a clearing reaching a healing crisis. Support the crisis, and allow it to continue to its natural end. Just calmly being present, not trying to change anything, maintaining unconditional presence, detaching and witnessing is enough to give yourself the support needed for the crisis to resolve. If it seems necessary to make an active intervention, go to the breath:

> Focus on your breath. Breathe deeply.

In addition, if needed (Give yourself time to do each suggestion, don't recite them off mindlessly, use just one or two):

> Relax your body completely on the exhale.

Ground down to the Earth.

Step back from your feelings. Go to *the Witness*. Witness the feelings.

Go to your safe place.

Go inside your aura. Bring in the Light, and feel yourself protected and safe. Put anything harmful outside your aura.

## safe place

Many people feel more comfortable approaching the subconscious if they have a "safe place" they can retreat to if/when the going gets rough. When it occurs to you that you're starting to lose it, meaning you have dropped out of *the Witness*, feelings are overwhelming, you're getting confused and tired, don't hesitate to withdraw to your safe place for as long as you need. Now that you are gaining some capacity on the inner psychic planes, you can effectively construct a safe place and shift to it when necessary. You just need to remember to do it.

The simplest safe place is the protection of the Light, with which you have been working. Surrounding yourself with Light, visualizing the aura around you being impenetrable to any and all negative forces, is a completely dependable form of safe-place psychic protection. Even though you evoked the protection of the Light at the start of the session, you can go back to it to re-stimulate it:

Drop all negative feelings. Visualize the Light all around you. See it extending to the edge of your aura, forming an impenetrable shield that no unwanted or negative forces can penetrate. Feel safe and protected. Keep breathing.

If you want, you can get more elaborate:

You're going to create a safe place. This is an inner, sacred place where you feel completely safe and protected, where you can go anytime negativity has become too much to process.

> Think of a time, place, or person, that is completely associated with safety for you. It can be something you recall from the past or a place in your imagination. As you keep re-visiting this place, you make it more real on the inner planes, and more effective. See yourself safe inside, and see negativity outside, where it can't reach you. Make the resolution that this place will always be available for you, whenever you need it. Keep breathing.

Make a point of creating your safe place and even having some fun in it during a few peaceful meditations so it is there when you need it and you instinctually remember to go to it. What kind of fun would that be? Pleasant memories, fantasies, dreamscapes, or imagination excursions.

### past lives

Past life regression has become a popular New Age endeavor. It is postulated that present-day issues can have a past-life basis, and that going back to the past can aid in resolution. My experience concurs with this. Our point of view would be that the suppressed subconscious with its unresolved feelings has carried over from the past to the present life and continues to affect us.

Our focus in past-life work is then on going back to those buried feelings and applying the process to them *while in the regressed state.* The feelings are cleared just as with any present-day feeling. If you are open to the idea of past lives, you can be alert to their appearance. You will notice hints of a past-life link, and you can go in that direction

But again, as with regression in general, I don't want to give you the idea that you *must* go back into the past to clear present feelings. Those past feelings are the same as the ones you are presented with now, and you can clear them by working with them now, in your present circumstances. As with childhood recall, allow the past life only if it arises spontaneously. I have found it's usually best to wait for spontaneous past-life appearances rather than setting out to purposefully uncover them, because they don't usually appear on command, and then there is the sense of failure. However, even with that reservation, an abundance of past-life references have come up with my counseling clients. I would say more than half have spontaneous past-life recalls. They often occur when I ask the subconscious to give us an image that corresponds to the current feeling.

The key element in past-life recall is the feeling involved. A strong feeling from the present life will be the *bridge* that connects to the past life when that same feeling was in play, and then the circumstances will come into view.

In the end, past lives may be seen to be a metaphor for the accompanying feeling. We don't really know if they are literally valid, but that does not detract from their effectiveness. We always validate them, just as with any other type of recall. The feeling is what's important, and when the past life scene supports the feeling and brings it into view to be processed, that's enough for us.

Usually, there is so much strong feeling during a past-life recall that it's obvious something important is being touched upon. But remember, when going back to a past life, all processing steps still apply. For example, if you go back to a past life but still don't take responsibility and are trapped in blame, there will be no releasing.

If you want to try to be more directive about accessing a past life instead of waiting for it to spontaneously appear you can try the following script:

> Select a present-day event you wish to explore further. Enter *Alpha*, and let the event bring up feelings. It's important to allow full feeling to come up, because that's the bridge to the past. Let the feelings build, then when you sense you are ready:

> Let the subconscious take you back to another life when you had that same feeling.

> See yourself in the new setting, as if it's happening now. Become that other person.

> Where are you? What year is it? What are you wearing? What's happening? Etc.

> Identify feelings and take them through the process.

There is a school of thought which theorizes that past (and future) lives are actually happening *NOW*. Since time and space do not exist beyond the three-dimensional Earth plane, from a higher point of view, everything is simultaneous. Past-life recall is then understood to be the bleed-through of other parallel, simultaneous lives. I feel this is a more accurate way of understanding metaphysical reality, even though our limited 3-D minds are not able to conceptualize this beyond an intellectual assumption. If you agree, you can substitute "past" with "another" life and all the same principles apply. When you heal yourself now, you are also healing other simultaneous lives.

# Kate

Kate contacted me because of a chronic fatigue condition. We met for 29 sessions. She was having medical attention and was taking adrenal and thyroid medication, but it didn't seem to help much. She reported often being angry and frustrated that she was too tired to do anything productive.

I've had several chronic fatigue clients throughout the years, including one serious case who reported being bedridden for 3 years. My starting assumption has been – just as in the general condition of *depression* – that there is extreme unconscious suppression of highly discordant emotional and feeling energies, causing a huge inner conflict and energy drain. This has always proven to be the case, and resolution has occurred as the negative subconscious has been cleared. I have condensed several sessions into the following:

> **John:** Hi Kate, how was your week? Did you do any practicing on your own?
>
> **Kate:** Yes, I did several sessions where I focused on the breathing and would bring in the Light and the Earth. I would try to breathe down deep into the lower abdomen.
>
> **J:** How did it go?
>
> **K:** It was difficult – it felt uncomfortable and restricted.
>
> **J:** OK, but that's what you need to do to eventually loosen up those lower body areas. Just keep at it. Did any feelings come up as you were doing the breath practice?
>
> **K:** I was quite angry and frustrated that I can't do what I want.
>
> **J:** I hear you, but remember those are most likely suppressed feelings coming up that are only attaching to your condition of not being able to do what you want. I would treat them as a projection, and not blame the condition. It may seem as if

you're frustrated because of the fatigue condition, but let's assume that the anger and frustration have been trapped inside from some previous time. Then you're not dismissing them as being irrelevant or being completely the result of your current physical condition. Besides, rather than the condition having caused the feelings, the trapped feelings have most likely contributed to the condition.

K: I see what you mean. I also had a lot of sadness come up, which seems to get in the way of the practice.

J: Again, make the assumption that it's coming from the subconscious for clearing, and stay non-reactive to it. Don't let it influence you or keep you from meditating. Treat it as an emerging feeling and take it through the process as you're sitting in meditation.

K: I'm getting better at just saying to myself that it's OK to have feelings, that not resisting them makes them better, and I try not to let them interfere with what I need to do.

J: Great. Anything else?

K: Yes, I had another episode with my boyfriend where I wound up feeling ignored, like he won't pay attention to me, like I'm not interesting enough for him.

J: Let's go into *Alpha*, and maybe we can go deeper into these experiences you're describing.

[I take Kate through the induction:]

Get comfortable, and close your eyes. Start by connecting to the body. Just feel yourself to be in the body. You're starting to move in the direction of being more in the moment, shifting out of the left-brain mind. Let that feeling develop – that sense of being present now, in the body. You're becoming more alert and awake, as the mind drifts into the background. You're focusing on body sensations, feeling more and more in the moment.

Let's deepen your *Alpha-State* with the breath. Assume a gentle, steady breath. You don't need a big breath necessarily, just steady and even, breathing deep into the torso. Put your tongue on the roof of the mouth and keep it there as long as you can. Follow my count – inhale to the count of four, and exhale to the count of four. Stay relaxed as you're breathing, especially on the exhale. Feel yourself letting-go on the exhale.

[We breathe for 2 minutes.]

On the next inhale, visualize Light coming from above, entering the top of your head, and going down to the solar plexus where it forms a brilliant energy ball. On the exhale, expand the energy ball out to the edge of your aura. Feel yourself energized, safe, and protected inside your energy sphere.

Visualize a connection from the base of your spine down to the center of the Earth. On the next inhale, bring up Earth energy. See it as being blue-green, warm and supportive, taking care of you, nurturing you, holding you. Let it fill up your entire body. When you exhale, see the energy turning red-black and going back down to the Earth where it becomes neutralized and dissolved. Feel yourself to be grounded.

Go up to the Third Eye. Look up into the middle of your forehead, straining your eyes gently, and feel yourself shifting over to what we call Witness consciousness. You're stepping back from lower-self feelings or thoughts or the body. You're detaching, becoming more awake and alert. Maintain a smooth, even breath as you look up. Then, lower your eyes. Allow whatever witnessing sense you experienced to stay with you throughout this session, so that you're feeling detached, safe, and supported.

Let's open the door to the subconscious under the guidance of your Higher-Self or personal spirit guides, and invite feelings to come forward.

Kate, start with a body scan. What are you finding?

K: There's constriction in my middle chest. Like I can't breathe. Like something heavy is laying across my chest.

J: Focus on that whole general area. Keep up a gentle breath and send it there. Keep feeling what's happening there. Stay conscious of the body and the breath gently going to that area. That's enough to awaken and de-constrict those energy blocks. Are any feelings coming up?

K: I feel quite sad.

J: Let's invite this sadness to come forward even more. Don't be afraid of it. Just be present with it with no thought of trying to change it or escape from it. Relax into it, and stay detached. Breathe into it. Witness the sadness. Go up to the Third Eye.

Release the Third Eye and keep witnessing. [after 30 seconds.]

[We stay here for 5 minutes.]

The sadness is an important feeling, that's why we stayed with it for a while, but I'm suspecting there's another feeling behind it that's resulting in the sadness. Let's ask the subconscious to present you with an image that corresponds to the core feeling behind the first-level sadness.

K: I see myself in school. I'm 10 years old. I want so much to do well, but I'm not good enough. My teacher doesn't like me, and the other students make fun of me. Even my Mom is critical of me. I feel humiliated and embarrassed and angry and frustrated and just no good.

J: That sense of being no good is a traumatic core feeling. It's the same as you described having with your boyfriend. Let's welcome it and invite it to come forward even more. Keep breathing into it. Relax into it. Let the feeling build. Use the memory to keep triggering the feeling if you need to. Go back as if you are in school now, as the child, and let the feelings come up.

K: I'm back in school, experiencing the feelings of being no good as the child. There's also the constriction in the Solar

Plexus and that sense of something heavy pushing down on me.

**J:** Keep your focus on the feeling of not being good enough, and also include the body feelings: the constriction in the Solar Plexus and the sense of something heavy pushing down on you. Breath into it. As you stay in the setting of the class, as that child, let's take the experience through the steps:

*Step 1, Awareness:* We've discovered a key core feeling – the feeling of not being good enough. Don't blame your teacher, or the other students, or your mother for the feeling. Own it, and move forward.

*Step 2, Acceptance:* Look inside and find the resistance to the feeling – the natural impulse of wanting to push it away. Replace the resistance with a sense of being OK with the feeling as it is.

*Step 3, Direct Experience:* Come into the moment. Go to an energy level. Experience the sense of being no good as an energy constriction in the solar plexus.

*Step 4, Witnessing:* Go up to the Third Eye, just like you did earlier. Feel yourself shifting even more into the altered-state Witness, just choicelessly detaching and watching.

Lower your eyes. [after 30 seconds] Keep focusing on the feelings. Keep gently breathing into them.

[We stay here for 5 minutes.]

Let's see if we can go deeper. I'd like the subconscious to give us another image that corresponds to the feeling of not being good enough.

**K:** I see myself as a young man. I'm around 30 years old. It looks like I'm in a town in the old West. People are riding horses. I'm a worker on a construction site, but there's been an accident. I'm lying on the ground. A heavy scaffold has fallen on me, across my chest. I'm pinned down and dying. There's severe pain in my chest. I'm panicking, feeling suffocated and squashed.

**J:** Go back into the life of yourself as this young man before you were injured. See yourself as if you are there now.

**K:** I can see that I'm not happy. I once loved a girl, but she rejected me because I wasn't good enough for her. I'm feeling tremendous pain over that, which I never got over.

**J:** Let's take this through the steps:

*Step 1, Awareness:* I'd like you to recognize that these experiences from this other life have been caused by suppressed negativity you had with you then. I want you to understand that your painful experience with the girl was a kind of projection, and that you must take responsibility for the feelings associated with the experience and drop any blame you may feel for the girl. Also, the tragic accident where you were crushed in the chest is a result of the build-up of suppressed negativity in the Solar Plexus. Try to take responsibility for that as well, and drop any blame you may have towards others or towards the accident. The negative energy has not been released, so it is manifesting now in your present life.

*Step 2, Acceptance:* Focus on the experience with the girl. Find any resistance to that feeling of being rejected and feeling no good. This both a Heart and Solar Plexus issue. Replace the resistance with a sense of allowing the feeling. Relax into it. Alternate between the Heart rejection, and the unworthiness.

*Step 3, Direct Experience:* Come into the moment. Find the feeling in your body and open to it. Feel it as energy in the body – either moving or being constricted. Keep breathing into it.

*Step 4, Witnessing:* Go up to the Third Eye again. Feel yourself shifting even more into the altered-state Witness, just choicelessly watching. Lower your eyes.

[We stay here for 10 minutes.]

Where are you now?

K: I'm overcome. I'm feeling very emotional, but it's a good kind of emotion – relieved and thankful.

J: Excellent. Now gently go back to the accident and let those feelings come up. Keep detaching, stepping back, breaking the identification with the pain and the experience of being physically injured. Let all the fear and pain come up and witness it.

[We stay here for 10 minutes.]

Where are you now?

K: It doesn't seem to be so terrifying any longer. As I look at it, I'm detaching and at the same time more accepting. It feels like the panic has mostly melted away.

J: There's one more thing I'd like to focus on before we stop. I've noticed that you most probably have boundary issues. This is reflected by your relationship with your boyfriend, and other things you have told me. Weak boundaries not only affect your personal relationships, but your affinity for undesirable psychic interference. Let's take a minute to strengthen your aura, and then I want you to practice this on your own, every day for a few weeks as part of your daily meditation, or until you can feel a difference.

You're still in *Alpha*. Visualize your aura all around you, and visually check for any weak spots or openings. Use your intuition and psychic sense of feeling. Look at your aura from the inside looking out, in all directions: start by looking up, then down, then to your left, then right, then front, then back. Visualize, or imagine, that any weakness is being made strong and impervious. Use the Light to help you. Bring in the Light on the inhale, and see it fortifying your aura on the exhale. Feel yourself safe and protected. You can ask for assistance from your spirit guides if you are comfortable with this.

Let's close with some positive imaging: See yourself as brilliant and successful, easily achieving your most important goals.

**K:** It feels good, much better than before, but I can see that I'm not ready to fully go there.

**J:** No problem, it will take some time to fully release the negative energies that prevent the positive imaging. We'll take it slow. Start to gently come back to normal, and let all negative feelings pass away. Close the door to the subconscious. Let's thank the subconscious for cooperating so beautifully with us today. Ground down to the Earth one last time to send down any negativity lingering around you. Bring in the Light once more to lift your vibration to a high level, and allow a protective energy sphere to surround you that will stay with you at all times. I'll now count you up: 1, 2, 3, 4, 5.

The anger and frustration mentioned at the start have been carried forward into the current life as first-level emotions, and have become associated with the illness and the inability to achieve goals, but the prime factor is the core level sense of inadequacy. Inadequacy and not being good enough, not respected or valued is a Significance/Solar Plexus issue. This chakra is associated with the adrenal endocrine gland, and so it makes sense that the adrenals are low. Low thyroid is associated with the Throat chakra, and although we didn't discuss it in the session, Kate also had issues with speaking up and being heard, which can be associated with the critical treatment she remembers as a child. The past/alter life of the young man became a major point of focus. We went back to it again and again, releasing the feelings associated with that experience, which center around both the Solar Plexus and Heart. This life appears to have been a critical experience, both in terms of negativity coming to a climax, and serving as a launching pad for the present life dysfunction. I would again mention that in the enlightened view of multiple incarnations, they are all happening simultaneously in a way that our three-dimensional minds cannot grasp. Healing the "past" then directly impinges on the present. Was this other life something imagined, or was it real? For me, the question is irrelevant. There was so much emotion connected with that other life that, from a psychological point of view, important feelings were stirred up and cleared.

# Addiction

In addiction, there is a desperate attempt to gain psychic energy for the purpose of suppressing pain. It takes energy to suppress, and this demand for energy becomes a huge drain when we maintain the unconscious habit of suppressing negative feelings. Without realizing it, we fall into addictive patterns in the attempt to acquire the energy necessary to keep feelings suppressed. The pain that we attempt to suppress arises from the negative subconscious. The subconscious has built up over time and is now constantly making itself known in the attempt to clear and balance itself. The appearance of the subconscious takes the form of painful feelings and experiences, and this is what the addiction is trying to control.

The addictive pattern itself is subject to dualistic swings. There's an alternating cycle of highs and lows. In the high, we feel good because of the energy boost and because the pain has been temporarily hidden, but then the low occurs as a result of the depletion of energy reserves used to maintain the high and we feel depressed. If we are unconscious, we turn again to the addictive substance/activity/pattern instead of trying to break it. We may also experience physical cravings for the substance which makes it even harder to break the cycle.

The addictive substance may be chemical, such as alcohol, tobacco, drugs, or food, from which we attempt to draw the psychic energy, or another person. Attempting to draw energy from a person is quite common, and you have probably experienced it at some point. Whenever you feel drained during an interaction with someone, there has been an uneven exchange of energy. This occurs, for example, when you are forced into giving your attention to someone who talks without allowing you to speak or who may be lecturing or even "entertaining" you. In giving your attention, you allow your psychic energy to be drained. In modern times, this behavior of drawing energy from another person has been sensationalized as the vampire phenomenon. Contrary to the popular notion, real-life vampires don't suck the blood of the victim. They do quite well by just siphoning off psychic energy through manipulative, coercive, intimidating behavior.

We can also become addicted to activities, especially those which give a surge of adrenaline, like sports, either as participant or viewer; performing, where we are up in front of an audience; TV, movies, video games, cell phones and computers; and of course the most obvious kinds of addictions such as relationships and sex. Almost anything can be used addictively – it's the intent that matters. The activity keeps the mind busy and engaged, preventing awareness of negative feelings and keeping them suppressed.

Addictive acting-out usually begins with *compulsive* behavior. When our behavior reaches the point where we are irrationally driven towards a certain object, activity, substance, or person, we can say that we have become compulsive. When the intensity of the drive increases to the point where we feel we just cannot live without that item, we have become *addicted*.

These behaviors are all a form of *self-rejection* because their purpose is to deny, reject, defend against, and keep from awareness a painful feeling. For example, if you are holding feelings of inadequacy in the solar plexus, you may become compulsive or addicted to success and recognition in the attempt to satisfy the inadequacy. If you are holding heartbreak and loneliness in the Heart, you can easily become compulsive or addicted to intimate relationships. The irony with compulsive/addictive behavior is that the urge is never satisfied, except perhaps temporarily, and in most cases actually builds so you are always looking for more.

As you work on yourself, you must eventually become aware of any compulsive/addictive reactive acting out. Our emphasis, however, is not primarily to modify behavior through an act of will, but to release the feelings that are motivating the behavior, so that the need for the behavior is outgrown.

## compulsiveness

Acting out in any of the chakras indicates an attachment to the positive in an effort to avoid the negative. If you are working with a compulsive impulse that has not yet reached the point of being an addiction, you may be able to defuse it by simply bringing your attention to the feeling behind the compulsion, of which you may not have been particularly aware. As you focus on the impulse to act out, the negative feelings motivating it will come into view to be processed.

> Look at the feeling that's behind the compulsive behavior you are concerned with.

> Bring your attention to the feeling and take it through the steps of the process.

## addictions

If acting out has reached the point of addiction, you may need a more elaborate approach. As you look inside, try to distinguish between the *addictive impulse* and the *core feeling* behind it.

The *addictive impulse* is the pressure or strong urge to go to the object of addiction, whether a drug, food, money, recognition, or certain activity like work, shopping, sex, TV, internet, cell phone, etc. The *feeling behind* the addictive impulse is the core feeling that you are unconsciously attempting to avoid through the addictive behavior. We work in two stages, first with the *addictive impulse* itself, and then with the *feeling behind* the impulse.

### addictive impulse

What follows is a special intervention for the *addictive impulse*. Although our primary strategy is always to release core feelings behind the addiction, we can do valuable work by addressing and applying reconditioning techniques to the addictive impulse (which occurs on the *mental* level). The addictive impulse is a type of *Reactive Emotional Impulse* and is therefore a product of the mind and can be reconditioned, while core feelings cannot be reconditioned and must be processed.

We start by reconditioning the addictive impulse on a *behavioral level*. You need to have ready an alternate behavior that you are going to substitute for the problem behavior. Find something more desirable than acting out in the usual destructive way, which you can recondition yourself to switch to. Having an *active, physical* alternative can be useful. Even if you just go to the alternative behavior for a short period before you must yield to the addiction, you are reconditioning yourself over time. Examples:

**addiction:** Smoking. **new behavior:** Practice with the breath. Take a walk. Stretch.

**addiction:** Shopping. **new behavior:** Go into the kitchen and cook something. Call a friend.

**addiction:** Sex. **new behavior:** Go for a run or the gym. Divert it into creative activity. Yoga.

**addiction:** Food. **new behavior:** Drink water. Eat something harmless. Yoga.

Then, work in *Alpha*. You are going to work first with your *addictive impulse*, not the core feeling behind the addiction. You can work on this during your regular practice sessions, when the impulse may not be necessarily coming up, or whenever you feel the *addictive impulse* strongly.

Enter *Alpha* using the standard induction.

See yourself in that setting where the impulse comes up.

Focus on and *feel* the impulse without trying to change it.

Using a conscious breath, breathe into the impulse.

Continue the breath for as long as desirable (2-10 minutes).

Keep witnessing and detaching from the impulse as you breathe into it. Break the identification with the impulse. Recognize that it's part of the lower-self.

Affirm that you will cease being motivated by the impulse. Visualize yourself going to your new behavior in place of the old.

Send this new behavior deep into the subconscious so that it becomes your automatic response whenever this addictive impulse comes up.

core feeling

After you have worked with the *addictive impulse*, you will turn your attention to the feeling behind it. While still in *Alpha:*

> Shift now to the core feeling that's behind your *addictive impulse*. The *addictive impulse* represents an attempt to escape from, to control or manage, a deep painful negative feeling. What is that feeling?

After you have found the feeling behind the addiction, you take it through the process. You may not immediately be able to go to the core feeling. You may be presented with first-level emotions. Stay with what you find, treating it like a regular processing session except that the steps are modified for an addiction:

> Step 1, Awareness:
>
> Recognize that the feeling is coming from the inside and is only being activated by any outside event or person.
>
> Take responsibility for the feeling, dropping any blame that might be present, to the best of your ability.
>
> Recognize that your resistance to the feeling has taken the form of_____(the addictive acting-out behavior).
>
> Step 2, Acceptance:
>
> In your mind, put aside the addictive acting-out behavior and allow yourself to be fully present with the feeling behind it, with no thought of changing it.
>
> Drop resistance to the feeling. Open to the feeling, accepting it. It's OK to have this feeling.

Step 3, Direct Experience:

Focus on the feeling. Come into the moment, and experience this feeling as an energy in your body.

Bring in the Light or Earth healing energy to the feeling/chakra. Let these healing energies replace the energy you get from the addictive behavior. Let your intuition suggest which of these energies you need.

Step 4, Witnessing:

Keep detaching. Step back. Go up to the Third Eye at intervals as you stay present with the feeling.

# Nick

Nick is a 32-year-old man. We met for 9 sessions. Nick was devastated that his girlfriend of 2 years had just broken up with him. He had fallen into negative patterns as a result, developing a severe porn addiction. He understood that the addiction was a futile attempt to cope with the loss, but he was unable to break it. As I got to know Nick, his personal history emerged: His father had left the family when he was 8 years old; his mother had raised him, an only child. He was never happy with his mother, but did not quite understand why. I have again combined and distilled several sessions into the following:

I lead Nick through the *Alpha* induction and we begin:

**John:** Bring your girlfriend before you, and allow feelings to come up. Tell me when you get something.

**Nick:** I feel terrible, depressed and despondent.

**J:** Breathe into those feelings as you relax into them. Don't fight them. Step back from them.

**N:** OK. It feels a little better.

**J:** Look a little deeper and see what feelings are behind that. What's there?

**N:** I love her and want her but she's left me. She's with someone else. I hate her for leaving me. I'm overcome with jealousy.

**J:** Jealousy is a valid, first-level, Heart-centered emotion. Let's take it through the process: Try to put aside blame, even if only for this session. Allow yourself to open to the emotion of jealousy, even though it may be painful. Feel it deeply, without trying to change it. Step back and detach. Breathe into it. Can you find any body feelings?

**N:** Yes, there's a tremendous emptiness in the middle of my body.

J: Stay with all that – the emotions and the body feeling. Keep relaxing and detaching from the jealousy. What about the hate? Let's invite that to come forward. Relax into it.

N: I'm raging and hating her, like I want to scream at her.

J: Put the impulse aside of wanting to scream at her and focus on the hate in your body. Relax into the hate. Allow yourself to fully feel the hate, and at the same time, disconnect it from your girlfriend. Assume it exists inside you and is only being stirred up by her actions.

Bring in the anger as well. Feel both the hate and the anger in your body. Detach and keep breathing into them. Look up into the Third Eye. [hold for 30 seconds.]

[We stay here for 10 minutes. Nick goes through visible stages of being stricken with severe rage, breathing heavy and fast, his body shaking, and getting red in the face. Then, this passes and he moves into a calmer, relaxed mode.]

What's happening now?

N: That was amazing. I think that's the first time I allowed myself to fully feel the hate without censoring myself. I just allowed it to come up without resisting it, and then it passed away.

J: Let's ask the subconscious to give you an image that corresponds to the hate and rage.

N: I see myself with my mother. I'm 8 years old. My father just permanently left and I want to snuggle up with my mother, but she won't let me. I feel rejected by her and deserted by my father.

J: Go back and become the child. See yourself in that setting and let the feelings come up.

N: I'm there. She keeps pushing me away. I want her warmth, but she doesn't have it to give to me. She's incapable of being a mother. I'm deeply hurt. Why won't she love me?

J: Let's take this through the steps:

*Step 1, Awareness:* This is a core feeling for you – an absence in the Nurturing center, which is behind the Heart-centered loneliness, jealousy, and hatred. I'd like you to understand that this feeling has been trapped in the subconscious and has attracted a parent who corresponded to it. Drop blame as best you can, and let's focus on the absence of nurturing that's at the core of your issue.

N: I've never thought of it that way, but now that you mention it, I can see that that's the exact same feeling I had with my girlfriend. She was never warm or supportive or caring, she would never comfort me when I needed her, even though I tried to always be there for her. That used to always get me furious.

J: That's an excellent insight. Let's go to *Step 2, Acceptance:* Now that you're aware of the core feelings, look inside and find any resistance you may have to them. There's an emptiness there, a hunger. Don't be afraid of it or try to push it away. Replace any aversion you may have to the feelings with a sense of letting them be as they are.

N: I feel a huge sadness.

[Nick breaks down in tears for a minute.]

J: You're doing great work, Nick. Let's keep moving.
*Step 3, Direct Experience:* Come into the moment. Go to an energy level. Experience the absence of Nurturing in the body, in the Navel center. Don't try to change it into something else. Just stay present with the sense of *emptiness* and *lack*. Breathe into it.

*Step 4, Witnessing:* Go up to the Third Eye. Look up into the forehead, straining your eyes gently. Feel yourself shifting into the altered-state Witness, just choicelessly watching the emptiness in the navel, and being present with the core feeling of emotional hunger and neediness.

[After a minute, I instruct Nick to lower his eyes, but we stay in processing mode for 10 minutes more.]

Where are you now, Nick?

**N**: The hunger inside has come more into view. I can see how it's been at the bottom of my search for a woman, and how I give my power to a woman once I become attracted to her. That's what happened with my girlfriend.

**J**: Those are excellent insights. Let's look at the sexual issue you mentioned when we started. See yourself as if you are going to be drawn into a sexual episode. Feel what's going on with you, and tell me what's happening when you get a clear picture.

**N**: I'm feeling despondent about my girlfriend not being there for me, and I think I can fix the feeling with sex. I'm feeling pressure in the sex center and I want to release it.

**J**: Step back and witness the sexual impulse. Go up to the Third Eye. Lift up your eyes as you stay present with the impulse without acting it out. Relax and keep detaching. Breathe into it. The sexual addiction is an unconscious attempt to alleviate the painful feelings of not being taken care of in the Nurturing affliction, and the related jealousy and hatred in the Heart. We're going to treat the sex impulse in this case as a *Reactive Emotional Impulse*. That means we see it as a knee-jerk, unconscious, reactive response to a deeper pain trying to emerge. There's no need to process the sexual feeling beyond basic witnessing. Your strategy is to witness the sexual impulse without succumbing to it, to detach from it, and put it aside as best as possible, as you focus on the core feeling behind it. As these core feelings in the Nurturing center are resolved, the need to act out in the sex center will diminish. I'd like to have you include an exercise for transmutation of sexual energy in your daily practice which will loosen up the sex energy and raise it to the upper chakras.

It only took Nick 9 sessions with me to fully take responsibility for the hunger within, to see how it had been driving him to give away his power to women by becoming emotionally dependent on them, and to clear away some major suppressed feelings. The sex addiction died a natural death.

# Sexual Transmutation

Excessive compulsive acting out or incapacity (can't perform, frigidity) in the sexual center is usually accompanied by an accumulation of energy in that center due to blocking, stagnation, and congestion. However, the energy that accumulates is not primarily sexual; it's the universal life-force, prana, or chi, which is neutral in itself. It assumes certain characteristics when it is expressed through any chakra. In the sexual center, it becomes sexual energy. If the energy can be directed from the sexual center into any other higher center, it assumes the characteristics of that other center.

To loosen the blocking, and to raise the energy, we perform a specific Yoga practice. This practice is usually reserved for advanced students, for several reasons: Those new to Yoga will not be able to understand or appreciate the value of the exercise; their body may not be ready for the exercise; they may not be able to actually perform the exercise. Nevertheless, I will describe it in the hope that it may benefit some people.

To start, look at the condition of your spine. Hatha Yoga in its traditional, pure form emphasizes flexibility of the spine as one of its key objectives. If the physical spine is flexible, energy can freely move up and down, and congestion at any chakra point is more easily dispersed. If the spine is relatively rigid, it's more difficult to move energy out of congested places, and aging of the body is accelerated. If you have any type of compulsive issue due to congestion in any chakra, a regular Hatha Yoga practice is therefore invaluable.

If you find that the exercise increases sexual desire, it probably means you are stirring up sexual energy but not lifting it up to a higher center. Back off on the contractions, but work on spine flexibility with Hatha Yoga, and concentrate on mentally visualizing the energy going up the spine to the Third Eye in conjunction with the inhale in your breathwork meditation. As you perform the exercise, expect that emotional feelings relating to the congestion will appear. Process them.

### exercise for sexual transmutation

Sit on the floor with legs crossed, on the edge of a firm cushion. If possible, place your heel under the perineum, so there's a gentle pressure on the perineum. You can also sit on the edge of a hard chair, but it's not as good. The exercise you are going to perform is known in Yoga as *Mulabandha*.

The perineum is the space at the bottom of the torso, between the anus and genitals, right in the crotch. Briskly contract, or lift, the perineum and immediately release. Your rate is about one lift and release for every heartbeat. As you lift the perineum, you will also be secondarily contracting and pulling in the anus, the lower abdomen, and arching the lower back outward, but the perineum is the main focus. All these motions together form the sacral pump that will disperse sexual tension and raise the energy up to the higher centers. You can do them gently or vigorously.

As you lift, take in a short burst of breath and let it out as you release the contraction. Keep the image in mind that you are shooting congested pranic/chi energy out of the sexual center with the contraction and drawing it up the spine with the in-breath. The feeling is like sucking the energy up through a straw, to the higher chakras. Any higher chakra will do, but the best is the Third Eye. Keep your focus on the Third Eye as you perform the contractions, just as you do in the induction. Look up with the closed eyes into the center of the forehead. Feel the energy shooting up the spine, accumulating in and stimulating the Third Eye. As you gain proficiency, you should feel the Third Eye tingling.

Perform 3 sets of 15 contractions, every day or when needed to move the energy, each set separated by 5 to 10 gentle, full breaths. At a certain point you will be able to draw up the energy by means of visualizations and breath alone.

# Attuning for Health

Negative feelings are composed of a kind of psychic energy. When these feelings are suppressed, the unreleased negativity accumulates on the psychic energetic level of our being. At a certain point, the negativity starts to overflow, manifesting on the physical level, resulting in illness, as well as ongoing emotional dysfunction. It is likely that all physical health issues relate to suppressed feelings, and that certain kinds of suppressed feelings will coincide with certain kinds of illness.

When we approach healing the body from a processing-metaphysical point of view, we are engaging in nothing less than what has been known for thousands of years as *spiritual healing*. There have been abundant historical references to the validity of spiritual healing throughout religious literature, of both modern day, with the Christian Scientist movement, for example, and ancient Pagan religions.

From *The Master Speaks* by Joel Goldsmith:

"It is Spirit that performs all healing work. It is not my reaching out to your thought. It is not my pumping thoughts of statements of truth into you. It is merely my ability to sit and become one with the Father, and then let the infinite invisible Spirit appear as whatever healing or corrective influence may seem to be necessary.

Do not set up a mental wall against it. Do not set up a mental rebellion against it. Do not set up a mental denial against it, but learn to wait in silence."

I believe you can discern that he is speaking of the exact same principles we have been employing in our work, except that he frames it in a religious context. The important point he makes is that it is not you who heals, but that you must get your *mind* out of the way. It is not by mentally *resisting* or picturing a mental image of health that healing occurs, but rather, by surrendering to the will of the Spirit.

I don't believe spiritual healing necessarily needs to be applied within a traditional religious context. Most of us in the New Age movement recognize a higher power, but we don't need to have it interpreted for us through traditional religious dogma. We feel that when we personally contact the healing energies of the universe, or the Higher-Self, or *the Witness*, we are connecting with the exact same benevolent forces that Joel describes. Nowadays this type of healing is commonly referred to as *Energetic Healing,* and is similar to what healers in all kinds of ancient, sophisticated civilizations have applied.

Those of us who develop the required skills can become healers for the rest of us, and now that you have been cultivating these qualities in yourself, you can, without question, direct your powers towards healing yourself as well as others. When I sit with a client and we both focus on healing them, my energy naturally goes there – there's nothing special I need to do aside from stilling my mind and directing attention to them. When I focus on myself, that's where the healing energy goes.

In working with health issues, our strategy is to apply processing steps to the experience of the health disorder. We seek to set the *inner* conditions that will most favorably allow natural healing forces to operate effectively and unimpeded. In order to stimulate these natural healing forces, we emphasize several elements of the *Emotional Clearing Induction:*

As you focus on the Light and Earth, the natural healing forces of the Universe are stimulated and brought to bear on the affliction. These forces come from both inside and outside you. As you stay in *the Witness*, being present with the physical symptoms, you are shifting beyond the mind, inviting intervention from higher spiritual forces.

The key here is to bring the mind to rest and apply heightened witnessing awareness to the experience of the health disorder. Witnessing awareness does not have any opinion or preference about how things should be – it is the mind that has these opinions. When you go beyond the mind, you drop the interference that prevents the healing forces from doing their job.

### body sensation

The first step in attuning for health is to move into a deep *Alpha* state and be present within yourself for a few minutes, as we normally do for any processing session. Use the standard *Emotional Clearing Induction:* Contact the healing energies and feel them in your body; contact and awaken Witness consciousness.

Then, since we are concerned with the physical body, focus on the *body sensations* related to the health condition. You could consider this to be an extension of the body sensation sensitivity we have been developing. You want to be able to differentiate the *illness* from the *body sensations* related to the illness. This is important for several reasons:

- You will move into feeling as you focus on body sensations.

- By focusing into the body, you move out of *the idea* of the illness and into the reality – the moment – of the illness, so that when processing, you are not in the mind, thinking or worrying about the illness.

- Body sensation becomes the energetic bridge from consciousness to the negativity. You should monitor yourself, sensing if you are in the body feelings or the mind, and continually bring yourself back to the body sensations whenever necessary.

If you can't find a body sensation, focus on the specific or general location of the affliction.


### chakra association

As you are processing body sensations, at some point you will want to identify the chakra that appears to be related to the affliction. You don't necessarily need to do this immediately, but as you keep working with the issue over a period of time, you'll eventually bring in the chakra, feeling it if you can along with the body sensations relating to the condition. Bringing awareness to the chakra:

- Adds another dimension to the work, helping to clarify the emotional component so you can process this along with the body sensation.

- You'll get a clue as to whether the body best responds to the Light or the Earth healing energy.

- The chakra represents the energy itself that has resulted in the affliction. Working with the chakra by breathing into it or just staying present can be helpful.

## emotional association

As you focus on the sensations of physical symptoms in the body, emotional feelings may arise. Include them in the processing work but keep shifting between them and the body sensations, and perhaps the chakra itself if there's strong feeling or blocking there. Let your intuition guide you about how much time to spend on each. You may be able to blend all of them together, so you are focusing on all simultaneously. Our basic stance is always that the emotional has built up and is manifesting in the physical, so we must give appropriate emphasis to the emotional work, but working with the body sensation or chakra can still be important. Just be sure to allow enough time on each area, physical, emotional, and chakra as you jump between them.

## healing energies: Light or Earth

As you are working with the affliction, bring in the healing energies, which correspond to the Light and the Earth. It seems that in practice each chakra, and therefore the affliction that is associated with it, has a preference for either the Light or the Earth energy. This could be said to arise from the basic nature of the chakra being Masculine or Feminine. A masculine center will want the Light; feminine, the Earth. Based on your knowledge of the chakras, you will have a feeling which healing energy will be needed, but still it is often good to let the chakra, and the affliction, decide for itself which it prefers, so usually we will introduce both energies and see if there is a preference.

### the steps

As you process the affliction, you will use the steps as usual, except that we modify the concept of *Acceptance* so that it will apply to physical health. We are usually in strong resistance to the affliction. This stance is reinforced by much of the healing community, which urges fighting the condition, as in "you can beat it." It often appears that fighting is what's called for, and what needs to be done to "combat" the illness.

Our position is that we fight differently. Fighting keeps you on the dualistic mind level, where healing does not occur. We are focused in *the Witness*, which enables us to detach from the affliction, and we invite the Higher-Self to direct the outcome for the highest good of all concerned. This surrender, combined at the same time with accessing the healing energies and moving into acceptance of *what is,* not necessarily what will be, brings about the healing. The surrender is the spiritual consciousness, and helping a client get to this place as they deal with their affliction is something I regard as a privilege. Some people spontaneously achieve this consciousness, and that's why they say their illness is the best thing that ever happened to them.

### the healing process for physical illness

You have entered *Alpha*, observing all the steps of the induction. When you are ready, start to work with the physical health condition. There are more options in the script below than you would want to use at any one session. You can bring in various techniques at different sessions to give you a variety of tools, according to what you think will work best for you. However, you should always start by sensing and processing body sensations.

In *Alpha:*

Quiet the mind, come into the moment, and look inside.

Look more closely at the_____( physical health condition).

Locate *the sensations in the body* that correspond to it.

Stay present with the sensations, with no thought of changing them.

If any emotional feelings come forward, stay present with them as well.

Give yourself enough time to relax into the sensations/emotions and to allow them to develop. You can breathe into them, and go up to the Third Eye if you start to get a strong experience. Use your discretion about shifting between the sensations and the emotions:

Focus on the body sensations alone.

Now, go to the emotional feelings.

When you feel ready, bring in chakra awareness:

Identify any particular chakra that relates to this condition. Breathe into the chakra while keeping your body as still as possible. Feel the expansion and contraction *in the energy body* as you breathe.

Light/Earth: Recall from the chakra table (page 216) the kind of energy the chakra is likely to prefer, but also give the chakra the chance to find out for itself.

Bring in the Light or the Earth.

Now that you have contacted the body, the emotional feelings, and the chakra, let's take it all through the process. The important step here is *Acceptance* – getting to the place where you are allowing the energy sensations in the body that have taken form in the affliction.

Let's take this health condition through the 4 steps:

Step 1. Awareness:

Be aware, or just make the assumption, that what you are experiencing in your body as illness is the overflow of negativity that has been stored on the inside. Drop blame, stop seeing yourself as a victim, *own* your experience. This is your opportunity to release the negativity. Your body is now cleansing and clearing negativity that has been stored in it for years. You can expedite this process by relaxing into it and allowing it.

Step 2. Acceptance (or *Acknowledgement*):

Relax into your condition, especially the feelings accompanying your condition – emotional and physical. Trust that relaxing and accepting will bring you out the other side.

Find any resistance, and gently reverse it through an act of will. Allow yourself to move into acceptance, even if only for this session.

optional additional:

You know that to release any condition, you need to accept it. Start moving towards acceptance of your health condition and in particular the body sensations, but understand that acceptance does not mean you are condoning or giving permission for the health condition to continue into the future. It just means acceptance and *acknowledgement* of *what is, now.*

When you resist or fight your condition, the mind is active. The ego is active. It is not trusting, not relying on the higher powers latent in the super-conscious. I know it seems intuitive to fight, and people even may encourage you to keep fighting, but this other way of acceptance is higher.

Step 3. Direct Experience:

As you stay relaxed, focus your attention on the body sensations, emotional feelings, and chakra points. You can rotate through them one-by-one, or sense them all at the same time.

Open to all the feelings. Perceive them primarily as *energy* in the body. Feel yourself to be *IN THE MOMENT* with this energy. Remember to keep breathing, easily but fully.

See both healing energies, the Light from above, and the Earth from below, coming in with the breath and going to where they are needed. See and feel the energies illuminating any darkness they find. Notice if your body prefers one of these energies over the other.

Step 4. Witnessing:

Keep the feeling present and look up into the Third Eye again, as you did in the induction. Cultivate the *DUAL AWARENESS* of staying present with the feelings and looking up into the Third Eye simultaneously.

Keep going up into the Third Eye for 10-30 seconds at intervals of 3-5 minutes to re-stimulate Witness consciousness.

Feel yourself stepping back, just watching the body sensations or emotional feelings, whichever is coming up for you now.

You will stay with this basic format for as long as seems desirable. It can be for as long as 30 or 45 minutes. All during this time, even if there are periods of rest, you are bringing in the healing energy, and maintaining the healing presence. You may repeat various steps as you see fit, re-emphasizing them, including going back often to the Third Eye as we have discussed.

## pain management

As you stay with processing body sensations, sometimes pain becomes an issue. In theory, applying the steps of processing to the pain can result in a form of pain management that can prove to be helpful. Relaxing into, accepting and not fighting the pain, and in particular, witnessing it results in a shift from being identified and immersed to being detached and transcending, and this results in a practical sense of relief.

This specific topic has been researched and developed more completely by Jon Kabat-Zinn in his work. His approach is from a Buddhist vantage point. He advocates applying mindfulness to the pain, and in his group studies, he concludes that significant reduction and management of pain can result. "Mindfulness" is exactly what we do with our processing steps.

# Elliot

There's been exciting news concerning one of my counseling clients. Elliot, age 55, has apparently experienced remission of a prostate cancer condition. This is exciting not only because of Elliot's success but because of how it came about – with alternative healing treatments in which *Emotional Clearing* therapy played a significant part.

Elliot's urologist suggested a biopsy after a routine digital exam. Of 12 biopsy samples taken, 2 came back positive, at 15% and 30% cancerous. Elliot's doctors considered this a successful early detection of low-level cancer, with excellent prognosis if treated immediately. Standard medical treatment would range from radiation to surgical removal, with a few other options, such as cryosurgery.

Elliot employed a 'medical detective' right from the beginning to advise him of the best doctors and procedures available. Several doctors were consulted. They all confirmed the presence of prostate cancer, including a leading prostate cancer specialist at Johns Hopkins, to whom Elliot's biopsy slides were sent.

Rather than rush into medical treatment, which Elliot was considering at a certain point – he just wanted to 'get it out and over with' – I urged him to wait 6 months, to make a best effort with alternative approaches, and then to re-evaluate. I pointed out that spontaneous remissions have been known to occur, why not here, with a focused, thought-out program? Even if we could just stop the cancer from spreading, this might be good enough.

After 5 months of weekly sessions with me and other treatment modalities, Elliot consulted another leading cancer specialist. He evaluated Elliot in-person using the latest 3D Doppler Hi-Resolution Ultra-Sound. This equipment is said to be able to detect any presence of cancer, including low levels, which is why it was recommended.

No trace of cancer was found. Elliot reports he was definitely able to feel something going on in the prostate at one point. Now, that feeling has gone – he feels nothing.

How did we get this result? Elliot was motivated and diligent, applying a spectrum of alternative approaches, starting with lifestyle rebalancing. He felt that 30 years of work stress was the main factor in the disease. He adjusted his work schedule. Next, diet – elimination of red meat and other sources of toxins, while adding healthy options. Then, *Emotional Clearing Process* work, naturopathic remedies, acupuncture, meditation, Yoga, and exercise. Elliot and I both feel that the *Emotional Clearing* work was the foundation of his healing process. This therapy is an inner guided process that can be self-administered, but for serious conditions it will usually be advantageous to work with a trained facilitator, who can induce the healing levels in the client through a kind of personal resonance, adding their own energy, allowing them to go deeper than they can on their own.

In my experience, it has not usually necessary to employ additional healing strategies along with *Emotional Clearing*. But if desired, and if the case is serious, additional strategies may be applied without conflict. In fact, the effectiveness of any healing technique is greatly increased when applied concurrently with the *Emotional Clearing* paradigm. The self-activated *Alpha-Theta* relaxation state is inherently healing and allows any kind of healing work to be more effective because the mind has shifted from its normal state of activity and resistance to calmness and acceptance, not fighting, but just being choicelessly aware of what is happening, with no thought of changing it. When Elliot underwent the acupuncture, he self-activated the inner *Emotional Clearing* protocol that he had learned with me. This allowed him to maximize the effect of these other therapies, to go to a deep level with them, and for them to work in harmony with the work we did.

When any legitimate healing technique is applied, it will tend to release psychic-energetic negativity from the subconscious into consciousness, which is then often experienced as distressing emotional feelings or memories. If these feelings are not correctly handled, which is what happens most of the time, the negativity just becomes re-suppressed into the subconscious and the healing benefit is diminished. The *Emotional Clearing* paradigm may be used anytime by the client to understand what is happening and to permanently release these feelings when they come up.

A recent paper from Johns Hopkins, which Elliot brought to my attention, suggests that sometimes the body never recovers from chemotherapy or radical surgery, and that alternative approaches such as diet and meditation might well be considered first in cancer protocols. This is excellent as far as it goes, but it must be understood that just as there are different types of diets and medicine, there are different types of meditative approaches.

Most meditative strategies used today are in the spirit of resisting, fighting, and defeating the negative condition. The *Emotional Clearing* format is radically different from this adversarial approach. It is based on bringing unconditional presence, acceptance and consciousness to afflictions, and this is the crucial factor that I believe accounts for Elliot's success.

When the mind fights, it is active. When the mind is active, deep relaxation cannot occur, and natural healing forces are not allowed to intervene. Plus, in fighting, the mind ultimately fights itself and only strengthens what it fights. By dropping resistance and moving into acceptance, suppressed negativity comes to the surface to be released, resulting in emotional/physical clearing and healing.

Applying these principles in the face of life-threatening illness is in itself a challenge to both client and therapist. But I and those of us who routinely work with these principles know of their effectiveness on psychological and physical levels. I am excited that Elliot's case has been so well documented, and that we can now offer something in the way of concrete evidence to validate the effectiveness of this approach.

Let's look at the specifics of Elliot's case. I felt this was an excellent example of how body-based afflictions can tie into psychological stress and chakra dynamics. Elliot felt tremendous anxiety at work. He had a high-pressure job in which he was financially quite successful, but he couldn't fully enjoy his success because of tensions on the job. The problem was that he felt he was being constantly corrected, controlled, and dominated by his boss, who he took to be particularly insensitive as to how he affected his immediate subordinates.

After talking it out with Elliot, we clarified his experience to be a second chakra Power Center issue: The constant controlling, the restriction of independent initiative, the constant put-down of his ideas, always having other priorities over himself, being constantly dominated, all led to energetic frustration and congestion in this center. Since this chakra is located in the perineum, it's an obvious connection between negativity stored here and the prostate cancer.

Although over the course of 5 months we covered a wide range of issues, I took the Power Center issue to be the main factor in Elliot's condition, and we spent most of our time focused on it. Here's a typical session:

> I take Elliot through the induction. We have decided in the preliminary dialogue to look at the prostate/Power Center congestion:
>
> **John:** Let's focus into the prostate. Try to sense, on a body feeling level, what's happening there.
>
> **Elliot:** There's a kind of faint tingling. It's not painful, but it feels foreign to my body – like it shouldn't be there.
>
> **J:** Let's focus on that body sensation. Allow yourself to relax into it. Breathe into it and see and feel that area gently expanding as you breathe. Go up to the Third Eye again – keep breathing as you look up. Put aside any agenda and move into the moment with the body sensation with a sense of choiceless awareness. Lower your eyes.
>
> [We stay here for 10 minutes.]
>
> You're doing quite well in focusing for so long. Take a few deep breaths to wake up if you need to. Let's move to an emotional level. Allow the subconscious to give you an image that corresponds to the body sensation we have been focusing on.
>
> **E:** I'm at work. I'm trying to present my ideas for a problem the company is having, but my boss is not taking me seriously and contradicts whatever I say.
>
> **J:** How are you feeling about that?
>
> **E:** I'm feeling frustrated and angry. Like I'm controlled and dominated.

J: Let's address those feelings one at a time. Let's start with the first-level anger. Welcome the anger. Keep breathing into it. Try to find the anger in your body.

E: It's in the lower abdomen, close to the prostate.

J: Good. Breathe into that area. Relax into it, and go up to the Third Eye again, just like you did in the induction.

Lower your eyes.

[We stay here for 5 minutes]

Let's look at the core feeling behind the anger. That's the sense of being controlled and dominated that you mentioned, of having no control, being helpless, powerless. Go to those feelings.

E: Yes, I can go right there.

J: Let that sense of being dominated and controlled build. Don't be afraid of it. Let's take it through the steps:

*Step 1, Awareness:* Let's assume that this experience represents an emergence of the suppressed subconscious. It has attracted these circumstances in order to make itself known for clearing. Take responsibility and drop any blame you may feel towards your boss, as best as possible.

*Step 2, Acceptance:* It's easy to be frustrated and impatient this experience, but try to put aside the resistance and allow yourself to open to the experience, on a body feeling level.

*Step 3, Direct Experience*: Stay with the feeling. Come into the moment with it. Find it in your body. Sense it as an energy.

E: When I do that, I go right away to the prostate.

J: Good. *Step 4, Witnessing*: Detach and watch the feeling of being controlled and dominated with a sense of *choiceless awareness*. Go up to the Third Eye. Keep detaching and witnessing. Keep stepping back as you allow the experience.

[10 minutes]

Let's bring in the chakra itself. Imagine an energy center in your lower body, a few inches above the perineum. Imagine the breath going to that center as you inhale, expanding it, and contracting it as you exhale. Feel it as if it's as much a psychic movement as a physical movement.

E: Yes, I think I can sense it, but it doesn't feel quite right. There's tension there.

J: Just stay present with it as it is. Keep sending the breath there. Visualize both energy streams coming in as you breathe, going to the chakra. Feel the Light, with its power, and then feel the Earth, with its warmth. Does the chakra seem to prefer one over the other?

E: I think the Earth feels better – it's comforting and supportive, like what I'm missing.

J: Stay with that.

[Our primary strategy is always to process the negative feelings. but as we are doing that, it's permissible to bring in the positive energies that the client is lacking.]

Go up to the Third Eye for a moment as you work with the Earth energy.

Now let's try to integrate all these elements we've been working

with. Go back to the body sensation, then rotate to the core feelings of being controlled and dominated, then go to the chakra energetics. Try to feel them all happening at once.

E: Yes, I'm doing that – it's no problem.

J: Excellent. Stay right there. Keep relaxing, stay in the moment. Keep breathing into the chakra.

We have spent 40 minutes in the *Alpha-State* mode, processing feelings. Exposing all the different aspects of the trapped negativity to the Light of consciousness has resulted in a releasing, but not all the work has been done, and we will return here again. Each time a different memory may be evoked, the feelings may take a new twist – it seems there is no chance of getting bored with the routine. Note that we never went to any past life or even significant childhood traumatic recall. Not everyone has the psychic sensitivity to connect to past events, but it did not impede the effectiveness of the work we did, by focusing on the present-day job situation.

# John

I'd like to wind down FEEL III by sharing a little about myself. If you've gotten this far in the book, you might be wondering exactly who is this guy John Ruskan who came up with all this material? Here's a short bit about me, relative to personal healing.

My health is pretty good. I have some minor issues, but nothing like what many people face as they advance in age. I attribute this to a lifetime of 1. Dedicated Hatha Yoga practice, 2. Meditation and breathwork practice, 3. Intelligent diet, 4. Sensible priorities, 5. Always doing for a living only what I was genuinely passionate about and which would directly assist my personal evolutionary goals.

I'm always getting caught up in ambitious, creative projects. One of these involved buying a 42-foot 1956 Chris-Craft wood power boat (no fiberglass for me) and renovating it. I did the majority of the work myself, but hired a few people to help me occasionally. I have a history with boats and a lot of experience with wood-working, so I know what I'm doing. This was over 10 years ago, and I'm happy to say that it turned out great, except for what I'm about to tell you.

I spend my summers living on board on the Chesapeake Bay, and in fact, that's where I am right now (!) typing at the computer with a charming river view in the background, visible through the salon windows. It's idyllic – I'm in a rural part of Virginia, I drive through cornfields to get to the marina. The boat is parked at the end of the dock, I sit on the back and look out over the water at the sunset in the evening. The marina is like a ghost town all week, it's a perfect place for a serious reclusive like me to buckle down to the literally mind-numbing back-breaking mental effort of knocking off this book.

Anyway, I'm digressing, but that's what this section is about. Working on the boat involved a labor-intensive epoxy coating of the decks and cabin tops, which called for a lot of sanding of toxic materials, which generated a lot of toxic dust. Even though I always wore a respirator and thought I was being careful, after working on the renovation I came down with a serious lung infection. I went to a doctor in New York, who took chest x-rays, and at the next meeting with the doc I was informed that it looked like I had lung cancer.

Now – I'm not afraid of dying, I don't think, since I know for sure that it's a big step up from the Earth plane, but it's still something of a shock. Oh, yeah dying, no problem, but – uh – you mean now? It was a shock not only from the dying standpoint but because here I was, an ultra-experienced yogi with a lifetime of esoteric breath practice, an expert on breathwork, a metaphysical – psychological authority of sorts, who had never smoked, who was in great shape, enough to tackle this grueling renovation job, who considered himself a master carpenter, a wonderful if largely unrecognized musical artist, a decent tennis player, and so on. How could I have lung cancer? It didn't make sense. I'm not in denial, but it's an insult to my spiritual breath practice and accomplishments. What kind of twisted irony is this?

I explained all this to the doc. Here's what he actually said: "See this big gray spot on the x-ray? That's what lung cancer looks like."

So, I was plenty pissed off – at myself, at the boat, for getting involved with the stupid boat to begin with instead of just building a house somewhere (I've always got to do things the hard way) in order to have a retreat place to go to out of New York City. It went on and on.

The doc was already starting to make plans for some kind of intervention. Since this whole episode was about 8 years ago, and since I probably blanked out parts of it to begin with, I honestly forget what the intervention was to be, but he finally relented and said OK, let's wait a month and then check in with another x-ray and see how it's been progressing. I agreed.

During that month I became a monk, doing all the things I have tried to teach you in this book. Mostly I just sat and came into the moment, beyond the acceptance or rejection of the mind, breathed into my lungs, visualized Light going to the big gray spot and a vibrant, dazzling energy ball building up around it and the solar plexus chakra, felt it, and tied into the subtle body sensations for a minimum of two 45-minute sessions every day, witnessed from Third Eye outer space, with lots of Hatha Yoga thrown in. I'm chagrined to report I didn't uncover many suppressed feelings associated with the infection, which of course I was looking for, and which I've uncovered at other times. I started to think this might be some kind of pre-emptive Karma, intended to humble me and a challenge I was to overcome as part of the ongoing onslaught of Earth negativity, to illustrate the power of Yoga breathwork. Or maybe it was a dark force attack in response to the enlightenment work I do. I still don't know.

After the month was up, I went back for another x-ray. Here's what the doc actually said:

"This is *miraculous!* The gray spot has dissolved by about half. Looks like you didn't have cancer after all!"

Or did I?

It's almost a completely happy ending, except that I was left with permanent lung damage, a condition called *bronchiectasis* in the medical trade. It doesn't seem to be getting worse, but my lung power is greatly reduced, even though the doc says my condition is relatively mild. As you might know, another of my passions is composing and recording, and my singing voice is shot to hell, although I'm able to squeeze by with my distinctive low-key style and ample yet surreptitious software-based auto-tune pitch control on the vocals. I'm like that movie where the country singer star loses her voice overnight. Yikes! But – now that I think about it – doesn't she somehow regain it down the road?

# Loneliness

A few weeks ago, I happened to catch the 1956 movie, *Lust For Life,* starring Kirk Douglas. For those who may not know, this is the story of Vincent van Gogh. The movie brilliantly portrays his emotional struggle and eventual defeat. I remember first seeing it as a teenager and being moved by it, and even reading the original novel on which it was based. Even then, the artist in me was being stirred. I could identify with van Gogh's torment although not with his self-destructiveness.

As I watched the film again, I found it quite interesting that it suggests that *loneliness* was at the root of his pain. Several times in the plot, he passionately cries out that loneliness is tormenting him. In the final scene where he shoots himself, he scribbles a note in which he says he can see no way out. It would appear he was suffering from what would be termed mental illness, but what is that? From his point of view, he appears to be rational most of the time, except when he gets pushed over the edge and irrationality takes over. We can all relate to that.

I wish I could have had him as a friend or maybe even a client. I would say something like, "Hey bro, I can see you are extremely right-brained emotionally based. I'm all in favor of an active right-brain, in fact I consider that one of my most valued possessions, but it's important to keep it under control. I would suggest first of all that you get more *grounded,* to give you an emotional foundation, so you're not being blown around so much by random winds. We all need some kind of emotional education or training to optimize ourselves; don't think of it as an embarrassment."

I would continue, "Apparently you have not heard of Eastern philosophy, but it contains insights I believe you would find helpful. It begins by pointing out that human consciousness is naturally subject to fits of isolation, anxiety, and loneliness. This is the result of being encased in what has come to be called an *ego.* Going beyond perceiving yourself as an isolated ego is a major objective of Eastern spiritual practice, and is said to provide relief from the ongoing torment. If you are not aware of this inherent, existential burden that mankind is born/cursed with, and if you struggle mindlessly against it, you will probably run into trouble."

"Then, there's the painting addiction. When you are high in the moment of artistic creation – which I know from personal experience is totally enchanting and known only to those of us who resonate with the artistic archetype, that's why we don't give a hoot for material things – you temporarily transcend the loneliness pain. However, you appear, again, unaware of the insidious dualistic nature of the human soul – that highs are always balanced by lows. The loneliness will come on strong after any episode of flying high with the art, especially when it is unconsciously undertaken as a means of escape from the lows."

"As you are battered by the negative lows of the cycle, you again immerse yourself in the creative high in an effort to feel better, and the vicious, tragic, artistic *manic-depressive* cycle is established. Nowadays it's called *bipolar syndrome,* and regular people, not only artists get drawn into it, for the same reasons. You probably have picked up some psychic entities that are attracted to these energies as well, and they amplify your pain and hunger, pushing you into moments of hysterical irrationality. When you are deep into the dualistic cycle, you can't see any way out, and that's not totally inaccurate. You need to understand the nature of the trap you are in and slowly withdraw."

But what about my art, will I be able to paint if I am freed from these demons?

"That's a good question. I suffered from the identical syndrome I am trying to enlighten you about except I was able to avoid cutting off any body parts.* I used my art to suppress my loneliness and other existential angst that had accumulated. Eventually, I liberated myself with Eastern meditative techniques combined with Western psychological insights. I now have a thriving artistic practice that regularly renews me and lifts my vibration, which continues to this day even though most artists I know who reach my age have long since withered up."

---

*Some readers may not know that van Gogh intentionally cut off one of his ears during a particularly intense emotional episode.

"But is it necessary for great art to be impelled by a touch of the irrational, by an infusion of universal pain with which all can consciously or unconsciously identify? Or can art still portray the dualistic nature of the human drama, the highs and lows, the beauty and the ugliness, can it still inspire and transcend without being itself motivated by pain? Is it worth it for a life to be shrouded in torment if that's the only way great art can be produced? There have been many, perhaps most, great artists who have not been overrun by manic-depressiveness, who may even have figured out that it is an occupational hazard to be intelligently dealt with, in the same way that is an occupational hazard for regular people encased in a human body."

"So, Vince, here's the formula in a nutshell that worked for me, and probably will work for you if you have any affinity for it: First, let me teach you some basic *traditional* Hatha Yoga postures. This starts to ground you, and does a lot to release body-held tensions that can build up and drive you over the edge. Then, let's learn how to practice with the breath. This will immediately calm you down even more. Whenever you feel yourself getting frantic, you go to a conscious breath. Then, there's learning to still the mind and its addictive impulses with what we call meditation, and most importantly, to detach from and witness any emotional pain that may be coming on instead of being overwhelmed by it or trying to suppress it with your art, including the most fundamental pain known to everybody, the pain that keeps us in the modern world searching, striving, struggling, grasping, the pain that's at the bottom of the human comedy, which can only be ultimately transcended by completely coming into the moment, stopping the mind, going beyond time, dropping the ego, and merging with the Higher-Self – the pain of loneliness."

## About the Author

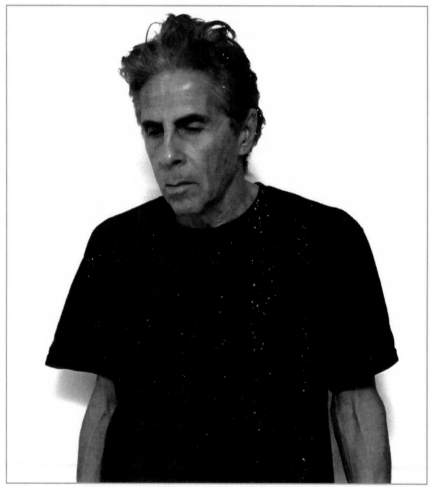

INTERIOR AND BACK COVER PHOTOS 2019

John Ruskan has been a life-long traveler on the consciousness path. He was initiated into a major Yoga tradition in 1968 when he was 26 years old, and has been a Yoga devotee ever since. Becoming deeply familiar with transformational work made him realize how essential emotional enlightenment is to personal spiritual evolution and well-being for all of us. Accordingly, he has focused his teaching efforts on introducing foundational truths about our inner feeling selves that are usually not understood in the modern world. His methodology draws upon esoteric Eastern philosophical principles and techniques as well as humanistic Western psychology.

Classical Yoga emphasizes pranayama (breathwork) as one its principle elements, and since John has had first-hand experience in just how effective breathwork can be in helping to resolve negativity, it has become a central factor in his approach.

John launched his counseling career in 1994 when his first book *Emotional Clearing* was published. Shortly after that, he started training other therapists in the *EC* technique. At this point, after more than 20 years, he has retired from personally working with clients, but continues to train others, and is focusing his efforts on other writing projects. The *Deep Clearing* book represents his evolved re-statement about his psychological process work.

John has been a life-long musical artist, working in the music field as a songwriter-singer-performer, recording studio owner, and independent record producer in the 80's in New York City before getting full-time into the holistic psychology field. He feels his artistic involvement has been instrumental in developing the right-brain soulfulness that has enabled him to successfully empathize with clients and formulate his vision. He continues to produce new creative work, which may be reviewed at **www.johnruskan.com**. His *Emotional Clearing* work is to be found at **www.emclear.com**.

John has a degree in Mechanical Engineering from Cornell University. Based in New York City for most of his life, he now spends 3 months of the year on his boat on the Chesapeake.

---

If you have found this book to be of value and would like to help in bringing this vital information to the attention of others who may desperately need it, and to participate in the movement towards individual and global enlightenment, please **post a review on Amazon.com.** Reviews on Amazon can be instrumental in encouraging others to make the leap to start working on themselves. Your efforts to post an **Amazon customer review,** as well as reviews on other book sites, are greatly appreciated by John and will make a difference.

**Join the emclear forum!** You can participate in a discussion, share about your journey, and get feedback directly from John on the free **emclear.com forum.**

Visit the **www.emclear.com** website for information on guided training programs, personal counseling with a trained *Emotional Clearing Facilitator,* and for professional training to become a facilitator. John no longer sees individual clients, but devotes his time to training facilitators and writing.

## www.emclear.com

## youtube: the Emotional Clearing Process

**Other books by John Ruskan:**

# Emotional Clearing
A Groundbreaking East / West Guide to Releasing Negative Feelings and Awakening Unconditional Happiness

# Emotion and Art
Mastering the Challenges of the Artist's Path

# Moon Walking
An Excursion into the Subconscious World of Emotion and Art

Made in United States
North Haven, CT
22 March 2023

34403580R00188